EDUCATION AS AND FOR JUSTICE IN THE GLOBAL SOUTH

Case Studies from Nepal, Perú and Uganda

Lizzi O. Milligan, María Balarin, Rachel Wilder, Expedito Nuwategeka and Mohan Paudel

First published in Great Britain in 2026 by

Bristol University Press
University of Bristol
1-9 Old Park Hill
Bristol
BS2 8BB
UK
t: +44 (0)117 374 6645
e: bup-info@bristol.ac.uk

Details of international sales and distribution partners are available at bristoluniversitypress.co.uk

© Lizzi O. Milligan, María Balarin, Rachel Wilder, Expedito Nuwategeka and Mohan Paudel 2026

DOI: 10.51952/9781529245172

The digital PDF and ePub versions of this title are available open access and distributed under the terms of the Creative Commons Attribution-NonCommercial-NoDerivatives 4.0 International licence (https://creativecommons.org/licenses/by-nc-nd/4.0/) which permits reproduction and distribution for non-commercial use without further permission provided the original work is attributed.

British Library Cataloguing in Publication Data
A catalogue record for this book is available from the British Library

ISBN 978-1-5292-4515-8 paperback
ISBN 978-1-5292-4516-5 ePub
ISBN 978-1-5292-4517-2 OA Pdf

The right of Lizzi O. Milligan, María Balarin, Rachel Wilder, Expedito Nuwategeka and Mohan Paudel to be identified as authors of this work has been asserted by them in accordance with the Copyright, Designs and Patents Act 1988.

All rights reserved: no part of this publication may be reproduced, stored in a retrieval system, or transmitted in any form or by any means, electronic, mechanical, photocopying, recording, or otherwise without the prior permission of Bristol University Press.

Every reasonable effort has been made to obtain permission to reproduce copyrighted material. If, however, anyone knows of an oversight, please contact the publisher.

The statements and opinions contained within this publication are solely those of the authors and not of the University of Bristol or Bristol University Press. The University of Bristol and Bristol University Press disclaim responsibility for any injury to persons or property resulting from any material published in this publication.

Bristol University Press works to counter discrimination on grounds of gender, race, disability, age and sexuality.

Cover design: Blu Inc
Front cover image: Stocksy/Clive Watts
Bristol University Press uses environmentally responsible print partners.
Printed and bound in Great Britain by CPI Group (UK) Ltd, Croydon, CR0 4YY

Bristol University Press' authorised representative in the European Union is:
Easy Access System Europe, Mustamäe tee 50, 10621 Tallinn, Estonia,
Email: gpsr.requests@easproject.com

Bristol Studies in Comparative and International Education

Series Editors: **Michael Crossley**, Emeritus Professor of Comparative and International Education, University of Bristol, UK, **Leon Tikly**, UNESCO Chair in Inclusive, Good Quality Education, University of Bristol, UK, **Angeline M. Barrett**, Reader in Education, University of Bristol, UK, and **Julia Paulson**, Dean of the College of Education, University of Saskatchewan, Canada

The series critically engages with education and international development from a comparative and interdisciplinary perspective. It emphasises work that bridges theory, policy and practice, supporting early career researchers and the publication of studies led by researchers in and from the Global South.

Also available in the series:

Rethinking Citizenship in Central and Eastern Europe
edited by **Nina Kolleck** and **Ireneusz Pawel Karolewski**

Learning through Collective Memory Work
by **Goya Wilson Vásquez**

Schooling, Conflict and Peace in the Southwestern Pacific
by **David Oakeshott**

Education for Sustainable Development in an Unequal World
by **Beniamin Knutsson, Linus Bylund, Sofie Hellberg** and **Jonas Lindberg**

Education and Resilience in Crisis
edited by **Mary Mendenhall, Gauthier Marchais, Yusuf Sayed** and **Neil Boothby**

Higher Education in Small Islands
edited by **Rosie Alexander** and **Holly Henderson**

Teacher Professionalism in the Global South
by **Leon Tikly, Rafael Mitchell, Angeline Barrett, Poonam Batra, Alexandra Bernal, Leanne Cameron, Alf Coles, Zawadi Juma, Nidia Aviles Nunez, Julia Paulson, Nigusse Weldemariam Reda, Jennifer Rowsell, Michael Tusiime** and **Beatriz Vejarano**

Find out more at:
bristoluniversitypress.co.uk/
bristol-studies-in-comparative-and-international-education

Bristol Studies in Comparative and International Education

Series Editors: **Michael Crossley**, Emeritus Professor of Comparative and International Education, University of Bristol, UK, **Leon Tikly**, UNESCO Chair in Inclusive, Good Quality Education, University of Bristol, UK, **Angeline M. Barrett**, Reader in Education, University of Bristol, UK, and **Julia Paulson**, Dean of the College of Education, University of Saskatchewan, Canada

Editorial advisory board

María Balarin, GRADE (Grupo de Análisis para el Desarrollo), Perú
Godfrey Baldacchino, University of Malta (from original Symposium series Board)
Michelle Bellino, University of Michigan, US
Maria Jose Bermeo, Universidad de los Andes, Colombia
Mark Bray, The University of Hong Kong (from original Symposium series Board)
Leanne Cameron, University of Bristol, UK
Fatuma Chege, Kenyatta University, Kenya
Artemio Arturo Cortez Ochoa, University of Cambridge, UK
Dave Gordon, University of Bristol, UK
Tigist Grieve, University of Bristol, UK
Eric Herring, University of Bristol, UK
Frances Koya-Vakuata, Human Rights and Social Development Division (HRSD), Pacific Community (SPC), Fiji
Mark Mason, The Education University of Hong Kong (from original Symposium series Board)
Simon McGrath, University of Glasgow, UK
Rafael Mitchell, University of Bristol, UK
Zibah A. Nwako, University of Bristol, UK
Nkobi Pansiri, University of Botswana
Marcela Ramos Arellano, University of Glasgow, UK
Tania Saeed, Lahore University, Pakistan
Robin Shields, University of Bristol, UK
Arathi Sriprakash, University of Bristol, UK
Lorraine P Symaco, Zhejiang University, China
Gita Steiner Khamsi, Teachers College, Columbia University, US (from original Symposium series Board)
Tony Welch, The University of Sydney, Australia

Find out more at
bristoluniversitypress.co.uk/
bristol-studies-in-comparative-and-international-education

This book is dedicated to the young people who took part in the JustEd study and all the educators, school leaders and policy makers working to advance justice in and through education.

Contents

Series Editors' Preface		viii
List of Figures and Tables		x
About the Authors		xi
Acknowledgements		xii
1	Education, Justice and Global Development Goals	1
2	Interrogating Education through a Multiple Justices Lens	17
3	Methodological Strategies to Investigate Education and Justice	41
4	Education and Justice in Nepal	60
5	Education and Justice in Perú	79
6	Education and Justice in Uganda	107
7	Education *as* and *for* Justice: Key Findings from across the Countries	128
8	The Central Role of Epistemic Justice in Education to Enable Sustainable Development	147
Appendix		157
References		163
Index		190

Series Editors' Preface

*Michael Crossley, Leon Tikly,
Angeline M. Barrett (University of Bristol) and
Julia Paulson (University of Saskatchewan)*

This is an important book. Theoretically rich and empirically grounded, it attends to the lived experiences of students in classrooms in three countries – Nepal, Perú and Uganda – and puts them into conversation with global educational policy debate in poignant and meaningful ways. The analysis speaks directly to the Sustainable Development Goals (SDGs) agenda, which sees education as a goal and as a driver for progress against other goals. This book argues that education's connections to and possibilities for contributing to various forms of justice – social, epistemic, environmental, transitional – matter for the SDGs and for possibilities of sustainable, flourishing futures more generally.

The book presents findings from the JustEd project, which set out to explore education *as* and *for* justice in Nepal, Perú and Uganda – three countries using a mixed methods approach, including policy analysis, surveys of students' understandings and intended actions around justice, and classroom observations. The study is original in the ways it extends well-established theoretical concepts around social justice and education to explore other forms of justice. This allows us to identify the ways that education imagines (via policy and curriculum, for example) its contributions to environment and climate; to diversity and multiple ways of knowing; and to peace, and, importantly, how these intentions land with learners. Three substantive chapters answer these questions in each country's context, highlighting particular realities tied to the histories, cultures and educational relationships of each place. The study's strong theoretical framing and mixed methods approach then allows for the elaboration of a set of cross-case conclusions that vividly show how the presence of multiple injustices in learners' daily lives, including at and in schools, shape the ways in which they understand and are able (or not) to imagine and act for justice into the future.

The book argues that shallow pedagogies, depoliticization of issues connected to justice, individualization of processes towards justice, and the failures of education to connect directly to learners' lived experiences all limit the ways that education acts *as* and *for* justice in these contexts. The book's findings are sobering, but its proposals are practical (as well as theoretical) and heartening. It concludes by highlighting the importance of attention to epistemic justice to social justice projects within and through education. Attention to epistemic justice centres learners' lived experiences and seeks to connect to them, engages them in multiple forms of knowledge and ways of knowing, and develops their capacities as knowledge creators – this is, the book argues, a pathway to education as justice and therefore to education contributing more richly towards justice.

Colleagues involved in this research have long been involved in, or connected to, the work of the Centre for Comparative and International Research in Education (CIRE) here at the University of Bristol, so as Series Editors we are collectively pleased to support this publication. The book joins others in this series that have made original theoretical contributions based on rich empirical investigation and puts forward new theoretical framings that will advance scholarship and understanding of education and social justice.

List of Figures and Tables

Figures

4.1	In-person creative activities conducted with learners in Nepal	69
5.1	Qualitative data generation sequence in Perú	94
6.1	The axis of miseducation across curriculum, time and classroom size	121
7.1	The JustEd framework	145

Tables

2.1	Different pedagogies and their core characteristics	37
3.1	Search terms to sample the textbooks and other materials	47
3.2	Qualitative methods used in each country	51
3.3	Research sites for qualitative data generation	53
3.4	Links between qualitative analysis and quantitative survey design	54
3.5	Iterative analysis towards theory development	56
4.1	Policy documents reviewed according to the three justices in Nepal	61
4.2	Curricular materials analysed in Nepal	66
5.1	Selected policies in Perú	82
5.2	Curriculum and textbook materials analysed in Perú	89
6.1	Policy documents reviewed according to the three justices in Uganda	109
6.2	Curricular materials analysed in Uganda	113
8.1	The 3Rs and the epistemic core	152

About the Authors

Lizzi O. Milligan is Professor of Education and Global Social Justice in the Department of Education at the University of Bath. She was Principal Investigator of the JustEd project. Her research particularly focuses on different forms of (in)justice in language-in-education. She holds a PhD from the University of Bristol.

María Balarin is Senior Researcher at Grupo de Análisis para el Desarrollo (GRADE) in Perú. She specializes in the political economy of education reforms in Latin America, especially on how global policy agendas interact with national contexts, often challenging social justice aims. She holds a PhD from the University of Bath.

Rachel Wilder is Lecturer in the Department of Education at the University of Bath. Her research explores the role of education in addressing complex, interconnected global challenges that may be understood as 'wicked problems' in education policy. This includes gender-based violence, reproductive justice, environmental crises and mental health. She holds a PhD from the University of Bristol.

Expedito Nuwategeka is Senior Lecturer in the Department of Geography at Gulu University, Uganda. He was a co-investigator in the JustEd study. He holds a PhD in Geography from Gulu University and his research focuses on Indigenous environmental knowledges and how they interact with and in formal education systems to influence (or not) transformative environmental education in the Global South.

Mohan Paudel is Associate Professor of Science Education in the Central Department of Education, Tribhuvan University, Nepal. He holds a PhD in Science Education from Tribhuvan University. In the JustEd project, Paudel contributed as a research associate from Nepal. His research focuses on (in)justice in education, accountability, and science education.

Acknowledgements

This book was developed from the 'Education as and for Environmental, Epistemic and Transitional Justice to Enable Sustainable Development' (JustEd) project. This was a collaborative, multi-country project based on the values of kindness, fun, collegiality, creativity, justice, rigour, transparency and respect. All project outputs represent the collective endeavour of the team, and we acknowledge all team members' contributions.

The international JustEd team includes Tina Aciro (Gulu University, Uganda), Patricia Ajok (Gulu University, Uganda), María Balarin (Grupo de Análisis para el Desarrollo (GRADE, Perú), Mrigendra Bahadur Karki (Tribhuvan University, Nepal), Daniel Komakech (Gulu University, Uganda), Lizzi O. Milligan (University of Bath, UK), Dorica Mirembe (Gulu University, Uganda), Carlos Monge (GRADE, Perú), Ainur Muratkyzy (University of Bristol, UK), Expedito Nuwategeka (Gulu University, Uganda), Alvaro Ordonez (GRADE, Perú), Mohan Paudel (Tribhuvan University, Nepal), Julia Paulson (University of Bristol, UK), María Fernanda Rodríguez (GRADE, Perú), Paola Sarmiento (University of Bristol, UK), Sushil Sharma (Tribhuvan University, Nepal), Robin Shields (University of Bristol, UK), Ashik Singh (Tribhuvan University, Nepal), Ganesh Bahadur Singh (Tribhuvan University, Nepal), Nese Soysal (University of Bath), Srijana Ranabhat (Tribhuvan University, Nepal), Alithu Bazan Talavera (GRADE, Perú) and Rachel Wilder (University of Bath, UK).

We acknowledge and are grateful for the time, insights and enthusiasm of all the participants in the study.

We also acknowledge the funding for the project from the UKRI Global Challenges Research Fund (project code: ES/T004851/1), without which this project would not have been possible.

1

Education, Justice and Global Development Goals

Introduction

The notion that education plays a significant role in enabling sustainable development – including social justice and equalities, climate action, and peace and security – is one that deserves thoughtful, methodical investigation so that we can better understand if and how education truly enables social change. Currently, formal schooling is widely expected to facilitate sustainable development (Bengtsson et al, 2018). This expectation often assumes linear trajectories, as though placing a topic into a school curriculum will be enough to bring about the individual, collective and systemic changes needed to enable such outcomes. Such assumptions can also underplay the essential role of pedagogy and experiences of schooling. To date, there is limited literature that considers the processes through which school contributes to multiple justice outcomes other than that for education itself (Vladimirova and Le Blanc, 2016; Kushnir and Nunes, 2022). This book demonstrates the complex trajectories between secondary education and sustainable development in the Global South through case studies of Nepal, Perú and Uganda and argues for far more attention to be paid to the role of education *as* justice. By this we mean the ways that educational experiences are just and also the ways that schools support young people to interpret and create knowledge and understand the multiple forms of (in) justice they encounter around them. When education is just, education can be *for* justice, as it can equip young people to contribute to more just societies.

In this chapter, we situate the study within the historical and contemporary global agendas about education and the contribution of formal schooling to development. We introduce our argument that education *as* justice is required to realize education *for* justice, and we explain why we have selected three of the Sustainable Development Goals (SDGs) to illustrate these arguments. From there, we share our definitions of the three forms of justice that we focus on: epistemic justice, environmental justice and transitional justice. Then, we outline the research methodology that was used in the research and the rationale for doing this research in Nepal, Perú and Uganda (see Chapter 3 for a detailed account). Finally, we provide a brief overview of each chapter and the key findings in the book.

Education, justice and sustainable development

Education has long been a central component of global development cooperation and has been seen as a factor which could advance human welfare, reduce inequities and inequalities, support economic growth, and enhance security and peace. Since free and compulsory primary education was established as a fundamental human right in the 1948 United Nations Declaration of Human Rights, there has been widespread and increasing recognition of the contributions that formal schooling can make to a wide range of development outcomes at the individual level, for families and communities, and for whole countries. The history of development cooperation is punctuated by pivotal moments when global actors across the politico-geographic spectrum have come together in rare unity to endorse inspiring visions of education as a transformative force for good, and to demonstrate the gravitas of these ambitions by backing them with enormous financial and political resources. Global campaigns such as Universal Primary Education (1960s), and the Education for All campaigns (1990, 2000, 2015), are revered for changing the daily realities and life trajectories of millions of children and young people all around the world. Extensive data collection and analysis has produced rich understandings of how participation and attainment in education have contributed to people's lives – from better health to girls' and women's empowerment to higher earnings and better employability, and more (UNESCO, 2020).

We also have a better understanding of how the collective impacts of increases in educational achievement have had substantial knock-on effects for households, communities and countries. It is estimated that every additional year of schooling raises a country's average annual gross domestic product (GDP) growth by 0.37 per cent and reduces the possibility of a young person engaging in violent conflict by 20 per cent; a child whose mother can read is 50 per cent more likely to survive past the age of five years, and it is estimated that if all women were to complete primary school, there would be a 66 per cent decline in maternal mortality (Global Partnership for Education, 2014). There is evidence that investments in education could have been used better and recognition that there is still much to be done (Miles and Singal, 2010; UNESCO, 2015; Unterhalter, 2019; Kakupa and Shayo, 2021), but few would disagree that global investments in education to date have been paramount in changing the world for the better.

Education continues to be seen as a vital mechanism for driving development forwards. The SDG framework (2015–2030) is the current, internationally agreed policy for global development, and many of the 17 SDGs explicitly identify a role for education. For example, in SDG 13 (Climate Action) the link is clearly made through target 13.3, which calls for improvements in 'education, awareness-raising and human and institutional capacity on climate change mitigation, adaptation, impact reduction and early warning', to be measured in part through the integration of these topics in school curricula, teacher training and assessments (UN Department of Economic and Social Affairs, nd). In SDG 16 (Peace, Justice and Strong Institutions), the emphasis on strengthened, inclusive and participatory institutions and mitigation of violence to children are underpinned by education assumptions. The UN (United Nations Suriname, nd) has stated, 'Education is the key that will allow many other Sustainable Development Goals (SDGs) to be achieved'.

As universal, free State education is rooted in human rights and social welfare, it is often assumed that more education and better access to quality education mean greater social justice and better futures for young people beyond the school walls. However, there are stories that belie this grand narrative of education, stories that falsify our expectations that progress in education is a linear journey forward for sustainable development. These stories tell us that the dominant model of public education does not serve everyone, or everything, equally. To approach questions of justice, we must ask, 'What is education for? Who is it for? Who benefits the most and who is left behind? Why is this?'.

The fact that education contributes to diverse areas of human and social development is one of its strongest assets. However, there is an evident hierarchy of development agendas that have shaped public education provision, which broadly correspond to the relative power and financial resources of their respective proponents (Bonal and Tarabini, 2009; Elfert and Ydesen, 2023). Powerful and wealthy actors such as the World Bank, regional development banks and the OECD have long championed education as a driver of economic progress (World Bank, 2018). Diverse forms of social development – including better health outcomes, gender equality, reducing socio-economic disparities and eliminating poverty – also have a lot of traction as arguments for investing in education. Multilateral groups such as UNESCO and global partnerships such as the Global Partnership for Education are staunch advocates for education and make visible its widespread contribution to diverse dimensions of social development.

Nonetheless, social progress due to education is still often instrumentalized as a vehicle through which economic growth can be achieved; indeed, the economic rationale – underpinned by human capital theory – is a ubiquitous, normative convention oft employed to appeal to powerful financial institutions. As a result, global campaigns for improving school 'effectiveness' and 'quality' treat as common sense that what schools need to be more effective *at* is delivering academic results, for example higher scores in standardized measures of mathematics, science and English abilities – those academic achievements which are correlated with higher-earning jobs and economic productivity. The *how* has then followed the *what*, with programmes for educational improvement modelling managerial approaches (Schweisfurth, 2023). Examples include fostering competition, narrowing the aims of education, and reducing teachers' autonomy to teach in ways that respond to learners' unique backgrounds, aptitudes and interests (Biesta, 2015).

In this context, justice in education is conceptualized as greater participation of marginalized groups – for example, those from lower-income households, girls, migrants, ethnic minorities and so on – and greater equality of educational outcomes across socio-economic groups. A 'just education' is synonymous with 'equitable education' and 'inclusive education'. By some measures, education worldwide is now more equitable than ever. For example, the rate of primary school completion has increased faster among rural children and among the poorest children compared to average improvements in primary school completion (UNESCO, 2020). However, we remain far from eliminating the disparities; 'the promise of reaching the further behind is not being kept' (UNESCO, 2020, p 8).

Evidence suggests that efforts to promote universal education without specifically taking action to promote equity can make education *more* inequitable, as the 'easy to reach' children progress and the most disadvantaged lag further and further behind (Chow et al, 2024). However, in global development cooperation ideas of what learners should learn and how schooling can contribute to sustainable development have changed very little over time. Increasingly, practitioners and academics are questioning the assumption that schools must prioritize academic achievements in order for education to deliver more justice and better development around the world (McCowan, 2010; Tikly, 2019; Unterhalter, 2019).

In parallel to the history of development cooperation, there have been a range of intellectual projects and alternative education provisions that have offered richer visions of a just education. These have emerged from a range of epistemic communities, including education scholars, social movements, Indigenous groups and environmental groups (Kopnina, 2020; Menton et al, 2020). They include child-centred approaches (for example, Reggio Emilia, Escuela Nueva), religious schooling (such as Madrasahs, Yeshivas) and experiential learning (for example, forest schools). These innovative models of education de-centre the economic objective to offer multiple nuanced and distinctive answers to the question 'what is education for?'. In diverse ways, they view education as an explicitly value-rich endeavour where care, community, planetary flourishing, democracy, faith, agency, play and/or ethical coexistence are positioned as its fundamental goals and where justice is a guiding principle. Questions of justice help to move education beyond the instrumental and beyond an intractable notion of stasis to encourage hopeful, future-thinking imaginaries of the world otherwise. At this time of unprecedented planetary crisis, uncertainty, conflict, movement and troubled anticipation, there has never been a time when a justice approach is more needed.

Powerful organizations and leaders around the world now recognize the urgency and scale of the global challenges we face. We are seeing the emergence of new policy visions for international cooperation for education that bear striking resemblance to some alternative models that have existed for many years in the subterranean. UNESCO's most recent manifesto – its new vision for education entitled *Reimagining our future together: a new social contract for education* – states,

> Knowledge and learning are the basis for renewal and transformation. But global disparities – and a pressing need to reimagine why, how, what, where and when we learn – mean that education is not doing what it could to help us shape peaceful, just, and sustainable futures. (UNESCO, 2022, p 6)
>
> And
>
> It is through millions of individual and collective acts of courage, leadership, resistance, creativity, and care that we will change course and transform education to build just, equitable and sustainable futures. (UNESCO, 2022, p 12)
>
> And
>
> Our energies need to focus on the risk-taking practices of empathy, ethics, solidarity, co-construction and justice, which need to be patiently taught and learned. (UNESCO, 2022, p 54)

In November 2023, UNESCO also adopted a revised 'Recommendation on Education for Peace and Human Rights, International Understanding, Cooperation, Fundamental Freedoms, Global Citizenship and Sustainable Development', which recognizes 'The important role of education in empowering individuals, communities and societies to address global challenges and to take transformative action for ensuring sustainable development and in implementing the 2030 Agenda for Sustainable Development' (UNESCO, 2023, p 123).

However, it is important to note that UNESCO's vision has been critiqued for being idealistic (Klees, 2022). It also stands in the shadows of more dominant, World Bank–led and problematic discourses of post-pandemic 'learning loss' and a 'learning crisis' (Sriprakash, Tikly and

Walker, 2020). While UNESCO's manifesto for transformative education (2022) and the Recommendation on Education for Peace, Human Rights and Sustainable Development (as known in short) (UNESCO, 2023) are welcome gestures towards educational futures that recognize justice as a core value and imperative in education, we anticipate increasing tensions between these movements and the more conventional, economic rationale for educational improvements as we progress towards the deadline for the SDGs and as negotiations for the next global development cooperation framework commence.

Introducing education *as* justice to enable education *for* justice

This book proposes that the current, narrow conception of justice in education is insufficient to deliver the gains it is expected to deliver for sustainable development. In particular, we argue that the manifestation of justice in education as the equal distribution of educational benefits is an insufficient and constraining view of a 'just' education and that a more complex, multiple justices understanding of education *as* justice is necessary.

The central argument of the book is that we need to pay far more attention to the ways that education is (un)just if education is to lead to a range of justice outcomes, notably the SDGs. We need education *as* justice – the concept that schooling is itself just – to enable education *for* justice – the idea that education generates justice in society, outside of the school. Throughout the chapters we will show the different dimensions of (in)justice present within schooling.

While we talk about education *as* justice and education *for* justice, it is important to note that we offer these as propositions – not unequivocal realities – and therefore suggest it is equally possible to perceive education *as* injustice and education *for* injustice. As we will argue in this book, the relationship between education and (in)justice is complex, and our research suggests education is simultaneously just and unjust, both contributing to and inhibiting wider justice outcomes.

Here, we outline three premises that are the starting points for our exploration of education *as* and *for* justice. The first premise is the expectation that education will develop particular kinds of knowledge, skills, attitudes, motivations and behaviours among learners that will equip them to contribute to justice outcomes. In acquiring these skills and capacities, it is anticipated that as individuals and a collective, these learners will become citizens who take actions to bring about more just societies. The second premise is that education – as a core social institution – facilitates broader social learning about what is valued in society, which contributes to justice outcomes. For example, the socially constructed roles, hierarchies and success that exist in schools and are observed by learners and their families shape understanding of appropriate and desirable relationships, aspirations and status, thus moulding their ideas of self-worth and likely/feasible futures. More broadly, the significance of schools in society shapes cultural understanding of what it is to be educated.

The third key premise of this book is that education *for* justice is inextricably linked to sustainable development. While the discourse of justice is often absent or superficial in conversations about the SDGs (Menton et al, 2020), we argue that it is in fact a profoundly important aim underpinning all of the SDGs, not least those that identify a clear role for education to deliver their aims. SDG 4 (Quality Education) includes as a target that all learners will acquire the knowledge and skills needed to promote sustainable development (target 4.7). '*All* learners' is a clear reference to equity and equality, signalling the work of Rawls (1971) and other philosophers who have argued that social justice depends on a fair and equal distribution of basic rights, goods and freedoms, including human and social capital. As suggested earlier, redistribution remains the dominant way in which justice is conceptualized in education (Tikly and Barrett, 2011).

We also focus on three additional SDGs where justice is a central concern: SDG 10 (Reduced Inequalities), SDG 13 (Climate Action) and SDG 16 (Peace, Justice and Strong Institutions). SDG 10 includes the following targets: reducing income inequalities among households/individuals (target 10.1); increasing political, economic and social inclusion (target 10.2); increasing equality of opportunities and reducing discrimination (target 10.3); and improving official development assistance, policies and other treatment of low-income countries to enable them to improve their socio-economic situations relative to higher-income countries (targets 10.4, 10.6, 10.a, 10.b, 10.c). Where these targets aim to redistribute wealth and opportunities, there is a clear link to distributional justice principles (Küfeoğlu, 2022) but they also connect with recognition as a justice principle, which suggests that many distinct groups experience diverse harms (for example, exploitation, oppression) as a result of their particular identities, circumstances and values not being 'seen' in policies, practices and in society at large (Young, 1990; Honneth, 1992, 1995). Target 10.2, about political, economic and social inclusion, also connects with the justice principle of representation (Fraser, 2009), which refers to equal opportunities for political participation and action. SDG 13 (climate action) includes two targets that specifically aim to equip low-income countries to respond to climate change, which are examples of climate justice. Climate justice recognizes that some groups around the world are experiencing disproportionate impacts from climate change, that some groups have disproportionately contributed to creating climate change, and that those groups and nations with greater resources have a duty to support those who have less and who are more severely affected (Sultana, 2021). It is clear here how the SDGs and their targets connect both to education and to different notions of justice.

In the next section, we delve further into theoretical understandings of justice that are especially aligned with SDGs 10, 13 and 16. These are environmental justice, epistemic justice and transitional justice. We share our definitions of these forms of justice and explain how we use them in this book.

Key definitions

A central argument of this book is that the contributions that education is expected to make to SDGs 10, 13 and 16 are extremely unlikely to be realized without education systems that embody multiple forms of justice. Here we offer our understandings and definitions of epistemic, environmental and transitional justice and how they are relevant to education.

We define *epistemic justice* as equality in the consumption, recognition and production of knowledges. This unique definition draws on Hall et al's (2020, p 35) writing about epistemic pluralism and knowledge hierarchies, where they propose that epistemic justice lies in 'equality in the production, recognition and consumption of knowledge'. When using this definition in our work, we propose two small but important adaptations: the explicit use of knowledges in the plural and a change in the order of words that we feel better reflects the processes through which we become producers of knowledges.

In education, epistemic justice refers to how schools enable learners to acquire the epistemic resources to engage with and contribute knowledge that helps them to understand themselves and others, their position in the spaces in which they live and their potential contributions to change. This relates to how different kinds of knowledge, experiences and perspectives – for example Western, Indigenous, local and children's knowledge – are included, taught and assessed in schools (Huaman, 2017; Manyike and Shava, 2018; Masaka, 2019).

Our understanding of *environmental justice* includes concerns for the achievement of justice for humans (an anthropocentric focus) and non-humans, including all living beings and the land and water that supports such life (a biocentric focus) (Schlosberg, 2007). Environmental justice in education responds to the environmental and social impact of climate change and other ecological crises, for example the unprecedented loss of biodiversity in contemporary times. It considers the extent to which education is or can contribute to the survival and flourishing of the natural environment alongside considerations of equality and fairness in how humans experience, benefit from and are held accountable for the natural environment. This might include whether education is contributing to the collective behaviour changes, and political action, that are needed to shift towards a low-emission economy which will bring both environmental and human benefits.

We use the United Nations' definition of *transitional justice* as:

> the full range of processes and mechanisms associated with a society's attempt to come to terms with a legacy of large-scale past abuses, in order to ensure accountability, serve justice and achieve reconciliation … [transitional justice] consists of both judicial and non-judicial processes and mechanisms, including prosecution initiatives, facilitating initiatives in respect of the right to truth, delivering reparations, institutional reforms and national consultations. (United Nations, 2010, p 2)

Within education, this focuses on the material and policy changes as well as the pedagogic and learning processes that are needed to recognize the dignity of individuals and groups, acknowledge past violations and injustices, and repair and redress the causes, effects and legacies of past violations (Zembylas, 2017; Sriprakash et al, 2020; Paulson, 2023; Walker, 2024). It also considers the multiple and complex ways that education contributes to past, current and future (in)justices.

In Chapter 2, we will go into further detail to explain how we bring together the dimensions of justice embedded in distribution, recognition, representation and participation with epistemic, environmental and transitional justice. We show how we integrate dimensions and concepts from across four distinct justices to develop a richer framing for understanding education in the distinct contexts of Nepal, Perú and Uganda.

Overview of the research study

Research aims and focus

'JustEd: Education *as* and *for* education to enable sustainable development' (JustEd, hereafter) was a large mixed methods study of secondary education in Nepal, Perú and Uganda. The central aim of the project was to broaden understandings of how education currently contributes to sustainable development and the implications this has for justice. We traced trajectories from policy to curriculum to classroom practice to learner knowledge, attitudes and intended actions. Our methods included policy and curriculum analysis, interviews with policy makers, classroom observations and teacher interviews, creative methods with learners aged 13–16 years and a large survey with learners. We used social, epistemic, environmental and transitional justice to design our research instruments, and to generate and analyse the data. In this study, we interrogated how:

- notions of justice are embedded in policies, curricula, and pedagogies;
- schools engage learners in the consumption and production of knowledge related to preventing violent conflict (SDG 16), fostering transformative climate action (SDG 13), and reducing inequalities (SDG 10); and

- learners' understandings and experiences of justice, within and outside of school, interact and generate action related to SDGs 10, 13 and 16.

We focused on secondary schooling because this phase of education is the time when young people are expected to engage in more complex learning processes (such as evaluation or evidence-based arguments) and when the topics related to environmental and social challenges tend to be introduced. Policies and agendas for education that address justice objectives for education – notably target 4.7 under SDG 4 (education to enable sustainable development) – are more likely to be addressing this phase of education and to be anticipating that young people will emerge from secondary education equipped and able to go on to generate societal change.

In Uganda, secondary education is split into lower secondary (also known as Ordinary level) for four years and Advanced level, which takes two years (up to age 18). In Nepal, it is for four years from Grades 9 to 12 (up to age 16). In Perú, secondary education includes five grades, and children are expected to conclude it at age 17. We decided to focus on learners aged 13–16 years in all countries because at this point in their schooling learners are engaged in regular learning activities that are grounded in the curriculum. In these years, learners are usually not engrossed in preparing for final examinations and assessments, which places pressures on them both in terms of anxiety and stress, and in a distorted emphasis on specific learning outcomes and curricular content.

Research design

The JustEd study took place from 2020 to 2023 and involved research partners in four countries – Nepal, Perú, Uganda and the United Kingdom (UK) – throughout the duration of the study. The study focused on Nepal, Perú and Uganda, which are distant and distinct countries. They nonetheless share some important characteristics in terms of the need for environmental, epistemic and transitional justice that made them each uniquely interesting as research sites for this study, both as individual studies and for comparison (see Appendix for more background information about each country). While these three countries are struggling with comparable environmental, social and political problems and legacies, they clearly are also different in important ways. Their varying political systems, ideologies and debates, values structures (including, importantly, religious and spiritual traditions), economic status and trajectories, and physical geographies undoubtedly have profound implications for education policies and enactment, and for learners' experiences of justice. While cognizant of these differences, we did not explicitly explore the differential impacts of factors such as those mentioned earlier on the experiences and practices of (in)justice in schooling. They did, nonetheless, emerge in our analysis to some extent, and this is addressed in the country-specific chapters especially. We anticipate that the findings and claims we put forward in this book will resonate with people located in many other contexts and countries around the world, particularly those that share some of the qualities of Nepal, Perú and Uganda. It is our hope that in sharing this work we can contribute to greater awareness, deliberate action and greater justice in schooling in the Global South.

JustEd was designed and delivered in four distinct but overlapping phases: (1) policy analysis; (2) curriculum analysis; (3) experiences of learners and teachers in schools; and (4) learners' intended actions related to the SDGs. Each phase had distinct research questions and research instruments. Here, we outline our approach and methods. More details can be found in Chapter 3, including about the research sites and participants, the precise documents we analysed, what the creative methods were and how they were implemented, and how we analysed all the data. For phase 1 policy analysis, we selected a small number of relevant policies, both education policies and those from other sectors relevant to SDGs 10, 13 and 16. We also conducted semi-structured interviews with a small number of policy actors in Nepal and Perú. We examined the policy documents and interview transcripts using a 'value critical' approach to analyse the values and criteria that are embedded in policies and policy-making practices (Schmidt, 2006; Jessop, 2010).

For phase 2 curriculum analysis, we selected a small number of relevant curricular documents, textbooks and teaching materials for three or four curricular subjects in each country. We chose curricular subjects based on their alignment with SDGs 10, 13 and 16. As JustEd took place during the COVID-19 pandemic, some of the materials were newly developed online teaching resources. We developed a common analysis tool and used it to analyse all the materials.

For phase 3 experiences of learners and teachers in schools, we decided to conduct in-depth qualitative research in four secondary schools in each country (12 schools in total). The schools selected by each country research team had some common characteristics (for example, they all included a large number of learners from lower-income households), but they also differed in some regards. In Perú and Nepal, the schools were located across a wide geography, incorporating rural and peri-urban areas, as well as regions that have had more exposure to environmental harm as well as social conflict. In Uganda, the schools were all located in one region in the north of the country, and participants were more homogenous in terms of their social backgrounds and environmental contexts, including the history of the region's 20 years of war. In Perú and Nepal, all four schools were State schools, whereas in Uganda there were two private and two public schools (although it is important to note this did not substantially alter the demographic composition of the school population, as private schools there are not synonymous with higher-income families).

Across the three countries, we generated in-depth data with 146 learners and 61 teachers and head teachers. Most of the time, we met the same small number of learners through a series of connected encounters which included interviews and focus groups that drew on walking, photography and art creation to generate knowledge, discussion and reflection on experiences of justice and injustice within and beyond schooling. At times, in some places, we met participants online, and a small number of participants engaged with us on only one occasion.

For phase 4 learners' intended actions related to the SDGs, we designed a survey that generated data on knowledge, attitudes and intended actions. Questions on knowledge, attitudes and intended actions were focused on aspirations for SDGs 10, 13 and 16, and incorporated key elements of epistemic, environmental and transitional justice. Some questions were based on scenarios, and these scenarios were tailored to each country context. The surveys were also translated into local languages (such as Nepali or Spanish). In total, 4,142 learners, in three schools in each country, answered the survey.

In line with a sequential mixed methods research design (Chesnut et al, 2018; Bailey-Rodriguez, 2021), data generation for these four phases was consecutive. The data analysis was ongoing, iterative, and accumulative (Srivastava and Hopwood, 2009), with data generated from each additional phase being analysed independently and then together with existing data and previous analyses. Data analyses of the previous phases contributed to the design of research instruments for the research that followed.

Further details about our research methodology can be found in Chapter 3. This includes information about which policies and curricula we analysed, profiles of the schools and areas where we conducted in-depth qualitative research, detailed accounts of the methods we used in each phase, the numbers of people who participated in each method, and how we analysed the data both separately and together.

The research team

The research within each country was led and implemented by their respective country teams, while the entire team worked together to agree the methods for each research question. We – the five authors of the book – co-led and managed the project. Our research collaboration also included discrete and important contributions from 20 further project team members from a range of disciplinary backgrounds and at different stages of their research career. Some had distinct experience of working internationally, for others this was their first professional encounter with researchers from other countries. Within the project, we saw our work as a collective endeavour, recognizing each person's individual contribution.

In alphabetical order – and not including us – these team members were: Tina Aciro, Patricia Ajok, Mrigendra Karki, Daniel Komakech, Gwadabe Kurawa, Silvia Espinal Meza, Dorica Mirembe, Carlos Monge, Ainur Muratkyzy, Alvaro Ordonez, Julia Paulson, María Fernanda Rodríguez, Paola Sarmiento, Sushil Sharma, Robin Shields, Ashik Singh, Ganesh Bahadur Singh, Nese Soysal, Srijana Ranabhat and Alithu Bazan Talavera. All these colleagues contributed to at least one of the project publications, including country profile reports (Balarin, Monge and Sarmiento, 2021; Nuwategeka et al, 2021a; Singh et al, 2021), background papers on each of the justices in education (Balarin, Paudel et al, 2021; Milligan et al, 2021; Nuwategeka et al, 2021b; Paulson et al, 2021), policy and evidence briefs (JustEd, 2023) and a secondary school teacher training guide (Soysal and JustEd, 2023). Most were also involved in at least one published article (Balarin and Milligan, 2024; Balarin and Rodríguez, 2024; Milligan et al, 2024; Nuwategeka et al, 2024; Paudel et al, 2024; Sharma et al, 2024; Shields et al, 2024; Wilder et al, 2024). These collaborative research outputs – including writing teams from within and across the countries – alongside a series of team meetings and reading groups have all been important in the development of our argument in this book. However, when we refer to 'we' in the text, we refer to the five authors who have conceived of and written the book.

Mkwananzi and Cin (2021) write that 'genuinely collaborative spaces require the removal of power injustices ... inclusive spaces, conversational thinking, open engagement, willingness to learn and transforming the hegemony of what is legitimate knowledge'. Put a different way, they are spaces that enable epistemic justice. One way that we aimed – within the project and the writing of this book – to develop such genuinely collaborative spaces was through a non-hierarchical approach to the intellectual leadership of the work. This was done purposefully to challenge the tendency in international research teams for Northern researchers to take on these roles, while Southern researchers take on the role of data collectors (Grieve and Mitchell, 2020). Team members' contributions were defined as much by their disciplinary and methodological expertise as their (still important) country-specific knowledge. We also developed and sought to embed collectively agreed values – kindness, fun, collegiality, creativity, justice, rigour, transparency and respect – throughout the project. This was developed through a collaborative, structured ethical reflection process, drawing on practices from practitioner inquiry and participatory action research (Stevens et al, 2016).

Mkwananzi and Cin (2021) also highlight how the coloniality of research funding priorities and higher education practices – including financial, ethical and due diligence processes – hinder many international collaborations in their attempts to enable equitable partnership working. The most significant of these during the life cycle of the project was the UK government's decision to cut its official development assistance (ODA) with nearly immediate effect, breaking commitments that had already been signed into legal contracts. As a project leadership team, we decided that the best way to minimize the impact of losing around 40 per cent of our 2021/22 budget on individual team members – including some whose income was dependent on their role within the project – was to reduce the length of time of the project from 3 years to 2.5 years.

There is no doubt that the ODA budget cuts together with the COVID-19 pandemic brought significant 'harm' (Nwako et al, 2023) and threatened the collaborative work that we had set out to do. For example, we had to delay all in-person meetings until near the end of the project, which meant a lengthier initial period of developing trust and understanding among the core team members. However, and perhaps ironically, the fluctuating and uneven impact of the COVID-19 pandemic in each of the countries during 2020, 2021 and 2022 also provided some unconventional challenges to typical hierarchies and demanded an accelerated process of trust and delegation. As we discuss in Chapter 3, we had to adapt planned data generation approaches in line with respective waves of COVID-19 and corresponding government restrictions and take the project forward as best we could. Without rigid reporting mechanisms or the need to replicate the same thing in each country, research leads in each country had greater autonomy to contextualize approaches in ways that still brought rich and broadly comparable data.

Structure of the book

In this book, we bring new curiosity to questions of how schooling might equip learners with the skills, knowledge, motivation and agency to take action themselves, and in collaboration with others, in ways that would contribute to a more just world and to the SDGs. We argue that through a greater focus on education *as* justice, there is a stronger likelihood that education *for* justice can be achieved. Our multiple justices approach to education helps to focus greater attention on how learners' school experiences shape their capacities to engage with the world around them and what it means for learners' relationships with their communities and the wider world.

Chapter 2 describes the different conceptualizations of social justice that have underscored global education agendas. We explain our reasons for choosing Fraser's multidimensional framework as a foundation for exploring justice in secondary education and demonstrate how notions of environmental, epistemic and transitional justice can be embedded within that framework to enrich analyses of education and justice. To show the interrelatedness of the four justices in education, we then consider the commonalities in the related literatures about curriculum, pedagogy and the school environment.

Chapter 3 provides a detailed overview of the methodology for the study. We discuss the different phases of the project and the ways this led to the theoretical development of our multiple justices framework. We also include detailed background to each of the countries and their distinct, and similar, experiences of environmental, epistemic and transitional justices.

Chapters 4, 5 and 6 are country-specific chapters (Nepal, Perú and Uganda, respectively) that follow a common format. We guide the reader through our key findings at policy level, through to the curriculum analysis, and then to school and classroom practices. Chapter 7 looks across these country chapters to present our main findings in relation to the conceptualization of education *as* and *for* justice. Here, we also present our multiple justices framework based on redistribution of environmentally and physically safe schooling, recognition of young people's lived experiences of different forms of injustice, and representation of all young people so that they can participate fully in the consumption and production of knowledge(s).

In Chapter 8 we draw our conclusions from the study's findings, situating them within contemporary global calls for transformative education. We raise important questions and make some proposals that should be considered in deliberations about the next international framework for global development cooperation. We particularly highlight the essential role of epistemic justice within education. This is because the consumption, production and use of knowledges are at the heart of educational practice. These are not only subject matter knowledges, but also knowledges about how to relate to each other and to the world around us. We conclude our arguments by showing how education can, thus, aim to enable parity of participation in justice-related processes beyond schooling, including preventing violent conflict, fostering transformative climate action and reducing inequalities.

We – the five authors of the book – are broadly representative of the disciplinary and nationality diversity of the wider project. We are all education scholars who also have distinct expertise in other disciplines, including environmental studies, development studies, policy studies and sociology. We collectively conceived of the book – including its structure and main arguments, some of which have developed beyond the key findings determined within the wider team when the project finished in November 2023. We note here the distinct contribution from Ashik Singh, who was involved in early discussions about the book and its central arguments but due to unforeseen circumstances had to step away from writing. We have each taken responsibility for different sections of the book. We are authors with five different nationalities and working in four countries with different writing conventions and versions of global Englishes. The book is purposefully polyphonic.

2

Interrogating Education through a Multiple Justices Lens

Introduction

This chapter describes and explains our multiple justices approach for exploring education *as* and *for* justice. We are minded of Anderson (2012, p 165), who set out to 'consider what it would be for our social practices of inquiry to operate justly' and we ask: what would it be for our educational practices and policies to operate justly? And what forms of justice are necessary for this to take place?

We are not the first to look across different forms of justice to explore education (for example, Novelli et al, 2017) and global development issues (for example, Mookherjee, 2023). The novelty of our approach is in the ways that we have integrated dimensions and concepts from across four distinct justices to develop a richer framing for understanding education in Nepal, Perú and Uganda. We first provide an overview of dominant approaches to education and justice, particularly in Global South contexts, highlighting some of the key debates and tensions that exist between economic, cultural and political dimensions of social justice. We introduce Fraser's (2009) 3Rs social justice framework and explain how it is the appropriate foundation for bringing in notions of environmental, epistemic and transitional justice into a singular model from which to address justice in and through education. Finally, we explore the parallels between the different justice theories, including through looking at the common arguments from authors drawing on these theories to explore different parts of the education system.

Education and social justice

Distributive models of social justice

Distributive models of social justice promote the idea of fairness, particularly in relation to the distribution of goods within any singular nation state.

According to Rawls (1971), every person has the same claim to equal basic liberties, rights and goods, with justice interpreted as fairness and equality of opportunity. Central to this theory is the difference principle, whereby justice is achieved through appropriate division of social advantages. Inequalities in wealth and social standing are just only if they are of the greatest benefit to the least advantaged individuals in society (Jencks, 2002).

Rawls' texts include minimal mention of education, but he does acknowledge that education is central to the development of young people's sense of justice and offers a route to a fulfilling life (Costa, 2010). Education scholars have drawn on his writing to argue that education can be both a good that needs to be distributed fairly, and one that enables access to other essential goods (see: Brighouse, 2004). This distributive model of justice has often been equated with a narrow conceptualization of education as a good that all learners have the right to access. As Kotzee (2013) explains, questions of justice in and through education have focused on distribution of a finite number of educational opportunities – for example, places at universities – which inevitably gives education to someone while denying it to someone else. Phillips (2004) further argues that the promotion of equality of educational opportunities is not enough without a focus on equality of outcomes and a consideration of the unequal starting points from which children from different backgrounds encounter existing opportunities.

One of the central debates about global education agendas, and their implementation in education systems across the Global South, has been related to the prioritization of educational access over quality (Tikly and Barrett, 2011). The almost exclusive focus on access in Millennium Development Goal 2 – the achievement of primary schooling for all – demonstrated a clear realization of distributive forms of justice. However, such critiques remain in the SDG era, despite the significantly broader scope of SDG 4 and the marked shift towards concerns for quality – albeit understood in narrow ways (Schweisfurth, 2023). For example, writing in relation to refugee children's experiences in England, McIntyre and Abrams (2021, p 29) state that 'there is a need to think about SDG4 in its entirety and move beyond simply focusing on access'.

Unterhalter (2019) identifies and critiques the differences in SDG 4 between the goal itself and how it has been enacted through a detailed and highly specific indicator framework for delivery. This is a helpful illustration of the ways that distributive ideas of justice continue to dominate global discussions of education. She argues that while the goal expresses a 'vision of equity', the framework, by contrast, focuses almost exclusively on distribution. Equity is 'portrayed as some kind of numerical relationship (parity or equivalence), but not an undoing of structural inequalities, such as those associated with charging fees for schooling or challenging racial or gender-based violence' (Unterhalter, 2019, p 49). Inequity is, thus, only understood in terms of how much certain groups have access to different stages of education. This supports McCowan's (2010) earlier arguments that universal rights to education need to be reframed in broader and richer terms. He suggests that the vagueness of how the right is conceptualized means that it is unclear if achieving rights to education means 'access to educational institutions, to a particular form of educational experience, or to some educational effect' (McCowan, 2010, p 62). The outcome is that access is often prioritized over questions of educational process and experience.

These arguments mirror many of the critiques of distributive justice by Young (1990), Honneth (1992, 1995; Fraser and Honneth, 2003) and Fraser (1995, 2009; Fraser and Honneth, 2003). They argue that understanding justice solely in terms of the fair distribution of resources lacks engagement with the injustices involved in the processes that create maldistribution. They, instead, centre considerations of recognition in a richer understanding of social justice. However, as we will see in the next section, these authors' conceptualizations of recognition hold some distinct differences.

Beyond redistribution: recognition

Young (1990) theorized the earliest, and highly influential, critique of the overemphasis on economic distribution as justice. Young (1990) argues for a refocus on the recognition of different social groups and the institutional constraints that prevent the redress of structural inequalities. It is a powerful case for attending to the variety of conditions that lead to maldistribution and widens understanding of justice to include a broad range of social and cultural factors. Here, Young (1990) particularly focused on (at least) five faces of oppression – exploitation, marginalization, powerlessness, cultural imperialism and violence. These interrelated faces are commonly obscured in distributive justice. Gewirtz (1998, p 482) helpfully offers some key questions that can be asked of education policies to analyse education's relationship to these five faces of oppression. How far do policies support, interrupt or subvert:

> Exploitative relationships (capitalist, patriarchal, racist, heterosexist, disablist, etc.) within and beyond educational institutions? Processes of marginalization and inclusion within and beyond the education system? … Practices of cultural imperialism? … Violent practices within and beyond the education system?

The writing of education scholars such as Freire (2013) and hooks (1994) further show the essential role of pedagogy for disrupting oppression. We discuss these further later in this chapter.

An alternative interpretation of recognition is put forward by Honneth (1992, 1995) who takes a more individual and psychological perspective. Honneth (1995) argues that recognition can be understood in terms of the necessary mutual recognition needed to enable self-realization and dignity for all individuals. He considers three spheres of recognition – self-confidence, self-respect and self-esteem – alongside the social conditions that could enable all individuals to live a life of dignity and self-realization. As Mookherjee (2023, p 21) explains, this is not only about self-interest, but rather it suggests 'that the dignity and esteem of others, even potentially of distant others, are vital for affirming one's own'.

Young's focus on group-based inequalities has been critiqued for limiting understandings of individual differences (for example, Wilson-Strydom, 2015). By contrast, Honneth's conceptualization has been critiqued for focusing too much on individual experiences and failing to look at the status-based processes of misrecognition (Fraser and Honneth, 2003). Both critiques are important and point to the necessity of considering individual experiences, particularly of injustice, alongside the broader structural transformations needed to address individual and group-based inequalities of opportunity and outcomes. Within education, a focus on the former may be more important in analysing classroom practice where individual interactions may be silenced with consequences for dignity and self-worth. However, the latter is essential in the analysis of educational policies and global agendas. The need to look across these levels is something we return to in our discussion of epistemic justice.

Despite their differing foci, the commonality between Young (1990) and Honneth (1992, 1995) is that recognition is the foundation of social justice. Fraser (1995), by contrast, argues that injustices and inequalities cannot be understood solely in terms of misrecognition. There is little doubt that in global education agendas and national policies, there has been an increasing focus on matters of cultural recognition alongside economic redistribution. We see, for example, the recognition dimension of justice in the ways that learning environments and materials are encouraged to be inclusive of diverse cultures, ethnicities, abilities and gender identities. Keddie (2020), writing about the Australian education system, explains that there is a dual emphasis on redistribution and recognition reflecting concerns for the inequalities in educational outcomes experienced by groups of learners, especially based on racialized difference.

However, it is important to note that in SDG 4, and in line with Unterhalter's (2019) arguments cited earlier, groups of children more likely to experience inequality in educational access, experiences and outcomes are only explicitly named in a target in distributional terms. This is SDG 4.5: *By 2030, eliminate gender disparities in education and ensure equal access to all levels of education and vocational training for the vulnerable, including persons with disabilities, Indigenous peoples, and children in vulnerable situations.* Recognitional considerations are mentioned in broader terms in the rather all-encompassing SDG 4.7, which includes 'appreciation of cultural diversity'. This shallow conceptualization of recognition is a long way from Young's (1990) notions of resisting different forms of oppression.

Beyond redistribution: the contribution of capabilities

Another significant critique of Rawls comes from Sen (1992), who argued that theories of justice need to shift from a focus on resources (what people have and the public goods they can access) to outcomes (what people are able to do with the resources they have). Sen (1992, 1999) suggests replacing the notion of primary goods with capabilities. The freedom of individuals depends on their capabilities to lead the kind of lives they have reason to value. In this framework, education receives special emphasis as both an input to and an outcome of development. However, Sen's work is noticeably silent on questions of what constitutes justice in education and how education relates to justice in society more widely.

While Sen (1999) places the focus on each individual's values, Nussbaum (2000) instead argues that a list of central human capabilities is needed as an analogue of primary goods in Rawls' terms. Nussbaum (2003, p 35) further argues that Sen's conceptualization of capabilities does not take us very far in thinking about social justice because 'they give us no sense of what a minimum level of capability for a just society might be'. Nussbaum (2000, 2011) has refined a list of ten 'central capabilities' which she contends are the bare minimum for the requirements of a 'dignified life'. These relate to life, bodily health, bodily integrity, senses and imagination, emotion, practical reason, affiliation, relationship to other species, play, and control over one's environment. While this list of capabilities is not a theory of social justice per se, it does offer a useful set of principles that may define a just society. However, the use of a strict list of capabilities – however flexibly – has been widely critiqued by Capabilities Approach theorists who deem it to be fundamentally inconsistent with the notion of prioritizing the values of each individual (Robeyns, 2017).

One particularly helpful aspect of the Capabilities Approach for critiquing distributive forms of justice within education is that of conversion factors (Sen, 1992; Walker, 2016). These relate to the differences in how individuals can make use of resources in their lives. Wilson-Strydom (2015) gives a very helpful example of two South African university learners who are from equally poor homes and similar schooling backgrounds, and with a similar student loan. Student A lives on campus and has a part-time job. Student B needs to take two taxis to travel home and has caring responsibilities that prevent her from additional work and bring additional costs. As

Wilson-Strydom (2015, p 146, emphasis added) explains, 'despite the fact that learners A and B both have a place at university, and have access to the same financial resource – an equivalent loan – student A is more able to *convert this resource* into successful university study than student B'. This example clearly shows how a focus solely on distribution for education purposes can mask important aspects of inequalities.

The Capabilities Approach has been widely used as an analytical framework for understanding justice and wellbeing concerns. This is particularly evident within education, where there have been a plethora of studies utilizing this approach to explore issues related to inequalities and wellbeing in countries across the Global South (see, among many others: Walker and Unterhalter, 2007; Tikly, 2019; DeJaeghere, 2020; Adamson, 2021). This is because it offers 'a compelling and assertive counterweight to dominant neoliberal human capital interpretations of education as only for economic productivity and employment and asks instead about what education enables us to do and to be' (Walker, 2006, p 164). This is through considerations of the intrinsic value of education, broadening the contribution of education in solely economic terms.

While Capabilities Approach scholars offer compelling critiques of a sole focus on distribution in theories of justice, there are also facets of recognition that are absent in their analyses. Mookherjee (2023, p 4) pertinently suggest that there are limitations in viewing the harms of poverty solely in terms of the 'lack of positive freedom', and not also 'in terms of the experiences of denigration and social suffering which arise from structural inequalities, issues which have been more central to recognition theories'. There are also clear tensions between this approach – which centres on individuals and their values, freedoms and dignity – and recognitional approaches that converge around group-based inequalities.

This approach also brings in another consideration for social justice – the role of public deliberation. This could be, for example, public debate on schooling and what capabilities are most centrally important within formal education. Robeyns (2005) offers some helpful principles for such public deliberations, including the ways that they are contextualized and how a balance is achieved between short-term priorities and longer-term aspirational goals. Representation and voice in public deliberations is also a central tenet of Fraser's (2009) trivalent model of social justice – alongside recognition and redistribution – and it is to this that we now turn.

Redistribution, recognition and representation as the foundational blocks for exploring education *as* and *for* justice

So far in this chapter we have discussed some of the key theories of social justice and shown how they have separately attended to different dimensions of justice, including in economic, political and cultural terms. We have identified some of the shortcomings in each of these theories, particularly the limitations that come with *focusing* on one dimension of justice (redistribution vs recognition concerns), or one unit of analysis (individual vs group-based analyses). Considerations of education and justice in Global South countries like Nepal, Perú and Uganda necessitates looking across these dimensions and unit of analysis. We see these dimensions as essential and interrelated foundational blocks for a holistic understanding of education *as* and *for* justice. Before turning to how environmental, epistemic and transitional justice concerns build on these foundational blocks, we first explain how Fraser's (2009) trivalent model of social justice is the most appropriate underlying framework.

Social justice is 'more than about *what material resources* people have, more than the question of the *what, when, and how* of resources, but [also] about *how persons are being treated*' (Pilapil, 2020, p 38, emphasis added), and how individuals and groups can participate in decisions that affect their lives. Fraser's (2009) writing explains these aspects of social justice through her three key dimensions of redistribution, recognition and representation. These three tenets are all necessary correctives for existing injustices. Redistribution is the economic element whereby resources are redistributed more fairly between both individuals and particular groups who have been economically marginalized and disempowered. The second dimension is cultural recognition, particularly within institutions that shape societal perceptions, of which education is a clear example. Representation, which was added later, is the political dimension and refers to the importance of inclusion in decision-making. Fraser's theory has developed through intellectual arguments with both Young (Fraser, 1995) and Honneth (Fraser and Honneth, 2003) and articulates the importance of looking at both individual and group-based injustices, shifting the focus onto the analysis of social conditions.

One important aspect of Fraser's theorizing of social justice is that the different dimensions are interdependent. For example, Fraser (2009) discusses how economic marginalization and status-based inequalities undermine an individual's capacity to participate equally with others in society. Keddie (2020, p 48) persuasively argues that it is this multidimensionality that means it provides 'a productive lens for thinking about and addressing some of the key ways in which different dimensions of injustice are currently hindering the schooling participation, engagement, and outcomes of marginalized learners'.

Regarding redistribution, Fraser is clear that socio-economic injustices are not only about the lack of material resources but also how this is explained within capitalist economic and political regimes. When first writing in 1995, she highlighted how maldistribution was associated with exploitation, economic marginalization and deprivation (Fraser, 1995). This has important implications for how scholars draw on Fraser's work for exploring educational issues. They focus not only on a shallow understanding of distribution in terms of access, but rather the range of provisions that are needed to enable all children to progress through a safe and high-quality education as a way counter their experiences of marginalization or deprivation (Tedesco, 2010; Vincent, 2020).

To understand status-based inequalities, there is also a central role for looking at misrecognition of maligned groups and their attributes, values and practices (and we would add knowledges). In education, misrecognition has often only been seen in terms of what is included in the curriculum, or considerations of how to redress educational underachievement of marginalized groups (Ndofirepi and Gwaravanda, 2018; Keddie, 2020). When thinking in Fraser's terms, recognition must also account for historical and contemporary power struggles. Leibowitz and Bozalek (2015, p 113) helpfully suggest some status-based inequalities that can be recognized in everyday educational practices. These include the degrading of learners' prior knowledge so that the 'values and attributes of certain other groups are backgrounded and rendered invisible in the curriculum'. However, they further argue for the need to incorporate some pedagogical theory to fully explore such issues in educational contexts. This is an argument that Leibowitz (2008) had previously taken up in also proposing the importance of looking at how agency and structure interact in classroom contexts. This brings in Freire's notion of the pedagogy of possibility to conceptualize a model for social justice education.

Representation, although added later, is a core tenet of Fraser's theory. Musara et al (2021), as part of their discussion of the relevance of Fraser's model for understanding educational inclusion in South Africa, highlight the important contribution of Fraser's critique of misrepresentation in both national and global decision-making. They discuss how multilateral organizations drive educational agendas with very limited involvement of teachers or parents (and we would add learners), who are ultimately the main stakeholders of that education. Musara et al (2021, p 47) conclude that for 'justice to prevail in these circumstances there is a need for all parties to find constructive ways to decide the extent to which different stakeholders like parents and communities can have a voice in the debates and decision-making about education'. The importance of the third dimension of representation for exploring education in the Global South is also demonstrated by Tikly and Barrett (2011). They bring together Fraser and Sen's Capabilities Approach to develop a framework for exploring educational quality. They particularly highlight the importance of including a wide range of stakeholders in deciding on educational quality. This is so that it is contextualized as an education system that provides beneficiaries with educational experiences and outcomes that they have reason to value.

Fraser (2009) argues that social justice can be achieved through these three dimensions, articulated as participatory parity: the ability of all individuals to participate in social life as peers with equal moral worth. She writes that to enable parity of participation, we need to dismantle 'institutionalized obstacles that prevent some people from participating on a par with others, as full partners in social interaction' (Fraser, 2009, p 16). We have found this a particularly helpful concept for considerations of education *as* justice. This is in terms of seeing education as one of these institutionalized sites of unequal participation, as well as a site where participation beyond schooling is shaped. We also find it useful for thinking about education *for* justice and the ways that injustices within education lead to a lack of parity in contributions to a range of justice outcomes. For example, young people may not have the skills and confidence to participate in such decision-making processes.

Through the 3Rs, Fraser's theorization of social justice provides a normative framework that is a helpful starting point for considering some of the practical ways that education systems can enable participatory parity within and beyond education. Examples include the redistribution of material resources, recognition in how individuals and groups are treated, and authentic representation in school and classroom decision-making. In the following section, we discuss each of the three justices – environmental, epistemic and transitional – that we suggest can enrich this social justice approach to exploring the multifaceted nature of education *as* and *for* justice. We demonstrate how we build on and extend the 3Rs with concepts from environmental, epistemic and transitional justice. We also show how the underlying principle of finding balance between focusing on individual interactions and broader structural transformations is essential to understanding justice in education.

The suitability of the 3Rs framework can be seen in the many education scholars that have used it (see Vincent, 2020), and in its flexibility in the ways that it has been used in conjunction with other theories of justice to explain educational issues (Tikly and Barrett, 2011). It is also a critical theory, rooted ideologically in feminism and anti-capitalism. Most importantly, we took inspiration from other scholars who have used it as a foundational framework – the building blocks – for adding other conceptualizations of justice (see: Schlosberg, 2007; Novelli et al, 2017).

However, our use of it in this foundational sense does carry some caveats – the most important being that it is a theory developed by an American scholar to understand the justice concerns of Western, liberal democracies. We developed our understanding of education *as* and *for* justice over four years, as part of ongoing team meetings between the authors of this book as well as with 12 other team members, through shared analysis sessions and a reading group. Discussions also continued between the five authors of the book and in the collaborative writing teams of other outputs. This included long discussions about whether to include additional dimensions or enrich the existing 3Rs. We also debated the relevance of using a Western scholar's work as a foundation for understanding education in three Global South countries, and the potential ways that this could perpetuate epistemic inequalities, since education takes place in different contexts. However, a consistent conclusion from these many discussions was a belief in some fundamental tenets of education and justice that apply across different contexts. We anchor our arguments on those.

Bringing other justices into a social justice approach

In Chapter 1 we introduced the three justices that we focused on in the research project that is the basis for this book. In this section, we discuss each of these justices and the ways that we understand them as related elements of the 3Rs framework discussed earlier.

Epistemic justice and social justice

Meredith (2024) usefully identifies two main strands to conceptualizations around epistemic injustice, both of which hold significance for considering a broader idea of justice in education. The first focuses on individual interactions and draws primarily on Fricker's (2007, p 44) epistemic injustice as being the processes in which one is 'wronged in one's capacity as a knower'. By contrast, Fricker (2015, p 6) argues that epistemic justice is when all can 'contribute to the pool of shared epistemic materials – materials for knowledge, understanding, and very often for practical deliberation' – a vision that can be articulated in imaginings of a just education system. The second of Meredith's (2024) strands is a broader critique of the injustices inflicted on whole traditions of knowledges. Here, Ndlovu-Gatsheni (2021, p 160) critically reminds us that 'it is not correct to credit Miranda Fricker's work ... as the pioneering work on the subject of epistemic injustice', and references the work of Ake (1979), wa Thiong'o (1986), Smith (1999) and Goody (2006) as exemplary texts that have dealt with knowledge-related injustices. There is also a significant contribution from Latin American scholars, such as Quijano's (2010) powerful argument about the coloniality of knowledge (see also: Walsh, 2009; Mignolo, 2011), as well as Spivak's (1988) earlier conceptualization of epistemic violence. All these authors remind us of the major and persistent structural form of epistemic injustice that was embedded in the global colonial regime. They also significantly show that these injustices still permeate geopolitical relations and internal societal structures in many countries through the dominance of certain forms of thinking, being and languaging. Epistemic injustice cannot therefore be separated from recognitional justice issues of marginalization, oppression and exclusion, nor from the broader structural and historical processes that cause them.

It is important to note that this understanding of epistemic injustice marks a departure from Fricker's writing, which has been critiqued for failing to account for the 'material conditions fuelling epistemic injustice' (Walker, 2020, p 275). Anderson (2012) offers a helpful contribution through the conceptualization of the epistemic virtue of institutions. Institutions – such as schools – are discussed as sites not only of unjust interactions but also work to reaffirm epistemic injustices in society. Anderson (2012, p 169) concludes that through differential access to markers of credibility, 'an original structural injustice – denial of fair opportunities for education – generates additional structural inequalities in opportunities for exercising full epistemic agency, which is an injustice to the speakers'. Put differently, maldistribution of educational opportunities affects the potential for epistemic justice in and through education.

In the language-in-education literature, there are several scholars who have argued for the potential to bring understandings of social and epistemic (in)justice together to theorize the impact of learning in an unfamiliar language, such as English, on different groups of children. Milligan (2022) identifies a series of questions that can be used to analyse the multiple injustices of English medium education policies at the global, national and school levels, pointing to the role of epistemic justice in achieving justice in distributive and recognitional ways. These include how far materials are fairly distributed to support learning in English medium classrooms, how non-dominant languages are (not) recognized in ways that could support children's learning, what values and knowledges are privileged in English medium curriculum and policy, and how English is deemed a marker of credibility. Phyak and Sah (2022) draw on empirical research in English medium schools in Nepal to analyse what they call the 'epistemic nature of social injustice' for minoritized learners and their parents. They particularly focus on the 'misframing' (Fraser, 2009) of non-English-speaking parents – the boundary-setting process by which certain groups of people are excluded from decision-making activities. This literature is important for demonstrating how multiple justices can be used together to provide a richer analysis of one aspect of education, which also points to the importance of considering injustices related to knowledges and languages across Fraser's 3Rs.

When we look at our definition of epistemic justice within education as *equality in the consumption, recognition and production of knowledges*, we see further overlaps with the 3Rs. We find this helpful for exploring the ways that education is a space that can be built upon such a definition of equality (what we consider to be education *as* justice). It can also be used to consider also in terms of the outcomes of education and how young people can access such equality throughout their lives (the role of education *for* justice).

Firstly, there is a distributional element to the ways that children can access education – whereby they can fully participate in meaning-making activities – and physical materials through which they can consume curricular knowledge, such as textbooks and workbooks, in which different groups' knowledges and languages are recognized. There is also a very clear epistemic misrecognition in educational systems through the positioning of knowledges as alternative or inferior (Medina, 2018). We invoke Fraser's richer understanding of recognition here and suggest that epistemic justice in education is not just limited to the recognition of multiple forms of knowledge or what Keet (2014, p 27) calls 'simplified arguments on knowledge inclusivity', but that it applies to how knowledge is accessed and taught. This has clear implications for how school curricula and materials are designed. It also implies rethinking pedagogies to 'ensure that the knowledge passed on to learners attends to the need for them to awaken their own destiny in life' (Masaka, 2019, p 299). This suggests the vital role of genuine epistemic inclusivity if education can support young people to consume and produce knowledges that enable representation in decision-making and meaning-making processes both within and beyond education. This goes beyond simply participating in class, since speaking does not automatically lead to epistemic justice. For example, their contribution may only be a repetition of what the teacher has said, or their words may be dismissed.

By bringing in a focus on epistemic justice into Fraser's 3Rs framework, we are better able to understand the ways that young people's capabilities to contribute, access knowledge and understand how knowledge works are necessary conditions for parity of participation. Education and schools are key institutions in which young people can develop such capabilities. For this to occur, schools need a clear focus and commitment to just epistemic practices.

Environmental justice and social justice

Our understanding of environmental justice includes concerns for the achievement of justice for humans (an anthropocentric focus) and non-humans, including all living beings and the land and water that supports such life (a biocentric focus). Biocentric conceptualizations of environmental justice focus on human relationality with the non-human world and in doing so recognize the rights of all living matter to survive and flourish (Borràs, 2016). They present 'a persuasive challenge to the ideas of human exceptionalism and nature as a utility for human development' (Wilder et al, 2024, p 4).

Distributional notions of justice are embedded in an anthropocentric focus because it is about equality and fairness in how humans experience, benefit from and are held accountable for the natural environment (Horsthemke, 2009). The concept of climate justice further draws attention to the disproportionate impacts of climate change particularly on lower-income populations in the Global South resulting from a combination of historic social and economic inequalities (Sultana, 2021). In terms of education, there is clear maldistribution in the ways that school closures due to climate change unevenly impact around 40 million children and young people whose schooling is disrupted due to climate-related emergencies, including severe heatwaves and flooding. The vast majority of these students live in the countries – and rural regions – most affected by climate disasters (Prentice et al, 2024). There are also distinct recognitional elements to considerations of climate justice. This is because the aims of such an approach are 'to reduce marginalization, exploitation, and oppression, and enhance equity and justice ... [and to understand] who benefits, who loses out, in what ways, where, and why' (Sultana, 2021, pp 118–119).

Education can help to redress resultant injustices through recognition of the human impact of climate change processes and through pedagogies that support young people to be able to be involved in decision-making processes that may be able to address the injustices. There are also clear links between the expectations of education for transformation between environmental and social justice approaches. Mbembe (2021) contends that transformations of what he calls a 'new planetary consciousness' are not possible without addressing the similar dangers of degradation of the biosphere and racism. Sultana (2021, p 119) further argues for the importance of critical climate justice that incorporates an emphasis on intersectional analyses and 'resisting extractive exploitation of natural resources, confronting racial capitalism and Indigenous erasure'. We see a significant role for education as a space where such learning for such resistance can happen, with positive outcomes for social and environmental justice.

Our deliberate use of environmental justice – to include both human and non-human considerations – is also inspired by the writing of Schlosberg (2007), who develops a framework for environmental justice based on Fraser's 3Rs and capabilities. Schlosberg argues that environmental justice has primarily been conceptualized in terms of maldistribution and suggests instead a framing that accounts for broader, and intersected, ideas of social justice. Crucially, he argues that there has been too much emphasis on humans within notions of environmental (in)justice. Instead, he frames justice as the combination of distribution, recognition, capability and participation in both human and non-human domains. His use of participation, rather than representation in Fraser's terms, highlights what he sees as participation by everyone, and not just representation in official decision-making and justice bodies. Schlosberg (2007) further acknowledges the influence of climate and social movements for this more holistic understanding of environmental justice, arguing that movements work on multiple branches of justice every day and at any one time, and that this plurality adds richness to their work.

We note how Tikly (2019, p 27) has also drawn on Schlosberg's writing to develop his own definition of education for sustainable development as 'socially and environmentally just education that facilitates the capabilities of existing and future generations and of natural systems to flourish'. However, the influence of Schlosberg's framework has been quite limited in the wider educational research. Notwithstanding, we see the emphasis on multiple and intersecting dimensions of justice to be very helpful for analysing environmental policy, curricula and pedagogies.

Transitional justice and social justice

While we have shown that epistemic and environmental (in)justices can be seen in everyday social interactions and structural processes, transitional justice differs in that it is usually seen as 'exceptional' – something that is needed in response to conflict and as part of post-conflict reconciliation and reconstruction (Destrooper and Gissel, 2023). This includes processes such as prosecutions, truth-telling, memorialization and localized processes of justice and repair. However, economic, cultural and political aspects of social justice are also important to these processes. For example, there is often more emphasis on transitional justice through education in redistributive terms. These are often interventions that focus almost exclusively on getting children into schools after periods of conflict and/or putting measures in place so children can access safe school environments (Bellino et al, 2017). At the policy level, education has often been seen as a tool for transitional justice, particularly in relation to cultural recognition claims. Transitional justice bodies repeatedly call for curriculum revision or reform and in certain cases this has happened, with curricula that acknowledges victims of conflict and includes human rights and citizenship content (Paulson and Bellino, 2017). Davies (2017) identifies the latter in terms of recognition, with victims of conflict explicitly being recognized as citizens and rights-bearers. This has implications for the incorporation of rights and citizenship within educational curricula and supporting young people to know the ways that, as citizens, they have rights to protection by law. This highlights a tension between how transitional justice may demand recognition for particular groups and a schooling system that may have only focused on access for such groups, and not on the teaching and learning processes that may be needed to enable a full sense of recognition. We thus see how shallow notions of both redistribution and recognition can lead to schooling in post-conflict societies retaining and reinforcing legacies of inequality and exclusion.

If we turn to the 3rd R, we also see distinct lack of representation in decision-making transitional processes. Here, it is important to understand the ways that educational policies can also reflect the silences in formal transitional justice processes, such as truth commissions (Paulson and Bellino, 2017).

We discuss later how education scholars have frequently shown how testimonies are often silent and/or silenced in classrooms.

Novelli et al (2017, 2019), based on research in Myanmar, Pakistan, South Africa and Uganda, bring a 4th R of reconciliation into a framework for education and peacebuilding analysis in conflict settings. Reconciliation is understood as a related but distinct part of the framework, with a focus on addressing historic and contemporary injustices and the analysis of how services contribute to social cohesion, public discussion and debate about the past and its relevance for the present and future. Like our work, they were particularly inspired by Fraser's commitment to transformations and argue that 'the transformative role education can play [is] inherently connected to and embedded in processes of social justice and societal transformation' (Novelli et al, 2019, p 71). They also helpfully highlight the critical way that politics is at play in the interconnections among the 4Rs (Novelli et al, 2017). This focus on the political economy of how educational policies is developed and enacted is of relevance for the three contexts that we discuss in this book.

The 4Rs is a powerful framework for considerations of social justice and pathways to 'positive peace' (Galtung, 1969). Pherali (2021, p 723), when using it to analyse education in Thailand, argues that it is helpful to expose injustices in education. However, he also argues that it does not help to offer 'solutions about how to enable change in contexts where authoritarian regimes monopolize power and resources; hegemonic cultural groups dominate discourses about national identity; elite political class resists representation of marginalized communities in educational decision-making; and the terms of reconciliation are hijacked by those who control power'. Similarly, Hajir (2023, p 438) critiques the framework, particularly in its basis in Western critical thinking, including Fraser, in that 'the current mode of thinking in Education for Peacebuilding can only have practical political currency in contexts where "democracy" and "liberalism" – two main pillars of proper governance according to liberal theory – are in place'. Furthermore, we also suggest that the framework may also be particularly well suited to contexts where a primary focus on peacebuilding is required. However, it certainly served as a source of inspiration – alongside Schlosberg (2007) – for how Fraser's 3Rs can be a foundation for a more holistic understanding of education *as* and *for* justice.

There is a further salient contribution from refugee education scholars who have argued for the importance of the affective and relational aspects of social justice. Miri (2024) develops a rich framework for analysing refugee educational experiences in the UK, arguing for a different 4th R. He argues that the 4th R could be the relational affect, which he maps as the missing emotional dimension in Fraser's 3Rs framework. This supports the earlier writing of Lynch (2012), who argues for considerations of feminist notions of care, love and belonging if parity of participation in public spaces is to be realized. It also echoes some of the elements of Honneth's (1995) focus on love and care as necessary components for recognition.

This focus on relationality and care can also be seen in the ideas of reparative education discussed in the next section. There is no doubt that added attention to relationality and repair are particularly important in contexts of historical and ongoing violence – such as the three countries that are the focus of this book – and could merit their own distinct category. However, rather than seeing these issues as a 4th – and so distinctive – R, we see them as concepts that cut across issues of redistribution, recognition and representation. We have drawn some inspiration here from McIntyre and Abrams (2021), who blend an 'operational' model with a 'moral framing', based on Fraser, to explore refugee education in the UK. The operational components come from Kohli's (2011) three necessary foci for 'the resumption of ordinary life': safety, a sense of belonging and success. For each of these to be achieved, McIntyre and Abrams (2021) argue that appropriate distribution of resources, recognition of cultural values and representation of different voices are needed. This focus on dignity in relational and reparative approaches is one way to enhance our understanding of recognition. Through this focus, we can also extend reparative processes beyond the specific realm of transitional justice to a broader conceptualization of the role of education in helping to repair multiple past and present injustices in young people's lives.

Intersections across the justices

The complexity and scale of the global challenges that young people face now and in their futures demands a reimagining of education on the grounds of a richer and more holistic understanding of justice. By looking across the justices we have discussed in this chapter, and at multiple parts of the education system, we can imagine an education system that has the potential to be transformative. This is in the place of the current trend for primarily affirmative responses to education problems, usually rooted in shallow notions of redistribution and recognition. As Fraser (in Hrubec, 2004, p 6) explains, a transformative approach 'aims to correct unjust outcomes precisely by re-structuring the underlying generative framework'. In an education system, there are multiple components to such a framework, and in this section we focus on three key areas of educational design and practice: curricula, pedagogies and the school environment. We explore the common themes related to these areas in turn from across the literature related to education and each of the justices. We suggest that transforming education on justice grounds could enable the sorts of social transformations that education is often charged with fulfilling.

Before turning to the areas of curricula, pedagogies and the school environment, we first note that the understandings and enactments of education that are discussed are not static and need to be contextualized and temporal – including tracking between the past, present and futures. The notions of transformations and reparations are important here – and both are central to UNESCO's new social contract for education (UNESCO, 2022). Although the ideas of transformative learning are certainly not new (Dewey, 1938; Mezirow, 1991), here we understand transformations particularly in the ways that education is both a space for learning about the causes of injustices and for shaping collective, shared futures. Walker (2024) further equates the 'reparative turn' (Táíwò, 2022; Sriprakash, 2023), with the calls in UNESCO's new social contract for renewal. She reflects that she likes the concept of repair 'for how it acknowledges past harms as various national Truth Commissions have sought to do while looking to futures' (Walker, 2024, p 8). This call for education for reparative futures echoes Davies' (2017) description of the 'dual gaze' of education as a space which looks back, through teaching the past, and forward, by shaping young people who will build towards their futures. The emphasis on multiple futures – purposively used by Silova et al (2020), Sriprakash et al (2020) and others – is also important for epistemic justice in what Mignolo (2011, p 275) describes as 'an open horizon of pluriversality'. Through the acknowledgement of pluriversal accounts of the past and visions for the futures, a reparative and just education system may become possible.

Curricula

Curricula and textbooks play an essential role in the education policy–practice nexus and so are an important site for analysing how education is enacted (Prøitz et al, 2023). A dominant critique of environmental education curricular content is that it typically does not engage sufficiently with political, economic and democratic interests in environmental damage and protection. This is particularly in relation to the local, regional and global practices and systems that contribute to climate and environmental crises (Reid, 2019; Singh, 2021). Glackin and King (2020), in their analysis of the environmental education policy in the UK, usefully frame this dominant approach to teaching and learning as *about* the environment, rather than *for* the environment. Eaton and Day (2019, p 458) provide an interesting conceptualization in their term 'petro-pedagogy'. They write that in Saskatchewan, Canada, pedagogical practices and teacher resources promote 'neoliberal environmentalism centred on individual actions that insulate fossil fuel industries from criticism and attempt to dissuade young people from questioning or understanding the role of corporate power in the climate crisis'.

This lack of emphasis on politics and power can also be seen in educational research about difficult histories. Much of this has focused on textbook analysis, highlighting the challenges in coming to agreements on particular historical narratives – and the injustices in what is omitted, obscured and misrepresented in the final agreed texts (Bentrovato et al, 2016). This leads to classroom practice where often 'the historicity, sources, and consequences of … dominant assumptions and arguments are underexplored' (Phyak, 2021, p 226). The collection of analyses in Vanner et al (2022) demonstrate the ways that it is not only in the teaching of difficult histories that textbooks reaffirm a dominant and sanitized narrative. These examples show how, across the humanities and social studies, there are only cursory nods to ideas of social change, and more often they reinforce dominant and 'neutral' perspectives on rights and citizenship. This mirrors the many textbook analyses that show how social inequalities are often reproduced and reinforced in the images and words used in textbook content (Durrani, 2008; Chisholm, 2018).

Gandolfi (2022, p 12) argues for a curriculum grounded in (environmental) justice which 'involves thinking about consequences, not only from a purely scientific or local viewpoint – or even in relation to future generations – but also from the socioeconomic, political, and historical perspectives of communities severely impacted by environmental issues for centuries'. Other authors have also persuasively critiqued the overemphasis on teaching about individual actions to 'save the planet' (Macintyre et al, 2020). These authors rather argue for the need to contextualize any actions within broader understandings of whose actions are most likely to bring about transformative change, and how existing actions unfairly impact some groups over others. This resonates with the arguments made by Rodríguez-Gómez et al (2016) in relation to how violence is portrayed in social sciences textbooks in Colombia and South Africa. The authors demonstrate that textbook content about violence – and peace – focuses on individual interactions without exploring the structural dimensions that shape and perpetuate violence in the two post-conflict contexts.

Sriprakash et al (2020) further suggest an expansion of the types of historical practices and sources used in education to include recording of life histories, public testimonies, performances of song and dance and visual sources. Such multilingual and multimodal ways of remembering and sharing memories of past and ongoing injustices point to a potential way to rupture the epistemic injustices and silencing that have often accompanied history education about conflict. Their argument is also relevant to considerations of environmental justice, and the types of experiential and material learning that can deepen learners' understandings of human and non-human relations.

The critique of a dominant narrative – and calls for a multiplicity of knowledges – in the curriculum are also seen in the growing body of literature that argues for the importance of Indigenous knowledge systems for understanding the sustainable (and peaceful) relationship between humans, non-humans and the land they share (Manyike and Shava, 2018; Odora Hoppers, 2021). Huaman (2017), for example, powerfully shows how such environmental knowledge is contextualized in the land and the peoples that live there, including the accumulation of such knowledges over time and through intergenerational learning. However, it is also clear that these knowledges have been persistently erased and rendered absent from formal school curricula in many different contexts (Masaka, 2019; Kezabu, 2022). This is another clear example of epistemic injustice whereby some worldviews are marginalized, perpetuating relationships of domination (Silova et al, 2020; Odora Hoppers, 2021). What we take from this literature is that genuine recognition of multiple knowledges is not just an issue for content on justice-related topics – such as environmental degradation or cultural diversity. Rather, it needs to be embedded across curricula so that multiple ways of knowing – alongside learning how to handle and reconcile such knowledges – are everyday occurrences in young people's learning.

Pedagogies

As we discussed earlier in this chapter, there can be a tendency for shallow enactment of social justice in the pursuit of educational goals, whereby issues of process and practice are sidelined in favour of a focus on that which can be easily measured, such as inputs and outputs (Schweisfurth, 2023). However, looking across the literature concerned with the multiple justices, a common thread is the essential role given to pedagogy to enact justice in and through classroom practice. For example, Cole (2007) argues that if education about difficult pasts can contribute to peace and coexistence, pedagogy and teacher training is more important than any curriculum review or new textbook.

Our understanding of pedagogy is aligned with authors who argue that pedagogy is not only 'what' is taught but also must include the 'how' of teaching and learning (Alexander, 2008). As Walker (2024, p 12) explains, pedagogy is 'not a thinned-out version of teaching methods, but rather relational, values-based processes which include who is teaching, how they teach, who is being taught, what is being taught, and the contextual conditions'. This understanding of pedagogy – as situated and relational – is also extended to critical pedagogy, based on ideas of justice and freedom (hooks, 1994), and thus a foundational and transversal approach across the justices. We agree with Giroux (1983), who asserts that education is always a political act, with formal schooling often reproducing oppression and marginalization; and that, in turn, critical pedagogy is needed to support learners' understanding of the causes of such injustices through engaging with critical texts and their world experiences. This aligns closely with Freire's (2013, p 17) notion of 'conscientization' – which is widely used in social justice education — whereby young people can learn 'to perceive social, political, and economic contradictions, and to take action against the oppressive elements of reality'.

These notions of critical pedagogy have been extensively used in critical approaches to environmental education, in different forms of ecopedagogy (Kahn, 2010), ecojustice education (Lupinacci and Happel-Parkins, 2016) and critical pedagogy of place (Gruenewald, 2003). These approaches highlight the intersection of the effects of structural oppressions on environmental degradation and the unfair impacts on human populations, while supporting young people to think and act critically in response to these injustices. As Cachelin and Nicolosi (2022, p 494) argue in the context of their undergraduate learners in the US, this means 'thinking critically about systems of oppression ... because it can challenge individual-level responses while igniting an investment in collective action and social change'. Recent authors have also argued for an emphasis on epistemic justice through the inclusion of Indigenous knowledges within a critical pedagogy of place approach to environmental education. This, they argue, is important because they can enhance learners' ability to connect with their local realities (Mbah et al, 2021; Ajaps and Forh Mbah, 2022) and support reflection on human–non-human relationships (Kopnina, 2020). However, we also note the concerns raised by Barrett et al (2025) that such engagement with place-based knowledge systems is dependent on language policies that allow place-based languages into the formal education space.

For Gruenewald (2003, p 9), a critical pedagogy of place aims to '(a) identify, recover, and create material spaces and places that teach us how to live well in our total environments ... and (b) identify and change ways of thinking that injure and exploit other people and places'. Gruenewald (2003, p 9) further conceptualizes 'reinhabitation', that is, 'learning to live well socially and ecologically in places that have been disrupted and injured'. There are clear links here to the literature on reparative pedagogies. Sriprakash et al (2020, p 9) describe education for reparative futures as an approach 'that fosters processes of reparative remembering; questioning received narratives and supporting histories that 'revindicate' the lifeways of the oppressed'. Reparative strategies include addressing learners' histories, memories, and past and present experiences of violence (Zembylas, 2017) while attending to dignity, truth-telling, multiplicity of truths and responsibility (Paulson, 2023). This literature has been developed with a focus on contexts with recent histories of violence and experiences of transitioning to peace. However, we would argue that given increasing socio-economic inequalities and levels of violence (as we discuss later), such pedagogies are necessary for all young people. This is because they can support learners to walk through the past, present and future and repair the memories or experiences needed to guide what sort of action they can take for the future.

Another clear thread across the justices literature is the role of pedagogies for developing critical thinking and supporting young people to critique and evaluate the knowledges that they are presented with in classrooms. We find Lai's (2011) definition of critical thinking as particularly helpful as Lai (2011) shows it is not only the ability to analyse arguments and knowledge claims, but also to make inferences using inductive or deductive reasoning to evaluate and make decisions and solve problems. Wals and Jickling (2002) argue that critical thinking is particularly important within environmental education. This is because it support learners to examine the relationships between human/non-human environments, societal power relations, and the causes and effects of everyday problems, alongside supporting learners to consider solutions. Wals (2019) and Lotz-Sisitka et al (2015) further place critical thinking as a principal component in transformative pedagogies (see Table 2.1). Lotz-Sisitka et al (2017, p 897) suggest that these can support the transgression of existing norms or the 'embedded practices which need to be reframed and changed in order for sustainability to emerge'. Pedagogies for critical thinking are also about developing skills to look at different knowledge claims. As Robertson (2013, p 306) writes, 'few educational issues are more urgent than teaching learners what sources of information to trust and why... understanding structural injustice and how it can affect education, the media, and knowledge production in scholarly communities is not only a matter of education for social justice but is also epistemologically central'.

Phyak (2021, p 219), writing from the context of Nepal, argues convincingly for the importance of 'building educational practices upon the lived experiences of the people, particularly Indigenous and

Table 2.1: Different pedagogies and their core characteristics

Transformative and transgressive pedagogy (Lotz-Sisitka et al, 2015; Wals, 2019)	Reparative pedagogy (Zembylas, 2017; Sriprakash et al, 2020; Paulson, 2023; Walker, 2024)	Critical pedagogy of place (Ajaps and Forh Mbah, 2022; Gruenewald, 2003)
Action-oriented	Healing (looking to the past) and anticipatory (looking to the future)	Leading to learners' actions for environmental conservation
Political and disruptive of the norm	Developing understanding of responsibility and truth(s)	Seeking to develop 'conscientization'
Critical, through questioning and dialogue	Recognizing and building multiple perspectives and knowledges	Critical, through challenging assumptions
Relational, ethical and caring	Based in dignity and empathy	Rooted in – and responsive to – the place where the learning occurs

ethnic minorities ... [which] could help us resist the destruction of languages, epistemologies, and linguistic/epistemic self-determination of communities'. Kalungwizi et al (2018), through a case study of tree planting in a Tanzanian teacher college, have highlighted the potential for such experiential learning to lead to positive actions related to environmental sustainability. This is just one example of how learners could be encouraged to bring their own experiences, testimonies and epistemic contributions.

The school environment

Central to the arguments we take forward in this book is the notion that for education to achieve the just outcomes expected of it, we need to focus much more on the ways that schools are sites of multiple and intersecting (in)justices. At a distributional level, this can be seen in the inequalities in terms of access to teachers, learning materials and water, sanitation and hygiene (WASH) facilities. It can also clearly be seen in the significant impact of environmental degradation and climate change on children's wellbeing and education.

Paulson et al (2020, p 431) also argue for the importance of viewing schools as sites of memory production. By reviewing a range of relevant educational research studies, the authors conclude that this research 'highlights the complex, multi-scalar and dynamic processes and relationships involved in teaching and learning'. This supports Sobe's (2014, p 313) assertion that schools are sites 'of contestation, negotiation, and cultural production', rather than simply sites where pre-agreed and sanitized narratives are transmitted. While these arguments are made primarily in the context of teaching difficult histories, we think the conclusions can be made more broadly to the ways that educational and social practices in classrooms – and wider school spaces – play a crucial role in the ways that knowledges are consumed and produced.

Violence and discrimination play a significant role in many young people's everyday school experiences, with implications for their wellbeing, participation in learning processes and the outcomes they can achieve from that schooling. Devries et al (2022) show that there are millions of children in the Global South who experience physical, sexual and emotional violence every year, with much of this violence happening in and around schools. Studies have consistently shown how these episodes of violence – particularly related to corporal punishment and gender-based violence – and discrimination are commonplace, part of the everyday experience of attending school (Vally et al, 1999; Parkes et al, 2016; Ssenyonga et al, 2022). This is determined by what Floresta (2021), in the context of post-conflict Philippines, describes as a culture of violence in schools. Recent studies in South Africa (Ngidi and Moletsane, 2023) and Uganda (Parkes et al, 2023) highlight the significant levels of gender-based violence in schools while also noting that shame and silence often mean that such instances of violence evade broader conceptualizations of young people's experiences of schooling. Given this prevalence of violence, we argue that transitional justice in education cannot only be about learning about looking back to histories of injustices and violence but needs to also consider the ways that violence, in all its forms, continues in the present and future(s). The prevalence of violence is also one of multiple ways that schooling can mirror and reproduce the inequalities and injustices – such as those related to precarity and gendered and racialized norms – found in the contexts where the schools are situated (Hoadley, 2017; Unterhalter, 2021).

While there is significant direct violence in schools, we also consider the injustices here of broader forms of violence. Paulson and Tikly (2023, p 771) define violence as 'any act of power, whether directly or via systemic and cultural forms, that results in physical, psychological, emotional, environmental, or spiritual harm and that has the effect of limiting the capabilities (opportunity freedoms) available to individuals, groups, other species and natural systems'. This broadened form of violence reminds us of the importance of reflecting on violence in both epistemic and environmental terms. For example, the previous discussions about the erasure of non-Western worldviews from curricula can be understood as a form of epistemic violence (Spivak, 1988) whereby postcolonial education systems exercise violence in the consumption, recognition and production of knowledges.

A final key point in relation to the ways that schools can be sites of (in)justice is also to recognize the important role of non-school sites of learning in the justice project. Environmental and social justice movements have long been the foundation of justice 'work', and we see these gaining momentum among youth in various parts of the world (Sultana, 2021). The global school climate strikes and student protests in relation to Israel's occupation of Palestinian land are just two examples of young people taking action to advocate for alternative, transformed futures. While not shadowing the complexities of learning in such spaces, the approach of these movements, grounded in hope and action, offers a glimpse of a different way that justice-oriented learning can happen. Here, justice is conceivable through young people's experiences, demands and actions, and in the process young people are not only making themselves visible as knowers, but they are also showing that they can become epistemic leaders.

Conclusions

In this chapter, we have shown how there are multiple intersections across environmental, epistemic, social and transitional justices within, and through, education. While there are clear distinctions between the justices (and often in how the justices are defined), we believe that the resonances warrant bringing them together into a single, integrated framing of education *as* and *for* justice. We believe that this enriches our understanding of (in)justice in education and can be a useful tool to analyse the ways that education can enable more just futures. As Schlosberg (2007, p 40) argues, 'claims for justice can, and must, be integrated into a thorough, comprehensive, and pluralist political understanding of the term'.

In exploring how education can contribute to 'thick justice', Walker (2019, p 169) writes, 'educational institutions should undertake hopeful if not perfect work, equipping learners with subject and professional knowledge and a range of public reasoning abilities that will enable them to participate fully and meaningfully in education, work and in making a democratic society'. Such hopeful and justice-oriented work may appear idealistic – UNESCO's transformative agenda has certainly been critiqued for being such (Klees, 2022; Elfert and Ydesen, 2023). However, the evidence, particularly from the environmental education literature, shows us that pedagogies of hope are vital for developing learners' self-efficacy and agency (Baldwin et al, 2023; Finnegan, 2023).

While we wish to end the chapter with this message of hopefulness, we also note some of the challenges that we need to be mindful of in the pursuit of a just education. These are:

- translating acknowledgement into validation of alternative narratives in pedagogic practice;
- how education can be both a site of memory, reparation and building towards more positive futures and a space where hegemonic values are taught that can fuel injustice and violence;
- the suitability of experiential and learner-centred models of education, especially in resource-poor settings; and
- the requirements for transformations of education systems in the current political economy of education.

These are challenges that are also clearly seen in the contexts of Nepal, Perú and Uganda – and it is to these contexts that we now turn.

3

Methodological Strategies to Investigate Education and Justice

This chapter provides an overview and justification of the research design that we undertook within and across the three countries in our study. This sequential, qualitative-quantitative mixed methods design was chosen since it 'allows for a variety of approaches to the process, recognizing the complexity of education policy problems' (Chesnut et al, 2018, p 308). We define our approach as qualitatively driven mixed methods, where the qualitative research develops core concepts and the quantitative is used to generate a broader evidence base for the qualitative research findings (Mason, 2006; Bailey-Rodriguez, 2021). It is an approach to mixed methods most commonly used when the research is multidimensional and the questions are exploratory.

Our analysis took place within Nepal, Perú and Uganda and was also comparative across the three countries. The country-specific analysis and reporting – presented in this book in the following three chapters – took the form of a sequential mixed methods case study of each country's responses to justice and education. There was also a comparative element at each phase of the design whereby we used common methods of data generation and analysis. We took inspiration here from the horizontal comparison aspects of Bartlett and Vavrus' (2017) comparative case study approach, paying attention to contextual differences as we responded to common questions and made key interpretations across the three countries.

The design was co-developed by the five authors of this book and other JustEd team members, with the aim of answering five distinct research questions:

1. What forms of justice are embedded in secondary school education policies and decision-making processes?
2. What forms of justice are embedded in secondary school curricula and textbooks?
3. To what extent do young people's lived experiences of secondary education reflect and embed these forms of justice?

4. How are learners' intended actions in respect to SDGs 13 and 16 mediated by their knowledge of, attitudes to and experiences of different forms of justice in education?
5. What are the key components of a multiple justices analytical framework that could be used to examine the relationship between education and justice?

The first three questions were qualitative, drawing on a range of critical and creative approaches as discussed in this chapter. The analysis from these stages informed the development of a survey to answer the fourth question before a final stage where data integration and analysis led to the development of the theoretical framework presented in Chapter 7. The methods were also chosen to support methodological triangulation of core concepts, particularly through survey questions developed to explain or confirm key themes generated through the qualitative stages. This chapter starts with a description of the research sites before providing an overview of each of the stages of the research design towards our theoretical development.

The research sites

Country overviews

Despite their significant economic, political and geographical differences, Nepal, Perú and Uganda share some important characteristics in terms of their histories and contemporary experiences of the different forms of justice (see Appendix for more details of each country). The countries are all multilingual and multicultural as well as being geographically diverse. They are also all prominently affected by the global climate crisis and environmental degradation, in both ecological terms and in the impacts on human development and inequalities. In northern Nepal, for example, many communities experience regular landslides that have devastating impacts on homes and ecologies, and there is often flooding in the southern part of the country (Vaidya et al, 2019). In Uganda, many rural and disadvantaged communities rely on burning trees for charcoal despite widespread recognition of the erosion and other negative impacts this has on the natural environment (Branch and Martiniello, 2018). There is also extensive wetland reclamation for subsistence agriculture. In Perú, the Amazonian rainforest, a key resource in both local and global climate regulation, is being harmed through legal and illegal logging, mining and agriculture; tropical glaciers are rapidly melting, affecting the country's water supply; air, water and land pollution are rife, affecting the population's health; and climate change is increasing the recurrence of the El Niño phenomenon, leading to both rains and droughts that affect people's livelihoods and the country's food supply.

Nepal, Perú and Uganda all have relatively recent histories of conflict that have inflicted immense human, cultural and political losses. The Internal Armed Conflict in Perú between insurgent groups like Sendero Luminoso and the army from 1980 to 2000 resulted in thousands of documented deaths as well as disappearances of people (CVR, 2010; Uccelli et al, 2017). Twenty years of war in northern Uganda between the government and the Lord's Resistance Army (LRA) forced people to evacuate some areas, and many farmers are still fighting to reclaim lands (Akello, 2019). From 1996 to 2006, Nepalese people experienced violent conflict between the Maoist Communist Party and the Nepal government (Selim, 2018). In all three countries, there is a need for affected communities, families and children to reflect and learn about these large-scale conflicts in reparative and helpful ways, but currently education does not prioritize learning of this nature.

These three countries are, thus, interesting case studies for exploring how different forms of justice are embedded in secondary education and are contexts where a justice orientation may be particularly important. There are also some significant differences between the countries. For example, from a purely economic perspective, Perú is still considered a middle-income country, and there is a substantial proportion of the population who can opt out of the type of schooling we consider in this book and attend private schools. By contrast, Nepal and Uganda are both low-income countries dependent on external aid agencies and face fundamental issues in relation to basic requirements for education, such as having enough teachers. The findings from across the countries, thus, offer a range of experiences about how countries have responded to the broader global agendas of quality, equity and justice in education.

Districts profiles

In Nepal, we researched in the districts of Rasuwa, Lalitpur and Mahottari, taking account of geographical diversity and different territorial realities (mountain, hills and Terai regions, respectively). These districts are also known for different cultural practices, linguistic and cultural diversity, urban and rural locations, and the impacts of the Maoist insurgency and the Terai movement (Paudel et al, 2024).

Rasuwa district, in the Himalayan region of Bagmati Province, borders the Tibet Autonomous Region of China to the north. The district is ethnically diverse. The 2021 census identified 26 ethnic/caste groups and 16 mother tongue–speaking groups, with Tamang speakers constituting 69 per cent of the district's total population. The district is characterized by the Himalayas and remote landscapes, biodiversity and lakes. The district is affected by the ten-year-long Maoist insurgency and faces the problem of rapid migration from the district. The district was one of the most affected by the earthquake in 2015; it is also at high risk for natural disasters including floods, glacier lake outburst floods and landslides.

Lalitpur district is one of the three districts in the Kathmandu Valley, Bagmati Province. It features numerous water bodies, including rivers, streams and ponds. The district is ethnically diverse, with 107 identified ethnic groups and 79 mother tongue–speaking groups. Newa is the main ethnic group in the district, speaking Newari language as their mother tongue, but there are also significant numbers of migrated populations belonging to different ethnic/caste groups. Due to rapid urbanization, the area is facing various environmental and social challenges, including water, air and noise pollution; water scarcity; lack of free space; environmental degradation regarding migration to the district; increase in crime; and violence.

The Mahottari district of Madhesh Province contains a blending of fertile flat land into rising hills with a diverse ecology. The district is impacted by increased deforestation A decline in forest-based income is disproportionally impacting forest-dependent households, low-income families and Indigenous peoples in the locality. The region is impacted both by a decade-long Maoist insurgency and the Madhesh movement, a political movement that erupted in 2007 in Terai, Nepal's southern plain.

In Perú we worked in schools in Ayacucho, Ucayali and Lima. Ayacucho is in the southern-central part of the country, in the Andean region, and was at the centre of Perú's recent Internal Armed Conflict. Today, the struggles for the collective memory of this period coexist with the stories and perspectives of old and new generations. In addition, Ayacucho is a socio-cultural and ethnically diverse region, with three dominant languages: Quechua, Spanish and Asháninka. Rural areas of Ayacucho have been contaminated by mines and gas extraction, and urban areas are affected by river pollution and poor waste management, which have caused environmental degradation and social conflict. Ucayali is the second largest region in the Peruvian Amazon, located in the central-eastern area of the country. It is a region rich in natural resources in terms of forest and rivers, but it faces significant challenges in terms of environmental exploitation and degradation. Ucayali is among the most ethnically and linguistically diverse regions of the country, and it has high rates of violence and social disorder due to both organized crime linked to illegal activities (drug trade, mining, logging) and cultural conflict.

The capital of Perú – Lima – is located on the central coast. The city has been fundamentally shaped by the inflow of large numbers of internal migrants, a trend that began in the 1950s but accelerated during and after the Internal Armed Conflict. Migrants have established informal and fragmented settlements around the city, giving rise to peripheral neighbourhoods, commonly known as 'asentamientos humanos' (human settlements). Over time, some of the older settlements have become major districts with some of the largest populations in the city. These districts share common characteristics: they are made up of families with different socio-cultural, ethnic and linguistic backgrounds; they have high levels of poverty and totally or partially lack essential services (for instance, electricity, water, schools, sanitation); they face various environmental challenges (for example, air pollution, lack of water, environmental degradation); and they occupy a prominent place in crime and street insecurity. These peripheral urban sites are quite different from those chosen in Ayacucho and Ucayali, providing possibilities for other or even unique expressions of epistemic, transitional and environmental injustices. The Lima localities included in this research are *San Juan de Lurigancho*, one of the oldest, largest and most culturally diverse peripheral districts, and *Huaycán,* one of the poorest districts dominated by Andean, Quechua-speaking migrants. They are both highly polluted, and Huaycán is also vulnerable to landslides.

In Uganda we conducted research in the districts of Amuru, Gulu and Kitgum in the northern part of the country. We chose to focus just on this region – rather than a broader geographical area as in Perú and Nepal – because it is a particularly pertinent case study for each of the justices in focus. The COVID-19 pandemic also restricted movement during the study. The insecurity in the region is partly responsible for the relatively high poverty level in the area, which stands at 64 per cent, significantly higher than the national average of 20 per cent (Uganda Bureau of Statistics, 2022). Notably, the sub-region of Acholi land stands out for two main reasons. On the one hand, it is the most under-developed part of Uganda and remains extremely vulnerable to shocks (security, environmental, political, transitional justice/traditional justice, health) (Nuwategeka et al, 2021a). On the other hand, there is a serious issue of land conflict within the Acholi community and the Madi community, as well as ongoing deforestation for charcoal production (Branch, 2018; Branch and Martiniello, 2018).

Kitgum, Gulu and Amuru are broadly homogenous (inhabited primarily by Acholi people). The districts were at the epicentre of a two-decade-long civil war of LRA rebels which led to a massive movement of people into internally displaced people's camps. However, the districts have different environmental challenges. Amuru is experiencing deforestation for charcoal production, while Kitgum is experiencing conflict over environmental resources between Sudanese refugees and the local host communities. The refugee-hosting communities feel the refugees are enjoying a disproportionately larger allocation of cultivable land to the disadvantage of the locals. This has led to land wrangles between the two groups.

Critical policy analysis

Our critical policy analysis explored how far justice was embedded in secondary school education policies and decision-making processes. It also provided the context that helped us understand what was enacted and what was absent in curricula and schooling practice. The analysis focused on explicit government statements of policy and frameworks related to education or to any of the three justices. We were interested in analysing policies because they represent what governments perceive as 'problems', and how they understand causal pathways and relevant actors both in the creating and solving of these problems (Bacchi and Goodwin, 2016). We conducted a 'value critical policy analysis' which sought to identify the discourses and goals of a given policy (Schmidt, 2006). This approach assumes that policies are based on and help to solidify specific narratives about social problems, and that 'all narratives are selective, appropriate some arguments, and combine them in specific ways... we must consider what goes unstated or silent, repressed or suppressed in specific discourses' (Jessop, 2010, p 347).

We followed Schmidt's (2006) step-by-step articulation for applying a value critical approach. This incorporated four methods: identifying and selecting policies, describing the context, describing the policy and policy area, and critically analysing the values reflected and embedded in the data. We also considered the content, discourse, context and actors that were involved in the elaboration of each policy. We complemented the analysis of policy texts with in-depth interviews with key stakeholders. These interviews helped us understand the processes, struggles and compromises that were made during the formulation of different policies. In our critical analysis, we specifically sought to determine the extent to which the policies had incorporated a justice focus and, if so, if they conceived of this in terms of redistribution, recognition and/or representation; we also examined the consistency of the arguments through which the policies were framed and how the policies distributed responsibilities for proposed changes among individuals, communities, commercial markets, or State jurisdictions and authorities (at different levels).

Analysis of curricular documents and textbooks

One of JustEd's core objectives was to shed insight on the extent to which educational policies for generating social change were in fact delivering on these aspirations, so we sought to trace the trajectory from policy to curricula to pedagogy to learner experience to learner outcomes and intended actions. As such, we selected curricular documents not only on the basis of their content related to environmental, epistemic and transitional justice, but also according to how closely they were aligned with and were designed to advance the objectives set out in the policies we analysed. We wanted to know how or if the design of the curricular documents was oriented around achieving the policy objectives.

To aid the comparability of curricula, pedagogies and classroom experiences, we decided to focus on the stages in education for young people aged 14–16 years. We selected these age groups with the knowledge that these learners would not be preparing for any high-stakes assessments, and therefore there would be fewer barriers to engaging them in the participatory methods (for research question three), but also that at these ages they would have the maturity and capacity to critically engage with diverse notions of justice.

To select the materials for analysis, researchers in all three countries did a broad scan of curricular frameworks and subject areas to ascertain which ones should be included in the analysis and where the most relevant curricular content was located. Country research teams identified up to three priority subjects for each of the three justices for the analysis of curricular materials. The COVID-19 pandemic resulted in diverse combinations and fragmented models of education provision, including in-person and online models. This was particularly the case for Perú. As a result, in Perú we decided to include a range of curricular materials that were newly developed and implemented specifically for the distance learning strategy that was set in place during the pandemic. In each country chapter, we give the full list of curricular frameworks, textbooks and other teaching and learning materials that were included in our analysis. To sample the textbooks and learning materials, we searched the texts using the keywords given in Table 3.1. The second step consisted in revising selected texts and identifying key sections that were relevant to our analysis. Selected excerpts were organized into a database where we categorized the material according to its relevance for the different justices and included details of sources.

Table 3.1: Search terms to sample the textbooks and other materials

Epistemic justice	Transitional justice	Environmental justice
Human rights	Conflict	Climate change
Gender	Genocide/mass violence	Environmental conservation
Language of instruction	National history	Environmental degradation
Indigenous peoples	Global/regional history	(Un)sustainable
Minority groups	Peace	farming practices
Cultural diversity	Religion/religious diversity	Natural resources
Intercultural education	Ethics	Global warming
Race/racism/ethnicity	Memorials and museums	Development/
Citizenship	Local/community histories	international development
Learning to live together	Conflict resolution	Climate crisis
Social and emotional learning	Terrorism	
	Violence crisis	
	Historical problems/processes	

In line with our approach to analyse policies, we considered curricular documents as political and philosophical statements: the narratives used throughout them define the policy 'problems', solutions and relevant actors, and illustrate what has value and what does not (Bacchi and Goodwin, 2016). This led us to conduct a critical content analysis to help us to explore how far each topic was approached through a justice lens. This approach is inspired by critical discourse analysis (CDA) but does not include the fine-grained and linguistic analysis that defines CDA (Fairclough, 2013).

In our work, to understand whether a justice approach was taken, we broadly asked: what are the problems and what solutions are offered? Who are the protagonists? What are the main discourses that are present in the text? What overarching frameworks are used to problematize the issues (for example, human rights)? We then asked specific questions depending on the justice in question. For example, in relation to epistemic justice, we analysed the ways that particular minority groups were portrayed in textbooks. Here, we asked whether the text included content about rights or inequalities and how far it addressed disparities in relation to this minority group (for instance, health, education, employment, land ownership). We critically analysed how the minority group was presented; for example, whether they were blamed for their inequalities or if structural aspects were considered, or whether they were presented as valued members of society. How far the group's knowledges, stories and languages were included was also analysed.

Data generation and analysis on learners' experiences of justice in and outside of school

With the results of the policy and curricular analysis in mind, we then set out to explore how learners' experiences of schooling and classroom practice reflected the ways that justice was conceived at the national level. In this section, we outline our methods, the sampling strategy for selecting the research sites and the research participants, our ethical approach, and an account of our data analysis methods.

Data generation methods

We designed, piloted and implemented a series of qualitative methods to generate insights about how learners learn about justice-related issues in school, their experiences in and outside of classrooms, and how/if their schooling is related to everyday experiences of (in)justice outside of school. We wanted to prioritize learners' own subjective accounts, but we also recognized the value and unique perspectives that teachers and head teachers could contribute (Bradbury-Jones et al, 2018). Teachers and head teachers could share insights on the enactment of policies and curricula, considering their understanding of objectives, their intentions, how they approach different topics, their observations on how learners engaged with their teaching and the materials, and circumstances beyond their control that inhibit education about the three justices. Finally, we wanted to incorporate methods that would enable us to be third-party observers and form our own views of what was happening in schools. These aims are complex, and accordingly the methods we designed incorporate diverse perspectives and are multi-layered.

The COVID-19 pandemic necessitated some adaptations from the original research design within countries, so the methods differed to some extent within each country. Nonetheless, these methods generated a substantial body of data within each country and furnished rich textual and visual accounts of learners' experiences of the three justices in and outside of their schools, with reference to past, current and anticipated events and action.

In each country, we developed a range of qualitative methods to explore both learners' and teachers' perspectives and experiences of justice in education. We provide more details of the specific methods that we developed and adapted in the country chapters. Here, we give a brief overview of these methods. In researching young people's everyday experiences of justice in and outside of schools, we designed a series of connected, participatory and creative encounters that aimed to engage a small number of learners in each school (6–8 learners in total) around the concepts of epistemic, environmental and transitional justice. This combination of mixed methods was chosen since they can generate new ways of exploring and understanding social phenomena (Mason, 2006). The use of these methods was also appropriate given the range, complexity and emotionality of the themes we were discussing with young people. As Bagnoli (2009, p 549) writes, creative methods can be used 'to enhance participants' reflexivity and to gather a holistic picture of the topics under investigation that could also take into account their different needs and expressive styles'. This mirrors our own previous experiences of doing arts-based and creative methods with young people (Balarin, 2011; Balarin et al, 2017; Alcázar et al, 2020; Milligan et al, 2023), where we have found that interviews in which young people can reflect on their produced work can support them to elaborate further around research topics. A carefully designed sequence enabled participants to move from general to more specific topics and deepen their thoughts and understanding of different issues both individually and collectively.

The choice of creative methods was also reflective of our project's values and ethics. As discussed in Chapter 1, two of the values that underpinned our work were fun and creativity. These were particularly important given the significant impact of school closures and COVID-19 lockdowns on the young people involved in the study. There is also a distinctly ethical dimension to using creative methods given our concern for epistemic justice and wanting to reduce power differentials between participants and researchers, as well as between children and adults (Bagnoli, 2009). The methods were designed with the hope that they would be enriching to participants, generating opportunities to learn rather than simply assuming an 'extractive' approach to getting information (Smith, 1999).

Apart from a small level of attrition, we had the same number of young people participating in each of the research activities. These included:

- walking interviews around the school grounds that focused on young people's experiences of environmental justice in and outside of school (Bartlett et al, 2023);
- semi-structured interviews based on object elicitation (Kahlke et al, 2024), where learners were invited to select from a range of images and objects that were considered to have connections with transitional and social justice, and then to speak about it and what it meant for them;
- photo/image-voice (Wang, 2006; Anderson et al, 2023; Azzarito, 2023), where young people were invited to create their own drawings, comics or photographs about environmental, epistemic or transitional justice following an initial conversation about this topic, and then to bring their image back to the group to present and discuss it;
- community mapping to learn about the different contexts and learners' local experiences of (in)justice (Amsden and VanWynsberghe, 2005);
- 'letter from the future' exercise to help participants reflect on justice-related elements of their current lives and identify potential areas for change (Balarin, 2011);
- focus group discussions with small groups of learners about their understandings and experiences of all three forms of justice.

We also designed methods to analyse how the topics identified in the curriculum analysis were taught in practice. We explored how justice elements in the written curriculum are taught, how learners respond to this content, what pedagogical approaches are used to teach about justice and how teachers interact with learners (Smit and Onwuegbuzie, 2018). This was through classroom observations and teacher interviews in Nepal; teacher interviews, focus groups and reconstructed lesson plans in Perú; and teacher interviews and focus groups in Uganda. We were particularly interested in including a focus on learners' experiences, something which is often marginalized in traditional observation schedules (Mitchell and Milligan, 2023).

We developed a template for both the classroom observation and reconstructed lesson plans so that the data collected were comparable and consistent. The teachers that were observed or took part in semi-structured interviews were purposively selected: they were the teachers for the school years and subject areas of the curricular materials we had analysed. The interviews and focus groups were conducted either in person, in the school setting itself or online using a mainstream video-call platform. The interviews and focus groups were conducted in the local language, audio-recorded and transcribed, and subsequently analysed (see later in this chapter an account of the data analysis).

In each of the country chapters, we outline the specific methods that were used. The choice of methods was very much dictated by the impact of the school closures and COVID-19-related requirements. This particularly impacted our work in the schools in Uganda, where these requirements meant we were only able to spend a very limited amount of time in schools and with individuals. We were restricted from conducting multiple encounters with teachers or more than two with young people. In this case, we instead conducted semi-structured interviews with a broader sample of young people on topics across the three justices. Without classroom observations or lesson reconstruction plans, we are more constrained in the conclusions that we can draw about pedagogy in Uganda. Table 3.2 lays

Table 3.2: Qualitative methods used in each country

	Interviews with teachers and head teachers	**Classroom observations or lesson reconstruction plans**	**Interviews and focus group discussions incorporating creative methods with learners**
Nepal	15 teachers 4 head teachers	62 classroom observations	24 learners took part in 4 encounters: • Walking interviews in nature • Community mapping • Object- and image-driven focus group discussions • Life journey storytelling through drawing ('River of Life')
Perú	17 teachers participated in 2 individual encounters and 8 group discussion 14 interviews with headteachers and local key stakeholders	18 lesson reconstruction plans in lieu of classroom observations	21 learners took part in 4 encounters: • 2 individual encounters using photovoice • 2 group encounters using community mapping and 'letter from the future exercise'
Uganda	4 interviews with head teachers 20 interviews with classroom teachers	No classroom observations or lesson reconstructions were developed due to COVID-19 restrictions	32 learners took part in 2 encounters: • interviews • focus group research activities, including object-based conversation and community mapping A further 98 learners took part in short interviews

out the methods that were employed in each country and the number of distinct research events.

Sampling

Our strategy was to conduct qualitative research in four non-elite schools in each country that reflected the mainstream educational landscape of the country. Table 3.3 includes a range of socio-cultural, geographic and administrative data about the schools that were included in the study. Further details about the geographical locations and communities of selected schools are given in the previous section. We collectively established criteria for selection of schools so that they would be broadly representative of the schools in each selected region. We then purposively sampled the four schools in each country. In Nepal, we sampled schools in Rasuwa (one school), Lalitpur (one school) and Mahottari (two schools). In Mahottari, we sampled one school in a rural area deep within the Madhesh region near the India border and one school in an urban area marked with mixed communities of Madheshi and Hill peoples celebrating different culture and rituals. In Perú, we sampled four schools from Ayacucho (one school), Ucayali (one school) and Lima City (two schools). In Uganda, we selected schools in two districts – Amuru and Kitgum, both in the northern part of the country. The districts were also chosen for practical reasons because they are around 100 kilometres apart, which ensures the same teachers do not teach in the different schools (there is a practice in Uganda where one teacher may be employed to teach in several schools). These districts were purposively selected because they have a blend of both rural and urban secondary schools. The Ugandan team also selected two low-cost private schools because of the high prevalence of these schools providing secondary education for non-elite learners in the area.

Data analysis

Our research teams conducted iterative thematic analysis (Srivastava and Hopwood, 2009) of the data using NVivo. This process began with an initial coding structure developed on the basis of ideas that emerged from the previous stages of the research, as well as from those that emerged from our fieldwork notes and discussions. It was refined throughout the coding process to include more analytics and theoretical ideas. We double-coded selections of interview material within each country to ensure triangulation and the alignment of coding criteria. We also held regular team meetings, both within and between countries, to update each other and exchange ideas about the developing patterns of ideas that emerged from the material.

METHODOLOGICAL STRATEGIES TO INVESTIGATE EDUCATION AND JUSTICE

Table 3.3: Research sites for qualitative data generation

Location	Languages spoken in the community	Language of instruction	Sector	Location
Nepal				
Rasuwa	Tamang, Nepali, Ghale, Tibetan and others	Nepali	Public	Rural
Mahottari	Maithili, Magahi, Urdu, Nepali and others	Nepali	Public	Rural
Mahottari	Maithili, Magahi, Urdu, Nepali and others	Nepali	Public	Urban
Lalitpur	Nepali, Newari, Tamang, Maithili and others	Nepali	Public	Urban
Perú				
Ayacucho	Spanish, Quechua	Spanish	Public	Peri-urban
Ucayali	Spanish	Spanish	Public	Urban
Lima – San Juan de Lurigancho	Spanish	Spanish	Public	Peri-urban
Lima – Huaycán	Spanish	Spanish	Public	Peri-urban
Uganda				
Amuru	Luo	English	State	Rural
Amuru	Luo	English	Low-cost private	Urban
Kitgum	Luo	English	State	Urban
Kitgum	Luo	English	Low-cost private	Rural

The comparative qualitative data analysis was also supported by data immersion by the UK-based researchers. We read and re-read the English-language analyses produced by each country team, through verbal online presentations and conversations as well as through text. Some of the data were translated into English and these were also read, but a substantial proportion of the data was not translated due to resource constraints. Through reading and listening, the UK-based researchers wrote their observations and reflections, noting similarities as well as discordances, stand-alone findings, surprises and outliers. We particularly attended to the requirements of horizontal comparison to seek to understand 'how historical and contemporary processes have differentially influenced different "cases", which might be defined as people, groups of people, sites, institutions, social movements, partnerships' (Bartlett and Vavrus, 2017, p 53). The comparative data analyses were written and shared with the country research teams and offered starting points for group dialogues that represented the first stage of our collective comparative data analysis. These dialogues took place largely online through a series of 'South–South' meetings, led by team members from Nepal, Perú and Uganda. Comparative analysis was also a key feature of the only in-person team meeting we were able to organize including representatives from all four countries, in September 2022 in Bath, UK.

By the end of the data analysis, we had a list of core concepts. These were primarily those that were common across the three countries, albeit that they were presented in different ways. There were also some important concepts that were included that were particularly prevalent in one or two of the contexts, and these were included to represent the strength of these data.

Survey design, data collection and analysis

A questionnaire survey method was used to investigate how learners' intended actions in respect to SDGs 13 and 16 are mediated by their knowledge of, attitudes to and experiences of different forms of justice in education. In line with a sequential mixed methods design, we drew on the emerging findings of the qualitative stages to build and develop the survey instrument (Creswell and Plano Clark, 2018). This allowed us to evaluate the prevalence of certain key concepts identified across the qualitative data (see Table 3.4 for examples of this).

We were also able to test the broader conclusion from the qualitative analysis that experiences of (in)justice were an important driver of young people's attitudes and actions in relation to different forms of justice. Here, we mapped multiple questionnaire items to underlying latent constructs (knowledge of and experience of justice, attitudes and intended actions for SDGs) so that we could analyse relationships between these constructs.

Table 3.4: Links between qualitative analysis and quantitative survey design

Examples of core concept	How was this represented in the qualitative data?	Survey questions
Violence in young people's daily lives as injustice	How young people experience violence in their homes, communities and at school	My school is a place where I feel safe My home is a place where I feel safe
Economic and human livelihood concerns over planetary concerns	Immediate livelihood concerns as a priority despite knowledge of environmental impact	This formed the basis of a scenario based on the potential development of a factory which would bring jobs to the area alongside environmental destruction

The questionnaire used an innovative methodology based on graphic scenarios that was tailored to each country to make questions on each justice contextually relevant (Shields et al, 2024). Different team members developed potential scenarios for the survey related to each of the justices and core concepts from the qualitative analysis. As a team, we then decided on one scenario per justice and adapted the scenarios to be contextually relevant for young people across the three countries and different urban and rural settings. A graphic designer in Perú developed the graphics that were used in each scenario, again seeking to include images that were as reflective of the range of contexts as possible. Team members from across the countries advised on the relevance of the images.

The questionnaire was administered at 30–32 schools per country (92 in total), in the same districts and regions as the qualitative work. The schools were purposively randomly sampled to include a range of categories that was appropriate to the secondary schooling landscape of that country. It was assured statistically that sample schools represented school types (public and private), geographical distribution, cultural and socio-economic diversity, and rural and urban contexts. In each of the sampled and participating schools, a convenience sampling technique was used to randomly select at least one class or grade which, at the time of data collection, was deemed available by the school administration to participate in the study. All the learners in the entire selected class participated in the study after being trained and given tablets to fill in the questionnaire, which were digitally designed with voice-over.

From 4,323 responses, 4,142 young people's responses were included in the dataset. These data were analysed by country and comparatively. The data analysis included structural equation modelling for the estimation of latent constructs and multilevel linear regressions to measure the effects of attitudes, experiences and knowledges on learners' intended actions in relation to environmental, epistemic and transitional justices (Shields et al, 2024). Participants' socio-economic status was determined based on their self-report on household possessions. In Chapter 7 we present some of the results from this structural equation modelling. We also report descriptive statistics. For responses to the scenarios and attitudinal questions, responses were given via the use of a slider, with 0 being totally negative in response and 100 being totally positive. When reporting on the survey results, the scores are presented as a mean of the point chosen on the slider rather than a percentage score. For example, a score of 70 denotes that this was the average place that respondents placed their slider, rather than that 70 per cent of respondents agreed with a response.

It is important to note that due to the time constraints imposed by cuts to our funding, we were compelled to develop the survey before the qualitative analysis was fully completed, as would be expected in a sequential mixed methods design. We sought to address this through a process of iteration whereby we further refined the key concepts from the qualitative data analysis and then asked new questions and queried relationships within the survey data. Similarly, where we found new insights from the survey data analysis, we returned to the qualitative data. This iterative process led to the theoretical development discussed in the next section.

Theory development

The final stage of our mixed methods design was the integration of analyses and conclusions from the three stages of qualitative and quantitative data generation (Fetters et al, 2013). We conducted this synthesis and framework development with three guiding principles of criticality, iteration and collaboration-through-dialogue.

We collaboratively and iteratively considered the common themes from across the data generation phases with broader constructs informed by the key theories of environmental, epistemic and transitional justice (see Table 3.5). The top-level finding from across the analyses was the essential role of justice within education to support the sorts of outcomes that we expect education to deliver, which we defined as 'education *as* justice' to enable 'education *for* justice'. This led to the development of the common framework presented in Chapter 7, which could be used to examine the relationship between education and justice across countries that face similar injustices as Nepal, Perú and Uganda.

Rather than seeking to draw out direct comparisons between country data, we critically reflected on the differences and considered explanations through understandings of the differing contextual and pedagogical

Table 3.5: Iterative analysis towards theory development

Iterative analysis moving between ...	Drawing on:
Core concepts generated from the analysis	• Datasets from each research question • Country internal reports
Understanding congruences and differences by country	• Team members' contextualized understandings of each country • Country profiles (Balarin, Monge and Sarmiento, 2021; Nuwategeka et al, 2021a; Singh et al, 2021)
Engagement with wider literature on the three justices	• Team members' theoretical and disciplinary knowledge • Background papers written on education and each justice (Balarin et al, 2021; Milligan et al, 2021; Nuwategeka et al, 2021b; Paulson et al, 2021) • In-person and online team meetings and reading group
Theoretical foundation of Fraser's 3Rs	• Reading group • Team reflections on its' suitability in Global South contexts

approaches. We took inspiration from the process that we used to critically analyse the policy texts (Schmidt, 2006). By working together as a team, we described the key findings and examined the underlying explanations for such findings. Here, the team members' knowledge of each setting and the broader political, social and educational landscapes was crucial, as were the critical questions asked by those less familiar with each context. The range of theoretical expertise and disciplinary backgrounds of team members were also important contributing factors.

Srivastava and Hopwood (2009, p 77) write that iteration in data analysis is 'a deeply reflexive process ... sparking insight and developing meaning ... [by] ... visiting and revisiting the data and connecting them with emerging insights, progressively leading to refined focus and understandings'. This happened in the analysis of each dataset and in moving between the datasets. However, the iteration continued into the framework development (see Table 3.5). Through a series of team meetings and reading group discussions, we progressively refined our findings into a single, coherent framing. As discussed in Chapter 2, we reached our decision to use Fraser's 3Rs model as the foundation for our framework collectively through a series of reading group meetings. Significantly, once we agreed that this was the foundation, we returned to the core concepts and our reading of the theories to develop stronger articulations of integration across the justices into one single model. The framework presented in Chapter 7 is the outcome of these iterative processes and the inputs of many members of the wider team.

It is also important to note that in developing this book, the five authors continued to refine and develop our theoretical contribution. This was informed by collaborative meetings, our engagement with a wider range of literature, and the further development of core concepts and theoretical arguments in other articles that we had written (Balarin and Milligan, 2024; Balarin and Rodríguez, 2024; Milligan et al, 2024; Nuwategeka et al, 2024; Paudel et al, 2024; Wilder et al, 2024). A central thread across this wider writing was the central role of epistemic justice in considerations of justice in education. We return to some of these extended arguments in our conclusions in Chapter 8.

Alongside these processes of theory development, another team member, Nese Soysal, was focused on translating our findings into practice through a secondary school teachers' guide for integrating a justice approach into secondary education (Soysal and JustEd, 2023). Here, the dialogue process worked between the core concepts and key literature about pedagogies related to the different forms of justice. For example, we identified reparative pedagogy – most closely linked to education and transitional justice literature (Paulson, 2023) – as an appropriate approach to potentially address the core concept of violence in young people's lives as injustice, and we designed a range of relevant teaching and learning activities. This teachers' guide has been adapted to be used in teacher training in Nepal and Uganda, and we present the six pedagogies that were identified in the conclusions chapter.

Ethical considerations

We sought to respect the diversity of institutional expectations and country-specific requirements for ethical approval. Ethical considerations and protocols adopted in this study were reviewed and approved by the University of Bath Social Sciences Research Ethics Committee in three stages (references S21-024, S21-110, S22-025). They were also reviewed and approved by the Gulu University Research Ethics Committee (GUREC-2021-60). In Perú and Nepal, ethical considerations were in line with, respectively, GRADE and Tribhuvan University's institutional protocols. In the qualitative research, written and signed consent was taken from all the participants, and signed consent was taken from the parents before involving the learners in in-person activities. The participants were informed about their voluntary participation, their right to withdraw from the study, anonymous treatment of information/data, the confidentiality of information, and the use of data for research purposes only. Across the qualitative and quantitative stages, all participants were assigned codes as identifiers with no individual names of the participants in the collection and storage of the research data.

As discussed in Chapter 1, at the beginning of the study we set out to nurture a mutually fulfilling and rewarding research practice that was based on a collaboratively agreed ethical code. This ethical code was developed in the first few months of the study through a process called 'structured ethical reflection' (Stevens et al, 2016). The initial 14-member core research team came together to share and reflect on our own personal values and commitments to research and partnership, and to recognize the common (ethical) grounds upon which we met. We also discussed and agreed values that were not part of everyone's usual lexicon for research or even academia (like fun!). Then, we explored what each of these values might look like at different stages of research and in a range of partnership scenarios in which we anticipated we would find ourselves (for example, collaborative writing, research design, data analysis, data generation). While our discussions of these principles were sporadic over time, this relational and instrumental work of listening to each other and agreeing how we wanted to work together helped us set intentions of care, appreciation of diversity, honesty and open-mindedness, and desire to support each other in our aims and hopes for ourselves and the project. Not least among these was an intention to see and mitigate legacies and ongoing systemic structures of power disparities in Global North–South research partnerships (Grieve and Mitchell, 2020; Mkwananzi and Cin, 2021).

Conclusions

JustEd was a complex, multi-stage and multi-layered research project and major investment in exploring how global agendas related to education's contribution to wider justice projects are experienced in implementation and in terms of outcomes. Our strategies incorporated multiple qualitative methods as well as a large-scale survey enacted through an intensely collaborative process of research design, testing and implementation. This design enabled us to generate rich insights not only on the topic of justice in education, but also on multi-country research processes and partnerships, not least because of the very particular bumps in the road that we encountered. Our research was punctuated by significant, unanticipated and unwelcome events – including a major budget cut partway through the research cycle and ongoing waves of the COVID-19 pandemic, which notably had a significant impact on the UK-based principal investigator. These necessitated frank discussion, rapid pivots and flexibility in research roles and implementation, both in timing and design adaptation. This has contributed to a better understanding of the realities of international and comparative education research, particularly how the results – varying in depth, number, quality and method – provide distinct but still comparable insights on the same object of study. While there were certainly many frustrations and disappointments along the way, the process has led to substantive learning and insight into how North–South research partnerships can be realized through humility, empathy and honesty.

The following three chapters present the main findings by country. These are presented through a staged narrative approach (Fetters et al, 2013), with the findings discussed by each phase, starting with the policy and curriculum analysis. In Chapter 7 we look across the findings to identify commonalities and differences by country and consider the key elements of 'education *as* justice' for enabling 'education *for* justice'. Here, we use a weaving approach (Fetters et al, 2013) to integrate the data from across research questions and country contexts into a singular narrative.

4

Education and Justice in Nepal

Introduction

Access to education is key to the translation into practice of constitutional aspirations for justice and inclusion in Nepal. To this end, Nepal's Constitution has guaranteed citizens' rights to compulsory and free education up to the basic level and free education up to the secondary level provided by the State (Government of Nepal, 2015, 2018). Likewise, every child is entitled to get basic education in their mother tongue. The State has prioritized education not only as a vehicle for human resource development, and economic growth but also as an indispensable tool for citizens' participation in and contribution to democratic practices.

In an effort to improve the quality and efficacy of education, the State has decentralized the education system. For this, the responsibilities and functions in the administration and management of education have been delegated to three tiers of government. In the current decentralized form, basic and secondary education comes under the local government tier, which is also responsible for disaster management, protection of natural resources, including watersheds, wildlife, mines and minerals, and protection and development of languages and cultures (Government of Nepal, 2015, 2017). The local and federal governments also share the responsibility for addressing issues related to utilizing natural resources, protecting biodiversity and responding to natural and man-made calamities.

The Local Government Operation Act (Government of Nepal, 2017) has delegated more regulatory powers and responsibility to local governments in framing local curricula and designing local textbooks. Despite such power-sharing, Nepal's school education system is still highly centralized, with the central administration exerting authority over most aspects of education, from policy to classroom pedagogy (Paudel et al, 2024).

In line with the global trend, Nepal has increasingly utilized school education as a vehicle for the protection of the environment and the equitable utilization of natural resources for sustainable development. To this end,

Nepal's secondary school education aims to produce environmentally aware citizens who (a) can contribute to sustainable development by protecting, promoting and utilizing natural resources; (b) are aware of climate change and natural calamities and respond to them wisely; and (c) can actively participate in the development of an inclusive, just and equitable society. These curricular goals are principally informed by the targets of SDG 4 that 'ensure inclusive and equitable quality education and promote lifelong learning opportunities for all'; achieving these envisioned goals will be difficult without the incorporation of environmental, epistemic and transitional justice in the curriculum and everyday classroom practices. Against this backdrop, this chapter reports the findings of the Nepal case of the JustEd study. Although the study was conducted in two sequential phases – qualitative and quantitative – this chapter focuses exclusively on presenting the qualitative findings of the study.

Education and justice in Nepal's policies

We reviewed educational and non-educational policies, focusing on how policies align with and promote the principles of environmental, epistemic and transitional justices in education. The reviewed policy documents are given in Table 4.1. Five policy makers were interviewed online via Zoom or Google Meet to understand the process, priority areas of educational policy development, and the incorporation of the justice landscape into educational policies. Two of the policy makers interviewed were representatives from the Ministry of Education, Science and Technology. The other three were Tribhuvan University professors involved in developing national education policies such as the School Education Sector Plan (SESP) (Ministry of Education, Science and Technology, 2022) and National Curriculum Framework (NCF) (Curriculum Development Centre, 2019).

Table 4.1: Policy documents reviewed according to the three justices in Nepal

Type of justice	Selected policies that were reviewed
Environmental justice	Environment Management Framework for SSDP Nepal (2017)
	Climate Change Policy 2019
All three justices	The Education Act 1971 (Seventh Amendments, 2001)
	The Constitution of Nepal 2015
	School Sector Development Plan (SSDP 2016–2024)
	School Education Sector Plan (SESP 2024–2035)
	Local Government Operation Act 2017
	National Curriculum Framework (NCF) 2007 and NCF 2019

Nepal's education system has undergone significant transformation through policies designed and focused on ensuring inclusivity, equity and fairness, and to increasing access, quality and efficiency in education. These efforts aim to provide equal opportunities for all learners regardless of socio-economic, geographical or cultural backgrounds. Nepal National Framework SDG 4: Education 2030 is targeted to achieve the goal of SDG 4 regarding quality education and guaranteeing equitable access (Ministry of Education, Science and Technology, 2019a). The National Education Policy (NEP) 2019 emphasizes ensuring equitable access to free quality education up to secondary level for all, expanding open and non-formal education to increase access, providing inclusive and special needs education, and establishing child-friendly environments in schools (Ministry of Education, Science and Technology, 2019b). Similarly, the SESP focuses on making the school system inclusive, resilient and accountable. The SESP is instrumental in decentralizing Nepal's school education to strengthen people's access to education. The plan aims at improving education in Nepal by aligning with both national goals and international commitments, like the SDGs. The Local Government Operation Act 2017 (Government of Nepal, 2017), another important document, grants powers to local bodies to manage schools, make decisions on framing local curricula and teaching–learning materials, conducting training, and more. The decentralization of educational governance under Nepal's federal system brings both opportunities and challenges. While decentralization can lead to solutions that are more tailored to local needs and encourage greater community involvement, it also risks exacerbating existing disparities if local governments lack the capacity or resources to effectively carry out national policies. As Nepal is still in the early stages of transitioning to federalism, the education sector, like many others, is navigating through this complex change. Making sure that decentralization doesn't weaken the impact of justice-focused policies is a significant challenge that will require careful planning and ongoing support from both the central government and international partners. However, the implementation of these plans shows several gaps that remain unaddressed.

Our analysis of Nepal's policy documents demonstrates that they have addressed directly or indirectly environment-related issues such as the impact of humans on the environment and the protection and equitable distribution of natural resources. However, these issues are not approached through the justices perspective. In what follows, we present a review of major policy documents to examine the place of environmental justice therein. Nepal's Constitution ensures the citizen's right to live in a healthy and clean environment, and the compensatory right of the victim of environmental pollution (Government of Nepal, 2015). Espousing this constitutional aspiration, the Environment Protection Act 2019 (Ministry of Environment and Forests, 2019) and the Fifteenth Plan 2019/20–2023/24

(National Planning Commission, 2020) emphasize sustainable use of natural resources and the protection of biodiversity and the natural environment for future generations. The Fifteenth Plan outlines strategies for climate change adaptation and disaster risk reduction to ensure sustainable development. The SDG 4 framework ensures that those who are vulnerable to environmental challenges should have fair access to environmental resources. The environmental concerns articulated in the Constitution are to some extent addressed in the Education Act, School Sector Development Plan (SSDP) (Ministry of Education, 2016) and SESP by considering education as a means to equip learners with the knowledge, understanding, attitude and skills to address local environmental issues. The Education Act, SSDP and SESP emphasize the incorporation of environmental sustainability, human values, inclusivity, diversity, human rights and environmental change in the curricula and learning processes. Additionally, they focus on supporting marginalized and vulnerable groups, including those impacted by crises, including natural disasters, thereby ensuring justice in education. The NCF (Curriculum Development Centre, 2019), a principal curriculum framing document, has also recommended the incorporation of environmental issues in the school curriculum (Government of Nepal, 2017; Sharma et al, 2024). It aims to develop conscientious citizens capable of supporting sustainable development while also protecting the natural resources and cultural heritage through education.

Our review reveals that although environmental concerns figured in Nepal's policy documents, they are yet to be linked with justice. For instance, none of the documents mentions the term 'environmental justice', nor do they speak about potential injustice incurred because of ongoing environmental problems. So, teachers and stakeholders must bridge this gap by integrating justice-focused practices into education and policy implementation in Nepal. Environmental justice has to do with the people's equitable access to natural resources and their right to live in a healthy environment, as well as a symbiotic relationship between humans and non-humans. Accordingly, environmental justice in education pertains to embedding these and other environmental issues in education policies, and teaching–learning materials and activities so future generations can participate in sustainable development while taking care of the entire ecosystem. Embedding environmental justice in education has a twofold goal. First, it enables learners to comprehend human interactions with the natural environment and devise effective measures to strengthen such interactions. Second, it develops understanding and awareness among learners about injustice resulting from overexploitation of natural resources and natural calamities and inspires them to play a proactive role in mitigating such injustice.

The Constitution values epistemic justice by recognizing local cultural experiences and knowledge and enshrining the citizen's right to have a voice in decision-making and equal opportunities to contribute and benefit from knowledge and education. The SSDP and School Sector Reform Plan (SSRP) (Ministry of Education, 2009) both highlight Nepal's dedication to providing fair and inclusive education. Over time, Nepal's education policies have increasingly focused on themes of justice, emphasizing fair access, equity, quality education and inclusivity. The SSDP places a strong emphasis on improving the quality of education, prioritizing equitable access to overcome disparities faced by disadvantaged groups, children with disabilities and those from remote areas. The NEP (2019) aims to provide mother tongue–based and multilingual education; ensures affirmative action, reservation, prioritization and incentivization to marginalized communities; and provides for inclusive and special needs education to mainstream people with disabilities in education. The Local Government Operation Act (Government of Nepal, 2017) guarantees opportunities to provide traditional education aimed at continuing, preserving and promoting the traditions, values, norms, culture, rituals and practices within the society; it allows for the operation of institutions dedicated to educating children in these aspects. Education policies focus on targeted programmes for the poor and marginalized and remote communities through scholarships, free midday meals, free education, free learning materials and more. Working towards ensuring equitable access to compulsory and free education, the Fifteenth Plan working policy arrangement was providing open and alternative education and establishment of residential schools to meet the educational needs of children from poor, marginalized and endangered communities, as well as inclusive education for children with disabilities.

When it comes to transitional justice, we critically examined the educational policies to discover how education is addressing historical events and (in)justices; advocating equity, fairness and peace; promoting reconciliation; and providing reparation to conflict-affected people. The SSDP emphasizes resilience within the school system and ensures that schools are protected from conflict through a comprehensive school safety approach. Furthermore, governance and management will adapt to accommodate the political and administrative restructuring of the education sector, aligning with the identified needs of the federal context (Ministry of Education, Science and Technology, 2016). Although the SSDP was developed and implemented after the settlement of the Maoist conflict and the major political transition in State restructuring, the policy lacked clear and specific strategies and programmes to address the educational needs of conflict-affected children and communities, address political transition and advocate for justice in post-conflict situations. The SESP (Ministry of Education, Science and Technology, 2022) prioritizes enrolling and retaining conflict-affected children – as well as children from vulnerable, disadvantaged, endangered and other targeted groups – in school education while also ensuring easier access, increasing participation and improving learning outcomes. The plan also considers the protection of school-going children from conflict, violence, natural disasters and diseases. Furthermore, the policy addresses the government's commitment to safeguarding children's right to education, protecting children during emergency and crisis situations caused by wars, conflicts, pandemics or natural disasters. It highlights the challenges of education in emergencies and crises, such as whether to provide education as a cross-cutting or separate subject, or whether to focus just on the risks from natural hazards or to also address epidemics and social conflicts.

While the SESP emphasizes ensuring social justice and education's role in the country's political transition, it notably lacks strategies, programmes, activities and outcomes aimed at addressing transitional justice within the education sector. During the time of the Maoist insurgency, Nepal had developed the Schools as Zone of Peace National Framework and Implementation Guidelines (Ministry of Education, 2011) aimed at keeping schools free from the impact of armed activities and other kinds of violence; party-based politics and other interferences; and discrimination, abuses, neglect and exploitation. This document addressed the negative impact of armed conflict, as well as other activities and incidents, on schools and children. The Local Government Operation Act (Government of Nepal, 2017) ensures the right to specific opportunities for children of individuals who were declared martyrs and those who disappeared as well as those who were injured or disabled during people movements, armed conflicts or revolutions. Furthermore, it ensures that children who were injured or affected by any incidents or events are provided education in a safe and secure environment. The fifteenth five-year plan in its vision focuses on creating foundations for a justice-oriented education system that guarantees equality, inclusivity, a dignified life and freedom from exploitation and discrimination, ensuring that the rights of individuals affected by past injustices are acknowledged or addressed (National Planning Commission, 2020).

Justice in the Nepal national curriculum and school textbooks

We critically analysed the curricular materials given in Table 4.2 using the critical content approach and keywords given in Chapter 3. Recent Nepal Government curricula for grades 9 and 10 comprise five core subjects – Nepali, English, mathematics, science and technology, and social studies – and two optional subjects. Following the elimination of Health, Population and Environment (HPE) from the core curriculum, environmental issues are partly included in science and technology and social studies.

Table 4.2: Curricular materials analysed in Nepal

Level/year	Document title and date
Secondary education (grades 9 and 10)	Social studies curriculum (2014) and textbooks, old
	Social studies curriculum (2021) and textbooks, new
	Science curriculum (2014) and textbooks, old
	Science and technology curriculum (2021) and textbooks, new
	Health, population, and environmental education (2014), old

Key environment-related objectives featured in the current curricula of science and technology and social studies (Curriculum Development Centre, 2021) are:

- to explain the interrelation between biotic and abiotic components in aquatic and terrestrial ecosystems;
- to define the food web and food chain in ecosystems and show the relationship between flora and fauna;
- to explain the concept, cause and effects of climate change;
- to discover measures to minimize climate change;
- to list endangered animals and measures for their protection;
- to list traditional plants through investigation of their utilizations,
- to analyse human–environment relationships;
- to understand sustainability and community roles in environmental protection;
- to learn about national environmental policies and challenges; and
- to emphasize responsible resource management.

The 2014 curriculum for grades 9 and 10 covered a wide range of environment-related topics, such as natural hazards, pollution and climate change (Curriculum Development Centre, 2014). It also emphasized the interrelationship between health, population and the environment. In contrast, the 2021 curriculum for science and technology focuses on ecosystems, food chains, ozone layer depletion and other issues. The removal of HPE as a subject has not only limited learners' exposure to environmental issues but also de-emphasized the urgency of environmental education in national and provincial policy documents, further creating a policy–practice gap. This has led to barriers in translating policy aspirations and goals into action for environmental protection and preservation. The analysis of secondary-level textbooks of science and technology, social studies, and HPE shows the dominance of theoretical knowledge of environmental issues. The areas covered in these textbooks include, among others, ecosystems; ozone layer depletion; effects of excessive use of insecticides and chemical fertilizers; the concept, causes, effects and mitigation of climate change;

acid rain; the greenhouse effect; pollution induced by industrial chemicals; chemical waste management; and conservation of endangered animals. These textbooks fail to include contents rooted in learners' local contexts or to link theoretical knowledge to learners' lived experience. Bridging this gap through experiential learning is essential for enhancing understanding and action for protecting the environment. Since HPE has not been recognized as a core subject in the new curriculum, there is no comprehensive textbook that can play a supportive role in carrying out the intended action.

In line with the national education aims as given in the NCF, local governments have developed their own curricula incorporating the diverse local environments and other issues. The local curricula should expose learners to a range of environmental issues at local and global levels, including pollution, climate change, natural disasters and deforestation, and their impact on their everyday lives. Such content allows learners to connect environmental problems to their contexts and find the measures to mitigate them. Bringing local environmental issues and experiences to classroom teaching can be counted as a sustainable way of promoting epistemic justice in and through education.

Although some content on culture, language, traditions and traditional music are included in the old social studies textbooks, learners felt that such content inadequately represents the diverse religious, cultural and traditional values of minority groups such as Muslims, Tharus and Chepang. A lesson on social problems discusses harmful traditional practices such as witchcraft, as well as the *Jhuma* and *Deuki* traditions of offering girls to monasteries and temples, respectively. These girls are not allowed to marry and have reportedly experienced sexual exploitation and violence (United Nations Nepal, 2020). The content covers discrimination in society in terms of gender, language, race, class and disability, as well as economic inequality. Additionally, it covers human rights and the UN Universal Declaration of Human Rights under the topic of civic sense. All this content is merely presented as information-sharing rather than critical engagement of leaners towards understanding the complex interplay of social issues. There is a dedicated lesson on rights related to women and *aadibasi janajati* (Indigenous nationalities). This makes learners become more knowledgeable about respecting and valuing diversity, as well as eliminating inequalities in society. The latest secondary-level curriculum includes several key concepts related to concerns of epistemic justice such as socialization; identification of social/cultural diversity and preservation of social unity; the importance of traditional knowledge, skill and technology; identification and preservation of cultural heritage; recognition and exploration of traditional arts; and exploration of social norms and values.

While the previous social studies curriculum had limited content on aspects of transitional justice, the new curriculum addresses the gap by incorporating some key aspects of transitional justice. However, the term transitional justice is not used in the old or new curricula or textbooks. The preface section of the new social studies textbook mentions that education needs to develop learners' competencies regarding their rights, promoting freedom and equality, practising healthy living, making decisions based on critical analysis, and more. Furthermore, it is expected that secondary education develops competencies so that learners demonstrate good moral character, sensitivity towards social cooperation and a commitment to sustainable peace through conflict management, among other things. The inclusion of chapters on social responsibility, domestic violence, identification of social issues and problem-solving skills, the role of international organizations in addressing social problems, and human rights fosters knowledge and understanding of (in)justice in society, recognizes and addresses past and ongoing injustice, and informs learners about where to report if injustice prevails in the society. Content coverage of various historical movements and conflicts from the time of the Rana regime to the recent federal republic system in Nepal and their positive and negative consequences highlights certain aspect of transitional justice within school educational discourse. For instance, an old social studies textbook for grade 10 (Curriculum Development Centre, 2017) describes a narrative around the Maoist insurgency and the formulation of the new Constitution in 2015.

The recent grade 10 textbook mentions that the current federal state system was established following the decade-long Maoist armed conflict, the 19-day People's Movement, the Madhesh protests and other significant events. There is discussion of the concept of a global brotherhood. It mentions that global brotherhood encompasses the sense of unity and the human right of every individual to live equally in peace and coexistence. Use of terms like social harmony, peace, coexistence, equality, end of discrimination, respect to other, human rights and sense of individual responsibility develop awareness among the learners towards maintaining cohesion and resilience in society. Similarly, use of terms like 'sacrifices of life during conflict' and 'violence and murder during conflicts' makes learners aware of the harsh realities faced by individuals and communities during times of conflict.

Although the content covers some important terms related to transitional justice, neither explicitly discusses how injustice prevailed during the conflict; nor about conflict resolution, reparation conflict healing; and preventing future conflict in the aftermath of large conflicts. When we asked learners about this, they suggested the incorporation of content on the causes and consequences of major conflicts in school textbooks. Likewise, a teacher emphasized the importance of equipping young learners with knowledge and skills in conflict management. It is difficult to see how curriculum and textbook content in its current form could contribute to building social harmony, reducing conflict, promoting peaceful coexistence and

Figure 4.1: In-person creative activities conducted with learners in Nepal

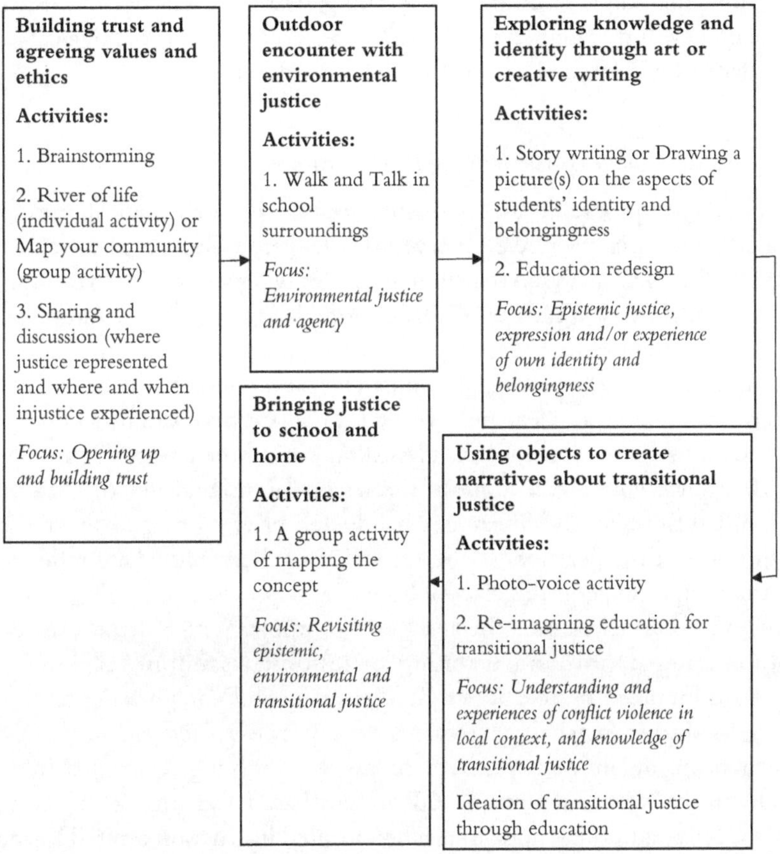

Building trust and agreeing values and ethics

Activities:

1. Brainstorming
2. River of life (individual activity) or Map your community (group activity)
3. Sharing and discussion (where justice represented and where and when injustice experienced)

Focus: Opening up and building trust

Outdoor encounter with environmental justice

Activities:

1. Walk and Talk in school surroundings

Focus: Environmental justice and agency

Exploring knowledge and identity through art or creative writing

Activities:

1. Story writing or Drawing a picture(s) on the aspects of students' identity and belongingness
2. Education redesign

Focus: Epistemic justice, expression and/or experience of own identity and belongingness

Bringing justice to school and home

Activities:

1. A group activity of mapping the concept

Focus: Revisiting epistemic, environmental and transitional justice

Using objects to create narratives about transitional justice

Activities:

1. Photo-voice activity
2. Re-imagining education for transitional justice

Focus: Understanding and experiences of conflict violence in local context, and knowledge of transitional justice

Ideation of transitional justice through education

fostering resilience in society, all of which are essential in the process of transitional justice.

Learners' experiences and classroom practice related to the three justices

We conducted a range of in-person participatory activities with learners, involving them in a series of individual or group tasks to explore their knowledge, experiences, skills and intended actions related to the environmental, epistemic and transitional justice concerns of the study. A total of 24 learners, comprising 6 secondary-level (grades 9 and 10) learners from each school, were involved in the in-person activities.

We also conducted face-to-face interviews with 15 teachers of 3 subjects and 4 head teachers (one from each school). Furthermore, we observed 62 classes for the selected subjects in the same schools to capture the classroom situation, including teaching and learning strategies, teacher and learner engagement, and assignment and assessment. This was followed by post-class interactions with three learners for each class observation.

How justice-related issues are taught in classrooms

The study found several cases of dissonance between pedagogical principles and classroom practices. We observed the delivery of lessons in the subjects for which we had analysed the curriculum. In this way, we aimed to capture the 'curriculum in practice'. We developed an observation template so that the different researchers engaged in the observations within and across the different schools produced comparable and consistent data related to classroom teaching and learning. The template was filled out by a researcher who either sat at the back of the classroom during the lesson or completed it while reviewing a recording of the lesson (audio and video). After the lesson had finished, the researcher conducted brief interviews on the spot with one to three learners in the class to gain their immediate reflections on their experience in the class.

In the observed classes, the teachers commonly entered the classroom without preparation and planning of lessons; classroom teaching was mostly dominated by teacher's talk; delivering and paraphrasing textbook contents; discrepancy between learners' everyday experiences and classroom instruction; and limited practice of problem-solving, critical thinking, exploration, experimentation and project-based learning (Paudel et al, 2024). This traditional mode of teacher-fronted instruction limited learners' learning opportunities and further restricted their abilities to access, process and share their knowledge and experiences (Adhikari and Poudel, 2024). We suggest that this is a significant epistemic injustice since it devalues learners' knowledge and experiences in teaching–learning resources and activities and does not recognize their capacity as knowers (Fricker, 2007).

Effective learning calls for learners' engagement in hands-on experiences, critical and appreciative perspectives on their surroundings, systemic thinking, a sense of responsibility and knowledge on wise use of environmental resources, environment protection and sustainability, and their involvement in decision-making (Piscitelli and D'Uggento, 2022). Despite this, such learner-centred and discovery-oriented teaching–learning activities were missing from most of the observed classes. For instance, the observation of an environmental lesson in grade 10 science in an urban Terai school showed that learners had very limited opportunities to engage in activities and put forward their ideas and experiences during classroom teaching and learning. The head teacher from the same school reported that the secondary curriculum has introduced the concept of sustainable development endorsed by the UN, but its effective delivery and practice rely heavily on teachers' skills, capabilities and commitment. The head teacher also mentioned that learners were not involved in activities beyond the school. This suggests a lack of external engagement opportunities for learners to go outside the school to participate in community awareness and environmental campaigns. Opportunities for learners to engage in community activities make them realize their position as change agents in the community. The issues of environment and episteme are directly associated with society and learners' everyday life experiences, calling for multimodal pedagogy (Sharma et al, 2024). Creating situations where learners share their stories and everyday experiences and connecting classroom practices to their personal experiences are vital for meaningful and experiential learning, thereby enhancing better educational outcomes (Nuwategeka et al, 2021b).

Lack of criticality in classroom instruction was another phenomenon that hindered learners' learning processes. We found that curricula, instructional materials and teaching–learning practices regarding all subjects were mostly informative and did not incorporate the critical approach to understand societal and environmental issues and problems from justice perspectives. Such issues cannot be addressed adequately through traditional teacher-centred pedagogy. The lecture method monopolized most of the teachers' classes with limited dialogic interaction (Adhikari and Poudel, 2024) that can leverage learners' place-based knowledge and experiences. Justice in pedagogical practices emphasizes the participation, recognition and representation of learners from different linguistic and cultural backgrounds, particularly those from marginalized and deprived communities.

A head teacher noticed no significant shift in pedagogical approaches and complained about the teachers' use of traditional approaches to minimized learner contribution to learning processes. In his observation, the teachers were not very aware of participatory learning and critical thinking. Another head teacher from a rural Terai school talked about his effort to create a stress-free teaching and learning environment in the school. However, as the interview data revealed, he was not clear what he meant by a stress-free environment and how it could be created, further suggesting a gap between his saying, understanding and doing.

We also found a lack of connection between learners' lived experiences and classroom teaching–learning activities. For instance, two of the learners shared observations of their surroundings. They complained about the lack of greenery and open space and wished to see more trees in their surroundings. Likewise, two learners from a rural school talked about floods and landslides in their area. However, the curricula and prescribed textbooks contain pre-selected and fixed content, allowing limited or no space for teachers and learners to discuss the impact of such adverse environmental events on their everyday lives and society as a whole. By the same token, the teachers were also found to be limited to the delivery of book content, failing to encourage learners to bring their place-based knowledge to the classroom discussion. It follows that lack of flexibility in the curricula and textbooks and teachers' inability to invoke learners' everyday experiences related to their surroundings could not address environmental and epistemic justice in the classroom.

We found that the lecture method is predominantly employed to teach lessons on social issues and conflicts, with teachers applying a similar approach to science and HPE. Learners from both an urban hill school and a rural Terai school expressed that teachers primarily rely on the textbook content, simply explaining and paraphrasing what is written, and seldom go beyond that; the use of critical and innovative approaches for engaged learning is lacking.

This was particularly evident from learners' interview data that they had never engaged in discussions about topics related to crime, violence and conflict, apart from teacher lectures and informal peer interactions. There is no teaching about the major transitions in the country dealing with the narratives, complexities and consequences of historical events. We found that teachers and learners have little knowledge and awareness of transitional justice and its processes and mechanisms. Learners were asked about their knowledge and experiences of past conflicts, including the Maoist insurgency and Madhesh movement, that had occurred in the country. Respondents mostly talked about redress of entrenched systems of domination, discrimination and inequality in society that they had experienced or studied in school. They reported existing caste-based and gender-based discrimination; social taboos like the dowry system, child marriage and witchcraft practice; and violence and crime adversely impacting social harmony, unity and peace. Only a fraction of learners had some knowledge and understanding of past conflicts and movements in the country, while the majority had little to no knowledge or awareness of them. A learner from rural Terai said, 'I think that Madhesh movement was for equality', while another learner from same school said, 'I am unaware of it'. Three learners and two teachers viewed the Maoist insurgency and Madhesh movement as a political issue. When rural Terai learners were asked about martyrs' memorials in their localities, learners were found to be unaware of the purpose of their construction, while a learner from a mountain school opined that a martyr's gate is to remember those who have been lost and provide justice for the family.

There was a distinct gendered dimension here. A female learner from a rural Terai school admitted she had no idea of the causes behind the Madhesh movement. She explained, 'in our society, political matters are not usually discussed with females ... they shut us out, even if we ask ... they say women don't need to know about political matters'. The learner's statement highlights the gender-based exclusion in society leading to injustice, inequality and reduced participation. This suggests a significant barrier to inclusive participation in decision-making and accountability mechanisms in post-conflict situations, as they often fail to critically examine the impacts of patriarchy and the distinct experiences of different genders (Billingsley, 2018).

Based on these findings, we argue that past conflicts and major political events need to be part of school curricula that help learners understand the context of society and foster the educational goal of informed citizenship. Critical and reparative pedagogy helps students learn and critically analyse the dynamics of conflict, promote empathy and tolerance, and foster decision-making capacity. Davies (2017, p 4), advocating for a justice-sensitive approach in education, highlights the 'need of structural reforms, changes in curriculum and institutional culture'. Education reforms offer the chance to initiate change both from the ground up and across various levels, involving key stakeholders such as educators, school leaders and administrators. They play a critical role in ensuring the successful implementation and broad dissemination of reform efforts to ensure transitional justice (Logan and Murphy, 2017).

Transfer of learners' learning into practice

Poor transfer of learners' learning into practice was another important theme that emerged in interviews and class observations. The curriculum teaching and learning covered the topics of environmental issues, and the learners were taught such issues in the classroom. One striking example comes from a rural Terai school. During our field visit, we noticed the school premises littered with plastics and other waste materials, which is indicative of the lack of use of learners' theoretical knowledge in keeping the environment clean. In other words, learners failed to translate environmental concepts learned from books into actions. This also shows that the theoretical knowledge could not bring about changes in learners' behaviour, which further highlights the need for effective teaching–learning activities to modify students' behaviours concerning the environment.

Several factors can be attributed to the learning–practice gap. The first reason is inadequate coverage of relevant content in curricula and textbooks leading to the lack of attitudinal and behavioural change. Secondly, there was low efficacy of what is taught and learned in schools. For instance, classroom teaching was predominantly lecture-based and required learners to memorize information, facts and figures rather than engage in interactive, problem-solving, project-based and critical thinking activities. Thirdly, learners had limited opportunities to engage in co-curricular, extracurricular and community engagement activities. Fourthly, there was inadequate coverage of social impact of environmental deterioration in curricula, textbooks and teaching–learning practices. For example, following the science and technology textbook, the teachers covered the 'what' aspect of climate change (definition, causes and effects) and the 'so-what' aspect (mitigation measures) but did not engage learners in the 'now-what' aspect (what learners can do immediately to deal with environmental issues at home and society).

School–community collaboration affords new and additional learning opportunities for learners, thereby solidifying, extending and expanding their classroom experiences. The learners in the study also highlighted the value of home and community engagement. They shared their experience of learning through interactions with parents, grandparents, relatives, neighbours and peers. At the societal level, they also learned through their involvement in clubs, campaigns, social work, volunteer services, and cultural and religious practices. This shows that the school should plan how to engage the learners in family and community activities, and accordingly that classroom instruction should capitalize on learners' family and community experiences related to the environment. Our classroom observations showed that the teachers mostly gave homework requiring learners to answer questions rather than collecting information from their families and communities. Classroom instruction should capture what learners have learned in and from their communities and encourage them to use classroom learning to solve their real-life problems.

The study revealed a lack of school–community collaboration, particularly in relation to environment protection and dealing with societal problems. A head teacher from rural Terai mentioned that his school planted a variety of plants on school premises. However, the villagers did not realize the importance of the initiative and let their animals graze on and damage the plants, which is indicative of the villagers' limited awareness of environmental sustainability. Another important issue related to this is the lack of community engagement in the environmental initiatives taken by the school. The head teacher from the urban hill school admitted her school did not create community engagement opportunities for learners. She further mentioned that her school is in the VIP area and that the children from this elite community do not enrol in this school. Consequently, the school remains isolated from the community. A head teacher from urban Terai reported that the school managed dustbins for waste disposal, started segregating the waste into biodegradable (organic) and non-biodegradable (other); constructed a well-managed garden; and built a child-friendly, plastic-free green school. Such school initiatives can serve as an example for the community, leading to substantial and transformative outcomes in society. School–community collaboration is instrumental in achieving SDG 4 Quality Education and SDG Target 13.3, which aims at improving education, awareness-raising and human and institutional capacity to meet climate change.

Schools as sites of diversity and peace

All four head teachers stated that their schools represent diversity in terms of learners' ethnicity, religion, gender, culture, geographical location, development and socio-economic status. For example, the head teacher from the urban hill school said that her school had learners belonging to the Tamang, Tharu, Magar, Brahmin, Kshetri and Dalit communities, as well as others from different parts of Nepal. She pointed out the multiple advantages of diversity in school education, where learners share with their colleagues their cultural, religious and other community practices and other place-based experiences. Learners from diverse communities grown in diverse geographical, social, familial, economic and cultural milieus can bring into the classroom their Indigenous and local-specific knowledge, ideas and practices of environmental conservation, along with Indigenous practices of dealing with natural disasters and ways to mitigate the environmental issues. However, we found that there were very few opportunities for learners to discuss and share their knowledge, experiences and skills connecting these with subject content. Furthermore, where there are disconnections between their experiences and what they are taught, these learning opportunities are unexplored (Paudel et al, 2024).

A learner belonging to the Muslim community expressed that Muslim knowledge systems and cultural practices have limited representation in the school curriculum or in its cultural programmes. The learner's statement reflects discriminatory epistemic injustice (Fricker, 2012), where certain traditional knowledges and cultural perspectives are marginalized or undervalued within the curriculum and knowledge-creating and -sharing spaces like school. In the same line, a female learner belonging to the Dalit community pointed out that 'when a community lives as a minority, there is a risk that their traditions, culture, rituals and language may face extinction if they are not passed on to the next generation through education. For instance, many younger people are unable to speak their mother tongue'.

All four head teachers stated that their learners were comfortable with Nepali or English as the medium of instruction. However, our interviews with learners showed a different story. Most of the learners expressed their discomfort with English as a medium of instruction. There were a few non-native Nepali speaker learners who experienced difficulty in understanding content taught in Nepali. For example, a Tamang girl learner from Rasuwa said that she did not participate in class discussions due to her limited proficiency in Nepali. A science teacher from a remote hill community also stated that he had difficulty making the Tamang-speaking learners understand subject content in English or Nepali. These learners often avoided classroom discussion or interaction with him, as on the one hand their proficiency in Nepali or English was limited, and on the other, he did not speak Tamang. Epistemic justice calls for recognition and participation of all learners – irrespective of their background, identity or cultural differences – in knowledge consumption, recognition and production (Balarin and Milligan, 2024).

Although schools are officially considered zones of peace, the influence of political unrest on education institutions in Nepal remains significant. Political activities disrupt the school environment, affecting learners, teachers and the overall learning process. During fieldwork, we witnessed a political campaign taking place on school premises during class hours, showing the intersection of education and politics. A teacher reported an incident in a rural mountain school where a dispute arose in the school as one group of learners supported a party-declared bandh while another group opposed it. A teacher from the urban hill school revealed a situation of fear and insecurity in schools during the Maoist conflict. He further said that at that time schools in remote areas were sites of Maoist activism, and education was regularly disturbed. According to him 'once in a school while Maoist parade and programme was happening army helicopter came to surveillance the activities, which made learners and teachers flee in panic from the school due to fear of bombardment'. Similarly, it was reported by a teacher that they were compelled to pay money from their salary to support Maoist activism. A head teacher from a rural Terai school reported that the Maoist insurgency and the Madhesh movement significantly disrupted teaching and learning. During the Madhesh movement, schools were closed for many days, and once normalcy returned, the school faced difficulties in locating and reintegrating learners into the classroom. Two teachers, from a rural mountain school and an urban hill school, respectively, said that there were learners who had lost their fathers during the Maoist conflict. The loss of a father makes it difficult for the family to sustain their lives and has severe, irreparable consequences for the children and the entire family (Billingsley, 2018). A head teacher from an urban Terai school reported significant displacement and migration of many learners from remote Terai and hill schools to their school due to the Madhesh Movement and the Maoist insurgency. During the Maoist conflict, teachers and others were targeted and victimized by both Maoist insurgents and State security forces, often due to suspicions of supporting and aiding the opposite side (Selim, 2018). Conflict in the country undermined and violated children's right to education, peace and security in school, yet it is a topic that is almost entirely absent across policy, curriculum and practice.

Conclusions

This chapter concerned the examination of justice in Nepal's secondary education system. The study reveals the marginal presence of justice issues in broader educational and curricular policies. There is lack of conceptual deliberation of justice in education in general, or epistemic, environmental and particularly transitional justice. These different forms of justice are implied peripherally and limited content concerning these justices are included in curricula and textbooks.

In principle, teaching–learning practices are supposed to be informed and guided by the nation's overall educational polices, thereby demonstrating their strong congruence between practices. The constitutional provisions for every citizen's right to live in a clean and healthy environment, sustainable practices for environmental conservation, inclusivity through equal participation of marginalized communities in decision-making, and equitable access to natural resources serve as a foundation for incorporating justice in education. It prioritizes equitable access to overcome disparities faced by disadvantaged groups, children with disabilities, and those from remote areas. Adequate infrastructure, including child-friendly, gender-conscious and disaster-resilient facilities, is a key focus, with an emphasis on providing WASH facilities. However, there is very limited consideration of a justice approach, for example including learners' knowledge of environmental issues such as disasters, pollution and climate change in day-to-day life. The SSRP and SSDP's emphasis on disaster risk reduction is at risk of not being realized in practice. One of the significant concerns raised by experts is a disparity in education quality between urban and rural areas. A policy expert mentioned that while the SSRP and SSDP emphasize inclusivity, disadvantaged regions like Karnali and other remote areas still face challenges in terms of infrastructure, quality teachers and access to resources. Experts argue that these gaps are the result of a lack of action-oriented policy and monitoring. Furthermore, there has been elite capture of reservation quotas, which were designed to uplift disadvantaged groups but are mostly utilized by those with better social standing, undermining the goals of affirmative action. Experts point out that the SESP, while addressing social justice, misses key elements of environmental, epistemic and transitional justice areas. Epistemic justice would promote the inclusion of local knowledge, languages and cultural practices in the curriculum, a critical area that the SSRP and SSDP overlooked. As such, while the SESP represents a step forward, experts believe that an emphasis on environmental and epistemic issues are necessary to fully address the challenges in Nepal's education system. This would ensure not only fair access but also create a learning environment that respects and integrates the diversity of knowledges and experiences across all regions and social groups.

Another key issue we identified was the translation of the policy aspirations into real practices. The Fifteenth Plan (National Planning Commission, 2020) identified the education sector's failure to ensure full access to quality education for all, especially for targeted groups of children. Furthermore, it highlighted disparities in access to educational opportunities and learning outcomes, underscoring the persistent issues of epistemic injustice. We found the curricula and textbooks lack an effective and functional structure. We found that the concepts of fairness, equity, inclusion, participation and collaboration in curricula and textbooks are neither framed within nor guided by the principles of the three forms of justice. Although the curricula recommend using general as well as specific child-centred and activity-based teaching methods for subject teaching, they lack clear guidance on applying these methods to specific topics and on developing learners' practical skills. Subject contents are mostly presented as abstract notions with little or no connection with learners' lived experiences, and teachers do not create opportunities for learners to link textbook content and classroom learning with their day-to-day lives or community life. Because of this, classroom delivery has also not been able to fulfil the concepts of justice in education. This requires teachers to adopt the place-based approach (Gruenewald, 2003; Ajaps and Forh Mbah, 2022) that affords opportunities for the learners to share their lived experiences with each other and fosters a deeper understanding and engagement with environmental and social responsibility.

5

Education and Justice in Perú

Introduction

In recent decades, concerns for justice have played an important role in Peruvian education policy agendas. Like in much of the Latin American region, educational access problems had been successfully addressed in Perú, with almost universal coverage in both primary and secondary education. Since the late 1990s, much of the policy focus in the country was therefore set on addressing problems of quality and the severe inequalities that cut through the education system – between urban and rural schools, or between schools catering for populations from different socio-economic backgrounds, or those that serve children who speak languages other than Spanish.

Most proposed solutions to these problems were redistributive in nature and included, for instance, building infrastructure or increasing funding for rural, intercultural and bilingual schools. In many areas, policies also sought to address some of the problems of recognition that lie beneath existing inequalities. In some cases, such as bilingual and intercultural education, comprehensive national policies and plans were put in place. A preoccupation with justice is also evident in recent revisions of the National Curriculum that have sought to promote gender equity and the appreciation of cultural diversity. This is fundamental not only in itself, but also to prevent future outbursts of violent conflict, rooted in social and cultural inequalities, like the Internal Armed Conflict of the 1980s and 1990s. Addressing violence and facing the history of violent conflict in the country, however, has been a fraught endeavour prone to politicization and disputes involving different groups.

Judging by the presence of environmental concerns in Perú's legal and policy frameworks – from the General Law of Education (MINEDU, 2003) to national and sectoral policies and plans – one might assume that environmental education plays a key role in the education sector. However, when considering the scant resources assigned to environmental education, it appears that the sectoral prioritization of environmental issues has happened more on paper than in practice. More importantly for the purpose of the JustEd study, the dominant approaches to environmental education have not incorporated a justice focus – that is, they do not seem to consider the unequal impacts and responsibilities for environmental changes and the role of education in addressing them.

Between 2000 and 2023, the year when JustEd ended, the education policy landscape in Perú showed a pattern that we describe as a 'rise and fall' of justice-related policies. The story behind this rise and fall is very much the story of the country's education sector: marked by economic growth and degrowth and by institutional reform and counter-reform. It is a story that began with the promise of democratization and ends (or continues) with an authoritarian drift and the co-option of public institutions by private and often corrupt interests, with grave consequences for the promise of a more just and inclusive education for all.

As we shall see, policy discourses on environmental and justice-related topics have not permeated the curriculum, school materials or practices in homogeneous ways. More importantly, justice-related issues are often approached in schools in formal, overly normative and at the same time superficial ways. Few, if any, connections are made between the kinds of attitudes and behaviours that schools seek to promote and the myriad injustices that learners and teachers face in their daily lives in a country marked by inequality, poverty, violence and weak institutions. This poses considerable limitations for the possibility of promoting justice through education and for the role that education may have in fostering the kinds of attitudes and behaviours that are required of young people to contribute to more just and sustainable futures.

The various aspects of the educational justice agenda covered by the JustEd study, together with the complementary methodological strategies that we used, resulted in a rich and complex picture of how concerns for justice have been addressed in Perú's education system. Beyond the idea of the 'rise and fall' of a justice focus in education policies, several key points emerge from our study. The first one is the degree to which justice concerns need to be rid of critical aspects, or of aspects seen as politically complex, to enter the national policy agenda. Depoliticization, therefore, seems to be a condition of possibility for justice agendas in education to flourish, but as we shall discuss, it is a condition that often goes against the grain of those same justice concerns, which are political by nature. The Peruvian case is also illustrative of the centrality of epistemic justice for educational justice agendas. As this chapter will explore, epistemic injustices cut across all the areas we explored in the study. This was evident in the lack of connection made in schools to the regular experiences of injustice that learners face, which deprives them of having a voice with regards to the often overly normative ideas they encounter in school, and it was noticeable also in the 'shallow pedagogies' (Balarin and Rodríguez, 2024) that seem to dominate classroom practices.

The chapter follows the stages of the JustEd study: it begins with a discussion of the policy landscape; it then analyses how justice concerns have been incorporated and addressed in the National Curriculum and selected school materials; and it ends with a discussion of findings from our qualitative study of school practices. Findings from the international learner survey will mainly be discussed in Chapter 6, but we will refer to some specific results from the Peruvian case that complement some of the ideas that emerged in the qualitative analysis. The chapter will include methodological notes regarding adaptations we made for the Perú case study. A more detailed discussion of the research design can be found in Chapter 3.

Education and justice in Perú's policies

During the democratic transition period that followed the fall of the Fujimori regime in 2000, there was a marked rise in policies seeking to promote justice in and through education. Such policies were considered central for strengthening Perú's democracy. In some cases, these policies were the materialization of years of advocacy by both grassroots movements and international organizations that had been championing equity aims in education. Two examples of this, which we selected for our analysis, are intercultural education policies and gender equity policies. The former had been promoted by grassroots movements in the country and in the region since at least the 1950s and became internationally sanctioned when in 1993 Perú signed the International Labour Organization (ILO) Convention 169 (ILO, 1989) that committed the country to recognize and cater to Indigenous communities (López and Küper, 1999; Trapnell and Neira, 2004). Gender equity in education had also been a key concern of feminist movements and became central to the policy agenda after the 1995 UN Beijing Conference on the rights of women (Muñoz et al, 2006).

The emphasis on equity acquired even greater centrality considering the recommendations of Perú's Truth and Reconciliation Commission, the Comisión de la Verdad y la Reconciliación (CVR). The Commission's Final Report (CVR, 2010) highlighted the deep-seated patterns of social and cultural discrimination and exclusion that led not only to the Conflict, but also to the extent of violence against Indigenous rural communities by both the terrorist movement Sendero Luminoso and the armed forces. Concerns for equity were enshrined in some of the broad policy frameworks that emerged in the wake of the democratic transition, like the new General Law of Education (MINEDU, 2003) and the first National Education Plan prepared by the recently created National Council for Education (Consejo Nacional de Educación, 2006).

The policies we selected to analyse how Perú's education system is addressing concerns for epistemic, transitional and environmental justice all emerged within this context. Except for environmental education policies, all selected policies incorporated a specific justice focus. They sought to promote recognition and inclusion of diverse groups and sought to address some of the root causes of their exclusion. Environmental education policies, as we shall see, are different from the others in that they seem to have responded mostly to an externally driven agenda – one promoted by international organizations and advocacy groups – but without strong local constituencies to carry the agenda forward.

Table 5.1 shows the policies we selected to examine what is being proposed to address each of the three justices that were the focus of the JustEd Study. There are two points worth mentioning about the selection of policies in Perú as compared to those of Uganda and Nepal. When considering epistemic justice, we chose to include policies that address not only cultural diversity, but also those that focused on gender equity. This responded to our understanding that the relevance of epistemic justice goes beyond injustices that emerge from cultural diversity (Balarin et al, 2021), but also to the importance of gender equity policies in Perú over the past decades. For transitional justice we included both a specific policy – the Educational Reparations Plan for Victims of Violence (MINEDU, 2016a) – and the Recommendations for Institutional Reform of the CVR's Final Report (CVR, 2003), which is not a policy per se but focuses heavily on actions required from the education system.

Table 5.1: Selected policies in Perú

Type of justice	Selected areas and policies
Epistemic justice	Interculturality and gender equity • Sectoral Policy on Intercultural Education and Intercultural Bilingual Education (MINEDU, 2016) • Gender Equality Policy (MIMP, 2019)
Transitional justice	Memory, truth and reconciliation • Recommendations for institutional reform in the Final Report of the Truth and Reconciliation Commission (CVR, 2003) – specifically the recommendations for institutional reform that emphasize the role of education in the development of peace and transitional justice • Educational Reparations Plan for Victims of Violence in Perú (MINEDU, 2016a)
Environmental justice	Environmental education • National Environmental Education Policy (Ministerio del Ambiente, 2012) • Environmental Education Plan (MINAM, 2016)

Justice-oriented policy trajectories

Our analysis of policy texts, available literature and interviews with policy makers and experts showed that while the selected policies coalesced at a similar time – between 2012 and 2016 – they followed distinct trajectories, with different combinations of push and pull factors that may help explain their (dis)continuity. The Sectoral Policy on Intercultural Education and Intercultural Bilingual Education (IBE) (MINEDU, 2016) realized ideas that had originated as far back as the mid-20th century but only made it into policies and programmes more recently in response to demands from both national and regional movements and global policy frameworks that emphasized the need to address the rights and needs of Indigenous populations (Aikman, 1997; López and Küper, 1999; Trapnell and Neira, 2004; Aman, 2015). IBE sought to recognize and preserve the pluricultural, multilingual and multi-ethnic nature of many countries in the Latin American region (Balarin and Escudero, 2018) and contrasted with traditional educational approaches that promoted the 'cultural assimilation' and 'civilization' of Indigenous populations. Teaching children in their mother tongue and valuing their cultural identity was seen as fundamental to their educational inclusion, as many children were lagging behind or dropping out early from the education system precisely because they could not learn how to read and write when taught in Spanish.

In Perú, IBE policies had two important antecedents: the Education Reform Law of 1972 (Ministerio de Educación, 1972), which led to the creation of a National Policy for Bilingual Education – this guided some actions in favour of rural areas but was inadequately funded and did not translate into concrete actions; and the National Intercultural and Bilingual Education Policy (MINEDU, 2002), which incorporated 'interculturality' as a guiding principle for sectoral policies and promoted the development of appropriate forms of educational delivery for rural and Indigenous populations. The impetus that IBE has received since the 1990s was, in no small measure, also the result of the external pull exerted by international organizations like the German Cooperation, UNICEF and UNESCO, which funded and offered technical assistance to consolidate IBE policies in a global context marked by a greater emphasis on educational rights and equity (McCowan, 2010; Unterhalter, 2019).

Gender equity is a comparatively recent issue in the education policy agenda: its origins can be traced back to the 1990s as a response to the push from feminist movements and the pull exerted by international agencies that focused on promoting girls' education (Muñoz et al, 2006; Muñoz, 2017). Although the efforts made during the 1990s were important, they did not consolidate into national policies and programmes. The return to democracy in the early 2000s generated a scenario of debate and citizen participation which, together with the recommendations of international movements such as UNESCO's Education for All, led to a stronger public commitment to equity and inclusion, including gender equity.

The case of education policies for transitional justice is quite different. While the CVR's Final Report was an internal push factor that emphasized the role of the education sector in addressing the root causes of the Conflict, the polarized way in which it was received by different societal groups made this a difficult area to tread. Apart from the educational reparations policy, which is quite specific in its aims, no other sectoral policy mentions the CVR's recommendations. Their influence, however, is evident in education policy frameworks that prioritized the rights and equity agenda (Tejero, 2014; Jave et al, 2018; Jave, 2021).

Environmental education policies constitute yet another type of case. At the level of policy intentions, there appears to have been a very decisive impulse in the years that led to 2012, when the policy was approved. In 2008, Perú created the Ministry of the Environment, which played a key leadership role in promoting the incorporation of environmental policies in all government sectors. In 2014, Perú hosted the COP20 Conference and played an important leadership role in international environmental debates. Until 2015 the Ministry of Education (MoE) had a specific directorate in charge of Community and Environmental Education, which was responsible for developing curricular guidelines and teacher training strategies. As an interviewed MoE official recounted, an organizational reform conducted in 2015 led to the 'demotion' of that directorate to a mere unit within the Basic Education Directorate. Units are not part of the organic structure of ministries and therefore have no specific budget and have little power to lead over other offices. As the interviewee said, the reorganization 'weakened' their role and 'reduced' it to its 'minimal expression'. The de-prioritization of environmental education in Perú seems to go beyond this ministerial reorganization. In the multiple attempts we made to find expert interviewees who could guide us in our understanding of the policies, we found there are few experts in this area.

What justice-related policies propose

We found significant differences in the extent to which selected policies incorporated a justice focus. The IBE policy clearly does, as it emphasizes the importance of 'recognising and positively valuing the country's socio-environmental reality and cultural and linguistic diversity' (MINEDU, 2016). It proposes two key strategies to do this: introducing a transversal intercultural approach in the education system and catering to Indigenous learners through intercultural and bilingual education. Our focus was on the former strategy, which led to the incorporation of an intercultural approach in the National

Curriculum and school materials for basic education.[1] Transversal curricular approaches are meant to guide classroom practice, ensuring that the work done in different areas involves certain desirable values, in this case respect for diverse cultural identities. An interviewed MoE official highlighted how this transversal curricular approach followed a 'functional' understanding of cultural diversity that emphasizes and celebrates the recognition of cultural identities without discussing how such identities may be linked to structural forms of material and symbolic exclusion, like poverty or discrimination. The interviewee contrasted this approach with 'critical interculturality', which explicitly seeks to address such structural forms of exclusion (see also Walsh, 2009). According to this and other interviewees, 'critical interculturality' has guided the work done in intercultural bilingual schools for Indigenous children, but it was not deemed suitable for mainstream schools. As the interviewees mentioned, the 'political' side of interculturality had to be compromised in favour of a less 'uncomfortable' approach to the subject.

In contrast, the Gender Equality Policy (MIMP, 2019) has a very articulate discussion of the structural inequalities that women face in Perú. The policy text outlines a historical, systematic and intersectional approach that highlights how social and cultural factors (race, ethnicity, poverty) deepen inequalities for some women, and explains how this has limited their access to fundamental rights. The text specifically mentions how inequalities are a result of the reproduction of gender roles, norms and stereotypes in the context of a patriarchal order, and it proposes to change such norms and to reduce violence and discrimination against women, guaranteeing their sexual and reproductive health and their participation in decision-making spheres. Among its proposed strategies is the transversalization of gender equity efforts throughout the State apparatus. In the education sector this has translated into the incorporation of gender equity as one of the transversal foci of the National Curriculum. The explicit political take that the policy has on the issue of gender inequality – which contrasts to the previous policy's mild and acritical emphasis – is at the heart of what we identify as the policy's strong justice approach. The latter may be one reason behind the strong political opposition to gender equity policies that we identified in our analysis. Our findings led us to focus on different political disputes by conservative groups that claim gender equity policies constitute a form of 'gender ideology' (Arellano Salazar, 2022). Such disputes have been constant, at one point leading to a halt in curricular implementation. While the policy itself has not been dismantled, efforts to promote gender equity have been

---

[1] The Peruvian education system has different models of service provision. Regular Basic Education is the main model; others, like Intercultural Bilingual Education or High Achievement Schools, cater for smaller population groups.

deprioritized in the Ministry of Education and have been undermined by legislation approved in more recent years.

The CVR (2003) recommendations are a somewhat similar case. The text provides an in-depth analysis of the causes of the Internal Armed Conflict, highlighting how racism and discrimination have been historically present in Peruvian society, and how they led to the inequalities in whose name the Conflict began. They are also seen to explain the atrocities that were perpetrated against rural peasants – both by the terrorist organization Sendero Luminoso and by the armed forces and the police. The report emphasizes the role of education in the development of a shared memory of the Conflict and of critical thinking skills among learners, which are considered crucial to prevent future outbursts of violence. No education policy other than the Educational Reparations Plan explicitly mentions or addresses the CVR's recommendations. The Reparations Plan is a very specific response to the consequences of the conflict that creates a programme of higher education scholarships for children of families that were victims of violence.

As we shall see, the National Curriculum did incorporate some content on the history of the Conflict, but there were no official teacher training initiatives to help teachers deal with the teaching of such a sensitive topic. We found no specific policy or curricular efforts to foster critical thinking among learners – an issue that we have elsewhere highlighted as giving rise to epistemic injustice (Balarin and Rodríguez, 2024).

In contrast to this, we found that the National Environmental Education Policy and the Plan Nacional de Educación Ambiental 2017–2022 (MINEDU, 2016c) do not incorporate a justice focus. Both documents are written from what we identify as a largely 'anthropocentric' perspective that considers the impact of environmental change on humans rather than on life in general (see Chapter 1). They highlight the importance of environmental sustainability and assign a central role to education in the development of an environmentally responsible citizenry and a sustainable society. The Plan proposes to introduce environmental education in the curriculum as well as in school management, focusing on climate change, health education, eco-efficiency and risk management. Both documents emphasize individual responsibilities for change without mentioning the need for systemic, institutional or structural changes, such as in patterns of consumption or economic organization. Neither, however, discusses existing inequalities in access to resources or in the burden of impacts and responsibilities for both environmental degradation and change. Maybe more importantly, our interviewees said that while these policies exist, environmental education is not a real priority for the education sector, as observed in the scant budget and small team of only two officials assigned to the area. These officials mentioned they no longer had sufficient resources for teacher training or producing school materials. Equally telling about the prioritization of environmental education in Perú was the fact that it was very hard to find experts willing to be interviewed for our study. Even those who had been involved in drafting the policy said they had not kept up their involvement with environmental education. It would seem that education is not a central concern for environmental researchers and activists in the country.

Depoliticization as a requisite for advancing justice-related policies

Our analysis of selected policy areas suggests that the priority given to different policies and their durability results from the encounter between the internal push from organized groups that have consistently fought for the expansion of rights and the pull exerted by various international organizations that have offered their economic and technical support. This is clear in the case of policies for the recognition of cultural diversity and gender equity. When policies have been advanced mostly because of an external pull – as seems to have been the case with environmental education policies – they have not always translated into relevant or consistent actions. In turn, when only an internal push has existed, as in the case of the CVR recommendations, support for relevant policies has been weaker.

Beyond push and pull factors, what seems to determine the adoption of certain courses of action is the extent to which policies adopt an explicitly political discourse and seek to change the structural causes of various inequalities and exclusions. The less overtly political and critical policies are – like in the case of environmental education and intercultural education for mainstream schools – the more likely to remain unchallenged. The more politically overt policies are – by questioning existing social, economic and cultural practices and pointing to their role in the reproduction of inequalities and social exclusion – the less likely they are to consolidate into actual programmes or to persevere in time.

The idea that depoliticization is a condition for policies to thrive has been suggested in some analyses of global education policies. Discussing the SDGs, Menton et al (2020, p 1622) suggest their condition of possibility is that they do 'not ... actually bind' us to anything. They are possible as long as they do not directly or fully address questions of justice that are unavoidably and inherently political in nature and require fundamental changes in existing power structures. But depoliticization compromises the justice focus of policies and the extent to which they can effectively address the root causes of current injustices.

In closing this section, we need to go back to the initial discussion of policy trajectories. Perú might seem like a country in which important policy steps have been taken to address justice concerns through education. This has been done not only through redistributive policies that have sought to improve the quality of services for the most disadvantaged groups living in rural areas; but also through policies that have emphasized the importance of recognition and representation, clearly articulating the ways in which society has excluded and marginalized people on the basis of their race, ethnicity, language or gender. However, the country's commitment to justice is somewhat relative. Our analysis of policy trajectories shows a pattern that in the JustEd study we came to describe as a 'rise and fall' of justice-oriented education policies. These policies received an initial impulse during the return to democracy in the early 2000s and peaked between 2011 and 2016, a period during which many policies coalesced into concrete plans and budgets and were carried into practice both through a new curriculum and additional funding. After 2016, however, there has been a shift in the country's political environment towards an increasing degree of political and policy instability and a prevalence of anti-reformist and conservative groups opposing the justice agenda in education (Balarin, 2025). This has compromised the implementation and sectoral prioritization of several of the policies that we analysed, with some, like gender equity, memory or even environmental education being substantially eroded or halted.

Justice in the Peruvian National Curriculum and school textbooks

Our choice of curricular areas and school materials followed from the policy areas we analysed. We searched the latest version of the National Curriculum (MINEDU, 2016b) and school materials for the last two years of secondary education, using a series of keywords to locate the sections that dealt with relevant topics. Given the diverse ways in which textbooks organized their content, we opted to characterize selected excerpts as 'lessons'. Following the methodological procedure discussed in Chapter 3, we identified a total of 394 lessons: 171 lessons for environmental justice, 144 lessons for epistemic justice and 79 lessons for transitional justice. Additionally, we revised available texts from the distance learning strategy *Aprendo en Casa* that the MoE developed during the COVID-19 pandemic. Table 5.2 shows selected materials for each type of justice and the keywords we used to identify relevant excerpts.

To understand the results of our analysis we need to situate them in the context of recent curricular changes in Perú. The publication of the 2016 National Curriculum (MINEDU, 2016b) was an important milestone in the country, as it consolidated the transition initiated in the mid-1990s towards a competency-based curriculum and away from content-focused curricula (Ferrer, 2004; Balarin and Benavides, 2010). While a previous consolidated version of the National Curriculum was published in 2008, its implementation faced important problems that cast light on the various

Table 5.2: Curriculum and textbook materials analysed in Perú

	National Curriculum for Basic Education 2016 (MINEDU, 2016b)
Selected materials	Science, Technology & Environment 4 (2015)
	Science, Technology & Environment 5 (2015)
	History, Geography & Economics 4 (2015)
	History, Geography & Economics 5 (2015)
	History, Geography & Economics 5 (2015 – Workbook)
	Personal Development, Citizenship & Civics 4 (2019)
	Personal Development, Citizenship & Civics 5 (2015)
	I Learn at Home 3rd & 4th (2020/21)
	I learn at home 5th (2020/21)

several internal contradictions that made it difficult for teachers to grasp what was expected (Caldani et al, 2013; Guerrero, 2013). In response to this, the MoE prepared several complementary documents to guide teachers, but there were inconsistencies between them and the broader curricular framework.

The 2016 curriculum sought to resolve these inconsistencies and presented a 'curricular system' that included several complementary tools with a unified conception of 'competencies' to clearly guide implementation (Tapia and Cueto, 2017). Every curricular area aims at the progressive development of desired competencies throughout the secondary education cycle. Examples of such competencies include: 'Lives together with others and participates democratically in the search for the common good', for personal development, citizenship and civics; and 'Responsibly manages the environment', for social sciences. Additionally, the National Curriculum includes seven transversal approaches that seek to develop learners' ethical and citizenship development. These approaches are meant to be embedded in the work done in different areas and include, among others, 'Interculturality', 'Gender Equity' and 'Environment'.

It is worth noting that between 2017 and 2020 there were two major disputes around curricular content and materials dealing with questions of gender equity and the Internal Armed Conflict. In the case of gender equity, an increasingly organized conservative movement has questioned the introduction of a gender focus in the curriculum, arguing that it constitutes an ideology that goes against traditional family values. The movement has specifically questioned the idea that schools should offer sex education or acknowledge and discuss gender diversity. In the case of curricular content focusing on the Internal Armed Conflict, increasingly organized political groups, mostly Fujimori supporters, have questioned the way that school materials have approached the history of the Conflict, including references to crimes perpetrated by the State and using the 'armed conflict' terminology, rather than referring to the period of violence as one of 'terrorism' (Portugal and Uccelli, 2018).

These disputes led to legal challenges that delayed the implementation of the 2016 National Curriculum as well as the production of school textbooks that respond to its guidance (MINEDU, 2016b). This explains why some of the materials we selected corresponded to the previous version of the curriculum. It also explains why, as we shall see in the next section, many teachers are not covering disputed topics in their classrooms. No similar challenges have emerged in relation to curricular content around interculturality or environmental issues.

All the topics we initially identified for selected curricular areas appeared in the textbooks. Some, like those related to environmental education, figured in extensive sections that were exclusively dedicated to cover environmental issues; others, like those relevant to gender equity or the Internal Armed Conflict, appeared in smaller sections that were usually part of broader lessons. We found important differences in the depth with which different subjects were approached, as well as in the extent to which the texts used a justice lens to frame different issues – for instance, by highlighting existing inequalities or the need for broad structural changes.

Environmental topics, as seen in the number of relevant pages we identified, were the most developed in the texts and often had sections exclusively dedicated to them – as opposed to being included as smaller elements of a broader topic or lesson. Selected lessons focused on several environmental problems (such as pollution, climate change or biodiversity loss) that have a negative impact on human beings as well as on the planet and which need to be confronted. As mentioned earlier, the 2016 National Curriculum also includes a transversal 'environmental approach' that is meant to permeate the curriculum. There was an interesting contrast between textbooks that followed the previous version of the National Curriculum and focused mostly on scientific descriptions of physical and biological processes (such as the effects of atmospheric pollution) and more recent materials prepared during the pandemic that have a greater emphasis on the impacts of environmental changes on humanity and the planet and the need to respond to the challenges they pose (MINEDU, 2016b).

All the texts employ concrete examples of environmental problems that are present in Perú, like contamination in the city of Lima and the problems generated by illegal mining in the Amazon. But they are rather imprecise when it comes to analysing the causes and actors responsible for these problems (for instance, one example indicates that 'sustainable practices should be developed' without explaining what this means). The materials also lacked content aimed at promoting analysis or an understanding of the complexity of different problems, and they did not incorporate a justice approach to deal with the different issues. For example, they do not establish links between environmental problems and the rise in social conflicts, nor mention inequalities in access to natural resources or the burden of impacts and responsibility for different problems. When considering solutions, they mostly point to the need for individual changes rather than structural changes that might require new policies or regulation.

Similar differences can be found in the case of materials that deal with themes related to interculturality and gender equity. While there is a general tone of condemnation about the disadvantages faced by women and Indigenous groups in the country, in the older materials these themes are rather interspersed in different sections and approached in largely descriptive ways (for instance, 'The role of women' in a chapter dedicated to 'The promotion of science and culture in Perú'). The more recent materials, in contrast, have sections exclusively dedicated to some of the themes (such as 'Sexuality and gender'), and these include more complex explanations of the causes and consequences of women's exclusion, as well as clear statements about the need for change. There is a key difference between materials that deal with gender issues and those that deal with interculturality. While the former emphasize the need to question traditional roles and stereotypes that help reproduce inequalities, cultural diversity is approached in a largely celebratory manner that extols different cultural expressions without linking them to the various forms of social exclusion that they give rise to. An illustrative example of this can be found in a discussion of the cultural dominance of richer over poorer countries in the context of globalization. As an example of harmonic resolution, the text asks us to imagine the fabrication of a surfboard – a foreign cultural artefact – with Andean designs. The example is not only simplistic, but also illustrative of the general tendency in the texts to benefit specific, individual and entrepreneurial action rather than State-led or societal changes. In the more recent civics and citizenship materials and in those prepared for the pandemic distance learning strategy, the term 'gender' disappears completely, possibly because of the disputes mentioned earlier.

Something similar happens to content related to the Internal Armed Conflict. Earlier materials that respond to the 2008 National Curriculum include a section on this issue in the history, geography and economics textbook. The Conflict is presented as a historical narrative that includes antecedents, key actors, causes and consequences and presents examples that seek to move beyond a simplistic 'good and bad' portrayal of the Conflict. In the more recent textbooks, mentions of the Conflict are almost completely missing – only one text makes a specific reference to it when discussing the process of national reconciliation – while materials prepared for the distance learning strategy include factually misleading information. In general, school materials foreground discussions of 'interpersonal conflict', emphasizing the need for dialogue to avoid violent 'solutions'. Here again, the emphasis is on individual attitudes rather than the need for broader State action or societal changes.

Like in the case of policies, less 'controversial' and more superficial approaches to the different topics seem to ensure their permanence in the curriculum and materials. Complex approaches that seek to problematize simplistic narratives or solutions are often rejected by groups who believe their actions or values are being challenged. In recent years, as conservative political groups have gained influence in Congress – often allied with actors that were responsible for violent crimes committed by the State during the years of the Conflict, and who often have interests in illegal industries (including those that predate the Amazon through illegal logging and mining) – the scope for justice agendas in education seems to have narrowed down. School materials have been specifically challenged by these groups, who have achieved important victories: Congress has now approved a law that mandates that parents should be able to 'veto' school texts in response to groups who have rejected 'gender equity' education; and it has also approved a new course on the 'history of terrorism' that explicitly seeks to 'redress' the supposedly warped narrative presented by the CVR.

Learners' experiences and classroom practice related to the three justices

Approaching school practices posed a real challenge for the JustEd study as our fieldwork coincided with the second year of the COVID-19 pandemic and adaptations had to be made for each country, where different degrees of school closures were in place. In Perú, schools were closed for two whole years. While we prepared for our fieldwork online, the Ministry of Education began to allow schools to open for some activities. The heads of the schools we selected were all happy and eager to allow us to do some of the work within the school premises, so we prepared to conduct our fieldwork through a combination of online and face-to-face activities. The biggest challenge we faced was how to grasp the nature of school practices when we could not observe them directly – most learners were learning through a combination of asynchronous distance learning sessions and direct interactions with their teachers via WhatsApp. We responded to this through a fieldwork design that combined online and face-to-face individual interviews and group discussions with teachers and learners with participatory activities. The central characteristic of this design was a carefully crafted sequence of activities in which participants were asked to engage in different tasks that enabled them to move towards deeper levels of reflection about different topics.

We worked in each of the four selected schools over a two-week period through a series of individual and group 'encounters' with learners and teachers – for details of the sites and sampling procedures, see Chapter 3. Participants included learners in their last two years of secondary schooling, as well as teachers who taught the courses we had chosen for our analysis of the curriculum and school texts for those years. We also conducted individual interviews with the headteachers of each school and with two key members of the local community who could help us understand local histories and current social dynamics.

We held group encounters with learners, using participatory techniques that included the use of prompts (videos, images) to promote discussion among participants and asking them to work in small groups to produce ideas. The sequence of activities, as illustrated in Figure 5.1, included four encounters: we began with an individual interview, followed it with a group discussion, then conducted a second individual interview and a final group discussion. In the case of learners, after the second and third encounters, we asked them to engage in two exercises: the first was a photovoice exercise in which they produced images that told the story of the places where they lived and what for them were key justice issues; the second was writing a letter 'from the future' to a current authority that could make necessary changes to ensure sustainability and people's wellbeing. We used the photographs and letters to deepen the discussion of the themes we had touched upon during the first and second encounters. Most of the work done with learners was face to face and in their schools.

We also worked with teachers through a similar sequence of individual and group encounters. In their case, we asked them to use a 'lesson reconstruction tool' to develop a written lesson to work on a relevant topic that we then discussed in detail in a final individual interview. During these interviews teachers explained the aims and relevance of the lesson, how they would approach the topic, how they had prepared the lesson, and the kinds of activities they would develop in class.

The sequential, iterative and participatory design that is illustrated in Figure 5.1 allowed us to move deeper into several ideas. In both cases the second encounter was used to explore participants' understanding of justice in general as well as of the justice issues that we identified in our analysis of the curriculum and school materials. Specifically, we explored their knowledge and ideas of cultural diversity and gender equality, sustainability and the environment; the country's history of violence; and their views on conflict prevention. Participants would first say what they thought about (in)justice

Figure 5.1: Qualitative data generation sequence in Perú

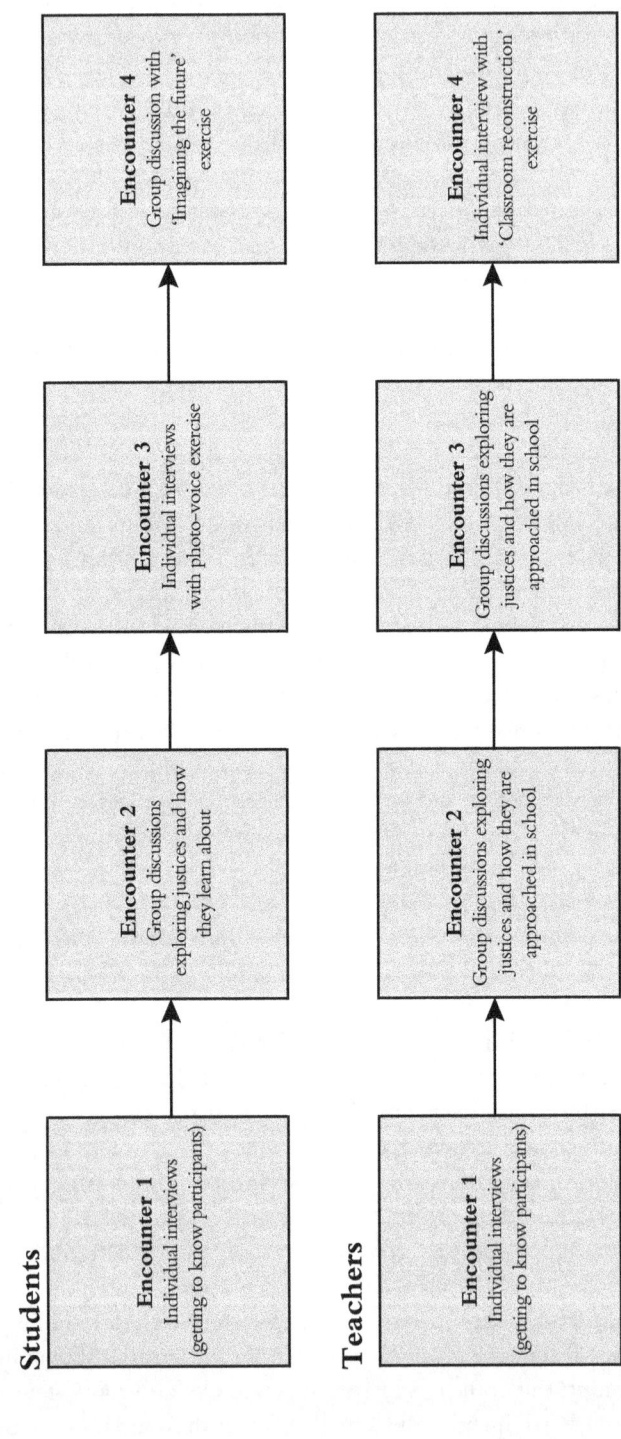

in these areas, and we would then discuss where and how they learned about them and how these issues were approached in their schools. In all cases we inquired about participants' thoughts on the causes and consequences of different problems. As we moved forward, the initial discussions would form the background for moving deeper into the different topics.

Data collected included fieldwork notes and recorded individual and group interviews, as well as pictures, letters and lesson reconstructions prepared by participants. In all, we had a total of 56 encounters with 24 learners, 45 encounters with 18 teachers, 6 interviews with school heads and 12 interviews with local actors. The data were analysed following the procedures described in Chapter 3.

Precarity and experiences of injustice as the common backdrop

The first encounters with participants made it clear that precarity and the injustices that it is associated with were the backdrop to learners' experiences and knowledge of different justice-related issues. When asked about what they understood by justice, learners initially gave formal definitions that expressed understandings of justice as equal application of the law and as equity in access to resources and legal protections. Learners would say things like justice 'is something that follows the law and injustice is something that goes against the law' (Ayacucho); 'For me it is equity. It is like … a scale' (Lima); 'justice is equality, to provide support in the right direction' (Lima).

As discussions progressed, learners began to contrast such normative ideas of justice with the everyday realities and experiences of multiple injustices that they, as well as their families and communities, were exposed to – from racial, social and gender discrimination to violence and abuses of power that led to the unfair application of the law, especially against the poorest and most marginalized people. They spoke of how 'people cheat the law', but also of how authorities regularly 'abuse the law' – how the police can 'stop anyone just like that, with no justifiable reason, and then they ask for bribes in order not to fine them' – and they mentioned also how 'many crimes remain unpunished' (Group discussions in Lima and Ayacucho). In general, the feeling of being unprotected against different forms of abuse or mistreatment was constant; and they especially emphasized the lack of protection by those in charge of enforcing the law, who would routinely bend laws in favour of those with more money or power.

When noticing such contradictions, it became clear that in school they learned about the normative ideas of justice, while their understanding of the realities of injustice came from their experiences and interactions outside of school, from the street to the home, and what they encountered in the media. Comparisons between what they learned in these two different spheres became central to our discussions and a way of deepening our understanding of learners' knowledge and attitudes in relation to the different themes we explored.

Knowledge, attitudes and reflections around diversity, the environment and Perú's recent history of violent conflict

Our approach to different justice-related issues began with broad discussions that allowed us to gauge learners' knowledge and attitudes around them, including how they had learned about different issues. Overall, learners appeared more comfortable and familiar with questions around cultural diversity, gender equity and the environment than with the recent history of the Internal Armed Conflict, about which they were curious but knew very little – a learner in a group discussion in Lima characterized their knowledge about the Conflict as 'an incomplete puzzle'. Learners in general were critical about discrimination based on racial or cultural attributes and in favour of valuing diversity. They mentioned their ideas on this matter had been formed both at school and in the context of their families and through what they learned through the media and social networks. While there seemed to be an important degree of consistency in what they learned in these different spheres, they recognized that the prevalence of discriminatory social practices in their daily lives contradicted what schools proposed and what they and their families believed.

Learners' positions were less homogenous when it came to gender equity. They all were aware of debates around the topic – especially in Lima – but female learners showed greater interest and participated more in discussions. Their rejection of gender-based inequalities, violence and discrimination was categorical, and they constantly mentioned societal changes with regards to equality between men and women. A female learner in Ayacucho stated:

> I think that's in the past, because before they used to say that men had more than women and they said that women should be in the home, they did things like cooking, those things, they couldn't educate themselves, I think these are things of the past and now we are all equal and we have rights.

At the same time, learners recognized that gender inequalities are still widespread in Peruvian society, something that, for them, was particularly evident in the constant news regarding violence against women. While our discussions focused mostly on inequalities between men and women, learners were eager and open to discuss gender diversity but stated that this was not mentioned in school and that they learned about it through their social networks. In contrast to learners' interest in this topic, most teachers said the official messages they had received about the meaning of 'gender equity' were confusing or contradictory, so they were reluctant to touch upon the matter in their classrooms.

While learners understood how cultural, racial and gender diversity were linked to inequality and exclusion, they found it harder to grasp how unequal access to the production and consumption of knowledges might contribute to the reproduction of those inequalities. As our discussions moved along, however, they were increasingly clear about their limited grasp of the complexity of some issues and their eagerness to learn more about them.

Learners were most comfortable and knowledgeable in discussions about environmental issues. They were generally aware of the impact of different environmental problems and considered it important to take action. This was also the topic on which they were able to identify a greater number of examples from their local environment (pollution, rubbish), with differences between areas, where the particular sensitivity to the topic among learners from Ucayali, in the Amazon region, stands out. Issues such as global warming or climate change were generally absent from their reflections, and learners did not seem to attach a sense of urgency to climate action; nor did they seem to understand the various (in)justices associated with environmental issues, like how environmental problems disproportionately affect the poor or those less responsible for them.

The hardest topic to discuss with learners was that of the Internal Armed Conflict, not because of any resistance on their part to do so, but rather because most learners knew very little about it. Although the extent of learners' knowledge varied in the different regions where the study was conducted – more knowledge in Ayacucho, almost no knowledge in Lima, and partial or distorted knowledge in Ucayali – we noted that learners, in general, had very little factual information about the Conflict, such as the years during which it happened or the actors involved, and had no minimally consistent narrative about what had happened or of the causes and consequences of the Conflict. This is what the learner from Lima described as 'an incomplete puzzle'.

In some cases, especially in Ucayali, the historical narrative of events and actors was mixed with references to even somewhat macabre elements linked to the acts of violence (references, for example, to a certain place where alleged terrorists were detained, tortured and killed) which, because of the very form of the narration – the gestures, distance and calm way with which they narrated specific elements of the torture – at times sounded like fictional horror stories that they did not feel were close to their experience or that of their families. In Ayacucho, on the other hand, although it was clear that the learners knew about the Conflict, they did not have much information about it either; on the contrary, they felt it was a very intimate part of their family histories which their families often preferred not to talk about. One learner in Ayacucho chose to focus her photovoice exercise on her family's experience of the Conflict. She prepared a video where she interviewed her grandparents, and she commented that it was the first time that she had heard them speak about those experiences.

These different, partial and contradictory stories are also indicative of the many versions of the Conflict that learners come to 'by hearsay' (for example, they used phrases such as 'I have heard', 'I have been told'). As they pointed out, this is a topic that they do not learn about or discuss at school or at home, and about which they learn about in a partial and fragmented way, in the media, through social networks and, mainly, in the experiential accounts of their relatives. According to them, what they do work on at school is the issue of interpersonal conflict and how to resolve it through dialogue rather than violence. They suggested that the messages about mediation and the importance of listening promoted in their schools, or about the need to punish learners who engage in violent acts, do not always work, either because teachers do not put them into practice or because learners learn how to avoid them.

Teachers' statements largely coincided with those of learners. They were clearly sensitized to the importance of respecting cultural diversity and caring for the environment and found it easier to deal with these matters in their classrooms because they had more clarity on how to understand and approach them. What they proposed was also aligned with the guidance available in the curriculum and textbooks: they generally embraced celebratory but uncritical narratives about the value of cultural diversity that highlighted the richness of cultural expressions, as seen in typical dances, music or food; in the case of environmental issues, these were largely approached in a topical, non-systemic way, with an emphasis on individual rather than institutional or structural changes. This was especially so in the context of the pandemic, where distance education did not allow for the development of experiential activities that were seen as fundamental to promoting environmental awareness. We also found that there was very little emphasis, in either case, on addressing these issues in ways that allow for the development of complex views, articulating learners' everyday experiences and the potential contradictions that might emerge from them in relation to the normative ideals proposed in classrooms.

When it came to the question of gender equality or the history of violent conflict in the country, teachers' accounts were rather different to those mentioned earlier. While most expressed critical views on gender-based violence and inequality, they also coincided in saying that they find the notions of 'gender equity' to be confusing and problematic, especially when it came to the question of sexual diversity, and said they often avoid touching upon this in their classrooms due to the lack of clarity and guidance. But they coincided that the history of the Internal Armed Conflict was an even more difficult subject for them to deal with, not just because of the lack of pedagogical guidelines and of current controversies surrounding the subject, but also due to fear of potential legal consequences. Some specifically mentioned their fear of being accused of defending terrorism, which is punished by law. As a teacher from Ayacucho mentioned:

> among us teachers, especially social science teachers, we have a certain fear that we will be branded as apologists and good-bye. It is for that reason [that we prefer not to talk about the history of the Internal Armed Conflict], not because we do not want to or because we do not know the history.

Earlier studies like that of Portugal and Uccelli (2018, p 22) similarly noticed that even when content on the Internal Armed Conflict was included in the curriculum and textbooks, teachers were resistant to teach about it because of their lack of guidance on how to do it and the 'absence of guarantees to do so freely, without being subject to reprisals'. From teachers' accounts it is evident that public disputes around the history of the Conflict and gender equity have effectively silenced many of them, who now prefer to avoid discussing these issues in their classrooms.

Comparing the findings for each theme, we note that for those subjects that make it into classroom practice – like raising environmental awareness or promoting respect for cultural diversity – schools *do* seem to contribute to the development of shared positive attitudes and dispositions among learners. As we shall see in Chapter 7, this was clear also in the survey results, which showed the widespread nature of such positive attitudes among Peruvian learners.

However, in our discussions with learners we noted that these positive ideas and attitudes are often superficial and function as slogans that learners incorporate and which might even guide their individual actions, but do not necessarily contribute to the development of critical stances on the causes and consequences of different problems, or the broader, collective, institutional and structural changes required for the establishment of more sustainable and just practices. Learners may believe in the importance of 'not polluting', 'recycling rubbish' or 'caring for plants', but they rarely reflect on how their positive individual actions or dispositions may be affected by other factors that could hinder the translation of those behaviours into sustainable changes – elements such as the unavailability of rubbish collection services or water in their neighbourhoods, or the poor State regulatory capacity and corruption that enable predatory economic activities like illegal mining or logging to thrive. Something similar happened in the case of cultural diversity: learners may value diversity and reject inequality and discrimination, but they show little reflection on the broader structural and institutional changes required to change the widespread forms of discrimination that they encounter in their daily lives. Such contradictions are usually not addressed in schools, and this makes it difficult for learners to articulate them and understand the complex and difficult choices involved in the establishment of sustainable and just practices.

In the case of topics that do not make it into the curriculum or classrooms – like gender equity or the Internal Armed Conflict – learners did not show such shared ideas and common dispositions. Some learners had greater knowledge and clarity with regards to these issues, but these were built through personal and family experience as well as through knowledge gained outside of school. Most, however, had vague knowledge and understanding, especially of the recent history of violent conflict in the country.

All this goes to show that the inclusion of content, topics or transversal approaches in the curriculum, textbooks and classroom practices plays an important role in developing such common dispositions or attitudes. Schools do matter and can make a difference. However, when certain topics become the subject of political disputes and teachers receive no clear guidance on how to deal with them, schools' influence weakens. Moreover, the positive influence that schools can make is seriously limited by the superficial nature in which many ideas and messages are dealt with. This is what we have elsewhere described as 'shallow pedagogies' (Balarin and Rodríguez, 2024) that do not foster critical thinking among learners – their capacity to explore and contrast different narratives, to delve deeper into different issues, to make distinctions and substantiate claims, to problematize and articulate the contradictions between the normative ideas they encounter at school and their everyday realities and experiences.

How schools approach complex issues

A very salient element in our discussions with learners and teachers was the difficulty that schools and teachers confront when they have to deal with complex, conflict-generating or contradictory themes. Similar observations have been made by scholars in very different parts of the world (Schweisfurth, 2011; Hoadley, 2017) and raise broader questions about the way in which schooling is conceived. While education systems often embrace critical thinking at a discursive level, in practice they tend to opt for sanitized and depoliticized accounts of the complex or divisive issues that are at the centre of just and sustainable transformations. Learners are therefore left with scant tools to articulate and confront the contradictions between the economic contribution of extractive industries and their social or environmental impact, or between the celebration of cultural diversity and the predominance of discrimination, racism and social marginalization in the country. The sanitized, depoliticized and often superficial ways in which different subjects are approached in Peruvian schools do not only translate into simplistic and slogan-like forms of learning, but also inhibit the articulation of justice perspectives on the different issues, as these crucially depend on the articulation of contradictions, the connection to unjust realities and the problematization of social, political and culturally sanctioned practices.

Environmental issues, for example, are presented as a homogenous reality that affects us all in the same way and for which we are all individually responsible. Issues are treated as specific problems that are the product of individual practices and attitudes (such as littering) as well as of certain economic practices (like illegal logging), but they are not addressed in a systemic way that articulates the interaction between different problems, or their multiple causes and consequences (individual, institutional, structural, global and so on). Nor is the contradiction, for example, between what is proposed regarding environmental care and the predominance of an economic system that predates the environment or relies on consumption practices contrary to its care – or the inequalities in the impact of environmental problems in different groups, areas or countries – made explicit and explored. Consequently, the responsibility for change is also focused on individual action and not on systemic changes.

Something similar happens in the case of cultural diversity, which is clearly a topic present in schools, and one that learners and teachers are aware of and address in the classroom. The way this topic is approached, through an emphasis on the appreciation and celebration of diversity and the exaltation of folkloric elements, does not allude to the unequal distribution of access to resources and opportunities or the prevalence of racist, discriminatory or exclusionary attitudes or practices that the celebration of diversity hardly helps resolve. Here, again, the responsibility for recognition is individualized and the institutional, cultural and social changes needed to transform society in line with the requirements of a sustainable future are left out of the discussion.

These depoliticized, often superficial and un-systemic views that fragment problems and emphasize individual responsibility for change are fundamentally consistent with what we find in the curriculum, materials and policies. Although with some variations – like in the case of a teacher from Ucayali who had been trained in 'community education' and had a more critical understanding of many of the issues – we found that teachers reproduce these discourses and narratives in their practice, promoting positive attitudes and behaviours towards the environment or cultural diversity but without articulating contradictions, problematizing, connecting to experience or fostering some understanding of the complexity of environmental and social problems. The more inherently political a topic is, the more difficult it is for it to make it into classroom practice. This was clear in the case of the Internal Armed Conflict, whose absence in the National Curriculum (MINEDU, 2016b) and the materials produced after its publication, as well as the polarization of the public debate on the topic, fully coincided with its absence in the classroom and with the lack of clarity that teachers and learners had on the subject.

Beyond this, we also found a general difficulty among the learners in noticing or articulating the contradictions that appeared when discussing the different themes. For example, the contradiction between the idea of valuing and celebrating cultural, ethnic and racial diversity and the widespread evidence, which they themselves mentioned, of how that diversity is associated with many of the social injustices (poverty, marginalization, precariousness) that they identify and often experience in their daily lives. Or the contradiction between the emphasis on individual change to improve the environment (such as not littering, not cutting down trees) and the nature and magnitude of environmental problems, which clearly exceed the scope of individual action. Or, even more so, the contradiction between the emphasis on dialogue and consensus building as a non-violent way of resolving interpersonal conflict, and the recognition that certain causes of violence in the country, such as inequality and exclusion, remain almost intact today; or the experience of violence implied by many of the injustices they recognize in their everyday lives.

What was most evident and clearly stated by participants during our meetings is that they are not used to participating in discussions of this kind. Schools, which are the predominant environment in which they learn not only information or content, but also how to think and reflect, generally do not present them with or expose them to minimally complex analytical exercises. What they get there, rather, is information and often simplistic narratives that do not articulate the contradictions between normative ideas of justice and sustainability with their own experiences of injustice. Both learners and teachers explicitly mentioned this and pointed out that their learning experiences at school and in their professional training (in the case of teachers) were rather formal and superficial, and contrasted them with the kinds of horizontal discussions we involved them in as part of the study, in which we sought to go deeper into the issues, approaching them critically and actively enabling participants' contribution to the development of ideas and explanations.

While it is possible that what we observed, especially the superficial treatment of issues, was also a product of two years of pandemic and remote education, participants' comments on this point suggest common practices in schools that go beyond this exceptional period. What we identify as shallow pedagogies is similar to what has been found in other studies that highlight how lessons are usually 'organized around thematic content that is dealt with in a very superficial way' and 'without providing learners with adequate feedback or opportunities to analyse, create or critique ideas' (González et al, 2017, p 233).

These shallow pedagogies can be seen as a cross-cutting epistemic injustice that hinders learning and above all learners' ability to understand their own experiences and the world around them. The partial, often superficial knowledge, the difficulty in discerning between true and false information and in basing personal opinions on solid information and consistent reasoning, as well as the difficulties learners showed in analysing the causes and consequences of the different topics – to contrast and articulate ideas, to deal with contradictions and to analyse the topics in depth – point precisely to a reality of profound epistemic injustice in education. Participants' reflections on the absence of spaces for discussion in their schools, which would allow them to contrast their ideas and build knowledge, also reveal the prevalence of the epistemic injustice at the heart of many contemporary education systems in the Global South.

Conclusions

The Perú case study has yielded several important insights about the way in which some countries in the Global South are approaching justice and sustainability agendas through education. Compared to Uganda and Nepal, Perú seems to have made greater progress not only in redistributive forms of justice in education, but also in terms of the recognition of diversity and gender equity. The Peruvian case, however, also illuminates some of the limitations that countries may face in the implementation of justice agendas in view of growing political challenges and in terms of their education systems' capacity to model and support more just and sustainable practices in education.

At the policy level, we saw how the turn of the millennium coincided with a favourable climate for the establishment and consolidation of different justice agendas that sought to promote equity, inclusion and recognition of various excluded groups. At the national level, the democratic transition after a decade of authoritarian rule and the work of the CVR created awareness about the importance of avoiding future authoritarian projects and consolidating democracy through changes in the institutional apparatus and sectoral policies, as well as through greater redistribution of resources and opportunities, citizen participation and recognition and respect for diversity. The emergence of this 'justice approach' in education policies was also influenced by several national and international processes and currents. International policy movements and frameworks – from the World Conferences on Women to the Education for All agenda, the ILO Treaty 169 (ILO, 1989) on the rights of Indigenous peoples and the COP conferences on climate change – created an important external pressure for Perú to address justice and sustainability issues.

This justice approach was reflected in the General Education Law (MINEDU, 2003) and in the National Education Project (Consejo Nacional de Educación, 2007), both of which highlighted the importance of citizen participation and the search for equity, and gave rise to important changes in sectoral governance that sought to facilitate a more equitable distribution of educational services and opportunities. But the justice agenda in education fully consolidated during the second decade of the new millennium with the approval of important policies for IBE, gender equity and environmental education. The existence of such policies, however, did not always translate into a real prioritization of the issues in the education sector, nor in the sustainability of some of the issues over time.

What we notice is a clear rise and fall of these justice policy agendas in Peruvian education, which peaked between 2011 and 2016 and then fell starkly to their near disappearance in the present day. The decline of these policies was influenced by opposition from conservative groups to certain issues (such as the treatment of the history of the Internal Armed Conflict or the inclusion of the gender approach in education), but also by the greater prioritization of a more narrow agenda focused on improving measurable learning outcomes that, perhaps unintentionally, shifted policies away from equity and justice concerns. This was compounded by the growing turmoil in the country's politics and governance, a chaos marked by increasing factionalism and political instability (6 presidents and 13 education ministers in just 8 years) as well as by the COVID-19 pandemic.

Our analysis of justice-focused policies also demonstrated the existence of significant differences in how policies approach justice aims, from more or less critical perspectives and with greater or lesser emphasis on causes, effects and structural or systemic changes. While some of the policies are developed on the basis of complex and critical discourses that point, for example, to the unequal distribution of responsibilities and benefits or the negative consequences associated with certain problems and aim at promoting social, cultural and economic transformations, others are characterized by presenting the issues in a fundamentally depoliticized manner, where these dimensions are absent from the discussion. These different emphases influence the approaches and content we found in the curriculum, textbooks and classroom practice, as well as the degree of political acceptance or rejection that policies face.

Maybe more importantly, we found that learners and teachers are not habituated to exploring the causes and consequences of different problems or do so only in superficial ways that do not foster understanding or learners' ability to grasp problems in their complexity but rather reduces them to simplistic readings that lead to equally simplistic solutions. A consequence of this is a general emphasis on individual changes to promote social or cultural transformations, and a lack of understanding of how such individual actions might be limited by institutional or structural factors.

In some cases, the depoliticization of justice-related issues – like we saw in the case of an intercultural approach to basic education – can be an explicit strategy on the part of decision-makers to get those issues into policy agendas. But depoliticization may also be an unintended result from processes of curriculum and textbook development, which in the effort to present issues in accessible ways may end up simplifying them to a point that does enable deeper forms of understanding, the making of connections and the articulation of contradictions.

This brings us to a point that emerges clearly in group and individual conversations with learners and teachers, who, when explaining how they work on certain topics at school, highlight the lack of depth, analysis, reflection and critical thinking that characterizes much schoolwork in Perú. This is something that has been mentioned in other studies on teaching practice (González et al, 2017) and that our study participants themselves pointed out when contrasting the nature of the work we did with them throughout our meetings. Many participants, both learners and teachers, mentioned that our work challenged them and pushed them to go deeper and beyond preconceived ideas around the issues we discussed in a way that they were not used to. Their descriptions of what they normally do in school, as well as their handling and ability to think about and discuss different topics, suggest a predominance of the 'shallow pedagogies' we mentioned earlier, which do not develop the capacity for critical thinking among learners (Balarin and Rodríguez, 2024).

On those issues with which learners were most familiar (environment and respect for cultural, ethnic and racial diversity), many of the ideas learned at school seemed to function as slogans or basic rules of behaviour ('it is important to take care of the environment', 'cultural diversity must be valued'). While this kind of learning may result in positive attitudes or dispositions towards these issues, they rarely translate into an ability to think independently, reflectively and critically (in the sense of adequately supporting arguments, identifying contradictions or articulating them into somewhat more complex ideas or explanations, among other things).

On the other hand, our study revealed a strong disconnect between learners' daily experiences, both within and outside of school, and the formal learning promoted in classrooms. School practices do not seem to connect with those experiences and do not articulate them to promote ways of learning that might be more grounded in learners' realities, many of which are characterized by injustices. Learners noted this disconnection and repeatedly mentioned their own experiences at home, in the street and in social networks that had led them to learn and develop certain ideas that they could not fully articulate and that could even contradict formal ideas about respect for diversity, care for the environment and other topics they were presented with at school.

If epistemic justice implies the possibility of accessing relevant knowledge to understand ourselves and the world around us, of having our ideas heard and valued, as well as of participating on equal terms in the creation of knowledge, not having this basic capability to know, think and make sense of our experiences and the knowledge that we encounter is undoubtedly an epistemic injustice at the very core of the school experience (Fricker, 2015).

The fact that schools can transmit some basic ideas that so obviously influence the way learners think, even if only through the transmission of basic messages, makes us reaffirm our belief in the potential that schools do have to shape the epistemic capabilities of learners. Schools are not irrelevant for attempts to promote more just and sustainable societies, but they could and should aim to achieve more ambitious learning goals than the ones that often dominate a learning agenda focused on narrow and measurable learning outcomes. The interest and enthusiasm of learners and teachers in our study to engage in more complex discussions – to learn to think and reflect together in more complex ways – also suggests that there is an unspoken demand for different and epistemically more just forms of education.

6

Education and Justice in Uganda

Introduction

Uganda has put in place significant measures to address equitable access to affordable, quality and relevant education in line with international, regional and national policies as well as legal commitments (Government of Uganda, 2018). Global calls for justice in education have been largely heeded by Uganda as the country is a signatory to various international conventions aimed at promoting justice in education. The country has ratified the SDGs (Office of the Prime Minister, 2021), specifically including SDG 4 (Ensure Inclusive and Equitable Quality Education and Promote Lifelong Learning Opportunities for All). It is also a party to the 1960 UNESCO Convention against Discrimination in Education (UNESCO, 2005).

Relatedly, the country is also a signatory to the Africa Agenda 2063, specifically Goal 2 for well-educated citizens and a skills revolution underpinned by science, technology and innovation. The SDGs have been domesticated in the country; and the National Development Plan (NDP) aligns with the SDGs and the Africa Agenda 2063. The NDP prioritizes education under the sector of Human Capital Development (National Planning Authority, 2020). Accordingly, universal access to education is being implemented through government programmes of Universal Primary Education (UPE), Universal Secondary Education (USE) and Universal Post-Primary Education and Training (UPPET) (Ayorekire and Twinomuhangi, 2012).

The 1995 Constitution of the Republic of Uganda (Article 30) provides for the right to education (Constitution of the Republic of Uganda, 1995). The operationalization of this right is supported by many Acts including: Education (Pre-Primary, Primary and Post-Primary) Act (Government of Uganda, 2008); Business Technical Vocational Education and Training (BTVET) Act (Government of Uganda, 2008); Universities and Other Tertiary Institutions Act (Government of Uganda, 2001); Uganda National Examinations Board (UNEB) Act (Government of Uganda, 2021); National Curriculum

Development Centre (NCDC) Act (National Curriculum Development Centre, 2000); Education Service Act 2002 (Government of Uganda, 2012); Higher Education Learners Financing Board (HESFB) Act (Government of Uganda, 2014); Employment Act (Government of Uganda, 2006a); Local Government Act (1997); Universities and other Tertiary Institutions Act (2001); Teachers' Professional Code of Conduct (Government of Uganda, 2012); Education Service Act (Government of Uganda, 2002); Refugee Act (Government of Uganda, 2006b); Public Private Partnership Act (Government of Uganda, 2015), among others.

This legal framework is targeted to include various educational actors – including learners, teachers, the general public and supporting institutions – for the attainment of desirable education standards in the country. Formal and non-formal education systems have been given equal recognition at basic education level as stipulated in Part IX Section 49 (1) of the 2008 Education Act (Education (Pre-Primary, Primary and Post-Primary) Act, 2008). The Act recognizes five non-formal education centres in the country in Schedule Six, and empowers the Permanent Secretary, Chief Administrative Officer or Town Clerk to identify and approve any centre in their jurisdiction.

Since these centres are at the basic education level, more needs to be done at secondary school and higher education levels. For example, various special interest groups whose lifestyles conflict with the formal structured education systems of the country have had special educational packages designed for them to fit their special circumstances. The Alternative Basic Education for Karamoja (ABEK) and the Basic Education for the Urban Poor (BEUPA) policies have been designed as non-formal educational programmes to fit the nomadic nature of the Karamojong pastoralists as well as urban poor youth in the slums of Kampala city, respectively (Nuwategeka et al, 2021a).

The ABEK and BEUPA programmes are enshrined in Uganda's Education Act (2008), which creates a framework for non-formal education. The Functional Adult Literacy educational programme has been developed outside the formal education system to equip adult learners with basic literacy and numeracy skills relevant for life in the community. All these programmes are an attempt by the Ugandan government to ensure equitable access to education for all its citizens. The educational policy environment in the country is broadly supportive in, for example, environmental and epistemic justice areas, but it is deficient in tackling transitional justice issues in education. Operationally, the curriculum and educational practices are characterized by inadequacies and inequities and rarely anchor a justice approach, as discussed later.

A combination of environmental as well as transitional justice issues therefore requires solutions that may be partly built in and facilitated by an education system which rallies the citizens to be active agents in environmental management and peace and reconciliation. This chapter

Table 6.1: Policy documents reviewed according to the three justices in Uganda

S/N	Type of justice	Selected policies that were reviewed
1	Environmental justice	The National Environment Act (2019)
		The National Forestry and Tree Planting Act (2003)
2	Epistemic justice	The Education Act (2008)
		The Alternative Basic Education for Karamoja policy (1998)
3	Transitional justice	The Amnesty Act (2000)
		The National Transitional Justice Policy (2019)

focuses on the role of education *as* and *for* justice in Uganda to achieve environmental, epistemic and transitional justice for sustainable development. We undertake a critical analysis of the education system, delving into how the Ugandan education system has (or has not) situated itself in the global agendas for justice in education, before exploring how the curriculum embeds (or does not embed) justice aspects. Finally, we analyse the teaching and learning of the justices as well as learners' experiences, aspirations and expectations regarding the justices.

Education and justice in Uganda's policies

The Ugandan environmental, educational and transitional justice policies that were reviewed as described in Table 6.1 have been developed due to the need for reforms occasioned by challenges facing the country. Firstly, environmental degradation in deforestation and large-scale wetland reclamation led to the development of the environmental policies. Secondly, the need to regulate education to be inclusive led to the reforms included in the 2008 Education Act. Lastly, the insecurity in the country occasioned by various armed groups and cattle rustlers formed the basis for the formulation of the National Transitional Justice Policy (Government of Uganda, 2019b) and the Amnesty Act (Government of Uganda, 2000) to deal with reconciliation and the reintegration of ex-combatants into society.

The National Environment Act (Government of Uganda, 2019a, p 1) is 'an Act to repeal, replace and reform the law relating to environmental management in Uganda'. This Act replaced the 2005 Environment Management Act. The National Forestry and Tree Planting Act was written in 2003, and some of the language used in it may reflect that it is over 20 years old. Across the National Environment Act (Government of Uganda, 2019a) and the National Forestry and Tree Planting Act (Government of Uganda, 2003), there is remarkable consistency in the view and language used. For example, objective B of the former and objectives C and D of the latter are coherent on the issue of the importance of sustainable use of environmental resources.

Despite the National Environment Act (Government of Uganda, 2019a) recognizing the environment as having rights and being entitled to protection, most of the language across the Acts reflects anthropocentric concerns. The National Forestry and Tree Planting Act (Government of Uganda, 2003, p 2) was written with the interconnected aims of facilitating 'the achievement of sustainable increase in economic, social and environmental benefits from forests and trees', conserving trees in a way that 'meets the needs of present generations without compromising the rights of the future generation by safeguarding forest biological diversity' and promoting 'the improvement of livelihoods through strategies and actions that contribute to poverty eradication'. The policies thus interpret the natural environment as a resource and service for human health, livelihood and enjoyment. Positioned in these primarily anthropocentric terms, we would argue that the key objective of the Acts falls short of creating 'environmentally responsible citizens'.

The National Environment Act explicitly states a key role for education in enabling such outcomes. It situates environmental education within the mandate of the National Environment Management Authority, which is supposed to work with the ministry responsible for education to ensure inclusion of environmental education in the educational curricular and materials. Point 148 of the Act – titled 'Integration of environmental education into educational curricula and programmes' – includes the following clauses:

1. The Authority shall, in collaboration with the Ministry responsible for education, ensure that environmental and sustainable development concerns are integrated into the national education system, including academic and non-academic programmes.
2. The Authority may provide technical support to the lead agency responsible for educational curriculum development to mainstream environment and sustainable development concerns in the national curricula.
3. The Authority shall, in collaboration with the relevant lead agency, initiate, promote and support nationwide environmental literacy campaigns through education, training and other forms of community engagement in the manner prescribed in guidelines issued by the Authority.

Accordingly, the National Curriculum Development Centre (NCDC), a body responsible for development of curricula for all primary and secondary schools in the country, has included 'environmental awareness' as one of the cross-cutting issues in every lesson that is taught in the newly revised lower secondary curriculum (National Curriculum Development Centre, 2019a). Whereas there are particular subjects with environment-related content like geography (25 per cent), biology (7 per cent) and agriculture (3 per cent) in the revised lower secondary school curriculum, other subjects are required to build environmental management aspects into their lesson plans as a generic skill. Whereas there is content included in the education curriculum, as we will show in this chapter, there is much less focus on the type of content and pedagogies that might be needed to deliver the objectives of the Environment Act through schooling.

However, it is also important to note that education is not consistently recognized as an intervention for environmental outcomes. While the National Environment Act (Government of Uganda, 2019a) connects to education, the National Forestry and Tree Planting Act (Government of Uganda, 2003) does not have any links to education. This is perhaps particularly surprising given that a central aim of the Act is to 'guide and cause the people of Uganda to plant trees' (Government of Uganda, 2003, p 4), but schools are not stated as important spaces where such guidance could be taught. This inconsistency may be both a cause and consequence of the limited attention paid to how education can bring about meaningful change.

The Education Act (2008) addresses aspects of equitable access to education, recognizing non-formal education to operate alongside formal education. It also legislates for UPE, USE and UPPET. All these are guarantees for citizens' access to education. The Act is noticeably clear on the regulation of education as a sector and guarantees citizens' access to (particularly formal) education. However, it is conspicuously silent about Indigenous education and the recognition of Indigenous knowledge as a component of the education system; nor is there any mention of which and whose knowledge(s) should be included in the education of the citizens.

When it comes to the policies related to transitional justice, we see that with this more contentious and political issue there is very limited attention paid to how the policy can actually be put into practice. This is despite both the Amnesty Act and National Transitional Justice Policy having aims that are broadly reflective of the transitional justice literature (Paulson et al, 2021). For example, the National Transitional Justice Policy (2019) aims 'to address the gaps in the formal justice system for post-conflict situations, formalize the use of traditional justice mechanism in post-conflict situations, facilitate reconciliation and nation building, address gaps in the current amnesty process [and] provide reparations for post-conflict situations'. The lack of attention to how this can be done in practice is especially seen regarding education. The Amnesty Act (2000) and the National Transitional Justice Policy (2019) do not have links to education. Unlike stipulations in the National Environment Act (Government of Uganda, 2019a), these two policy documents do not compel the ministry in charge of education to include issues of transitional justice in school curricula.

In contrast to the silence from national policies, attempts to undertake peace and justice education in Uganda has been spearheaded by civil society organizations where newsletters have been printed and circulated to schools as well as facilitating the formation of peace clubs. For example, the Beyond Juba Project supplied 47,000 copies of their newsletter, supplementing the *New Vision* newspaper's pull-out called *Jazz Peace* (Batanda, 2009). However, teachers are experiencing significant challenges integrating peace education programmes with other subjects (Tito, 2013).

It is worthwhile noting that both the 2008 and the 2020 curricula for the lower secondary school contain aspects of transitional justice in the history and religious studies syllabi. This is a case of school curriculum content not backed by policy recommendations. Whereas transitional justice content is in the curriculum, it is neither treated as a generic skill nor a cross-cutting issue to be included in every teaching and learning situation, as is the case for environmental management issues (National Curriculum Development Centre, 2019a). Secondly, Langole (2010) elaborates that the strands of peace education seem to lack holism and are generally optional, not made attractive enough and not diffused at all levels as to engender a philosophy of peaceful living.

Justice in the Ugandan national curriculum and school textbooks

We analysed the old and new curricula, alongside a range of textbooks (see Table 6.2) using the analysis process outlined in Chapter 3.

In line with the higher expectations of education for environmental concerns outlined in the relevant policies discussed earlier, of topics related to the three justices, environmental issues take up the largest proportion of the secondary school curricula. However, despite the observance of global calls for inclusion of environmental content in educational materials and the domestication of such calls by Uganda, the current reforms in the lower secondary school curriculum have witnessed a significant reduction in environment-related content. The subject of agriculture has witnessed the greatest reduction, from 11 per cent to 3 per cent for the topic of ecology in the 2008 and 2019 curricula, respectively. This reduction would be understandable if a cut in one subject were compensated for by an increase in another as a way of reducing repetitiveness across the subjects. However, this is not the case. Similar reduction in content is observed in biology and in geography, although geography has the least percentage reduction, from 21 per cent to 20 per cent.

The formal school curriculum content on environmental education in geography, biology and agriculture is taught under different topics, including climate change. References are made to it in terms of global warming and greenhouse gases in Senior 2 in the 2020 geography curriculum, while it was framed as atmospheric pollution in both geography (S.2) and biology (S.4) in the older 2008 curriculum. However, despite significant content,

Table 6.2: Curricular materials analysed in Uganda

Subject	Environmental justice			Transitional justice	
	Geography	Biology	Agriculture	History and political education	Christian religious education
Curriculum documents	Geography teaching syllabus – Senior 1–4 (2008)	Biology teaching syllabus – Senior 1–4 (2008)	Agriculture teaching syllabus – Senior 1–4 (2008)		Christian religious education teaching syllabus – Senior 1–4 (2008)
	Lower secondary curriculum –geography syllabus (2019)	Lower secondary curriculum –biology syllabus (2018)	Lower secondary curriculum –agriculture syllabus (2019)	Lower secondary curriculum –history and political education syllabus (2019)	Lower secondary curriculum – Christian religious education (2019)
Textbooks	MK ordinary level geography: North America (learner's book 2)	MK secondary: biology (learner's book 1)	MK secondary agriculture (Senior 1)	A primary history for Uganda (Book 1)	MK ordinary level: Christian religious education
	MK integrated secondary: geography (learner's book 1)	MK secondary: biology (learner's book 2)	MK secondary agriculture (learner's book 2)	MK ordinary level history: East Africa; 1000 AD–independence (learner's book)	
	MK ordinary level: geography of East Africa (learner's book 3)		MK secondary agriculture (learner's book 3)	MK ordinary level history: East Africa; 1880–1971 (learner's book 3)	

the topic is not framed as an issue of justice, as indicated in the learning outcomes of biology S.4 and geography S.2 of the 2020 curriculum. For example, the learning outcomes for the topic 'climate change in East Africa and the world' focuses on understanding the causes and effects of climate change, then mitigation measures, with no mention of the disproportionate distribution of the costs of climate change to communities which have a negligible contribution to its causes (Wilder et al, 2024). There is no mention of how rich and polluting countries do not or should compensate poor and non-polluting countries which suffer from this environmental injustice. Similarly, we see a consistent focus on how human beings are faced with the climate crisis without considering how the environment itself suffers the consequences, which points to an anthropocentric lens, only seemingly trying to care for the environment so that humans live comfortably.

The 2020 new curriculum geography syllabus for Senior 2 dedicates 12 per cent of term two class work to the topic of climate change. It has five sub-topics, and there are eight periods (a period is a unit of time for instruction, and one period is 40 minutes of class work). This inclusion of such content aligns with SDG 4's target 4.7 of global calls for education to ensure that all learners acquire the knowledge and skills needed to promote sustainable development. Impressive as the inclusion of environmental education is in the curriculum, how far it goes to impact the learners towards being agents of environmental management is discussed later in this chapter. This is because teaching practices may or may not be supportive in transforming learners.

Unlike the topic of climate change – which is not framed as a justice issue, as seen from the suggested learning activities, sample assessment strategies and learning outcomes in the geography syllabus (National Curriculum Development Centre, 2019b, p 32) – the topic 'Humans and the natural environment' in the biology syllabus is framed as a biocentric justice issue with the human impact on the environment expounded. It introduces learners to the concept of ecosystems and the injustices being done to the environment. One of the learning outcomes is that the learners should 'appreciate and describe natural factors and human influences that may have an impact on ecosystems and make suggestions about how to preserve the natural environment for all living things'. The environment is central to the topic, and the suggested learning activities all focus on how to manage environmental waste (through recycling and re-use) for a clean and healthy environment (National Curriculum Development Centre, 2019b, p 64). In the geography textbook for Senior 3, environmental justice is mainly discussed from the point of view of environmental restoration, such as afforestation and reforestation. Much as the scenarios mentioned earlier point to justice for the environment, the curriculum and textbooks do not present issues of justice to people or communities that are negatively affected by environmental outcomes of powerful economic agents in society. For example, there are no aspects of reparations, compensation or environmental clean-ups being proposed to ensure justice for the affected communities.

When it comes to content related to epistemic justice, we see a distinct lack of content in this regard. There is extremely limited consideration for Indigenous knowledge aspects in the teaching and learning materials. Western formal knowledge is the only knowledge considered. Another key finding from our curriculum analysis is the distinct lack of locally relevant case studies that relate to the experiences of the learners. In the new 2020 competence-based curriculum for lower secondary school, only 4 per cent of the prescribed learning activities in the geography syllabus relates directly or indirectly to locally relevant activities that may bring in learners' Indigenous or local knowledges. This epistemically disenfranchizes the learners and the entire community, whose knowledges and experiences are marginalized by the school system. Save for the 4 per cent, the rest of the learning activities are in conventional teaching and learning activities typical of formal educational practices based on Western knowledge.

Whereas there are no European and American case studies in the syllabus and textbooks, the African case studies are drawn from countries like Zambia, Congo, South Africa, Gabon, Egypt, Nigeria, Ethiopia and Ghana. These countries may have peculiar differences from the local Ugandan settings, and no indication is given of how the case studies are relevant for local realities. Epistemic justice issues do not only focus on knowledge content, but also the how of knowing. We also observe that the syllabus is not emphatic on using bridging pedagogies like fieldwork methods which exhibit both formal and Indigenous knowledge attributes. In prescribing field-based learning activities, the 2019 geography syllabus elaborates: 'If possible, learners visit an area where fishing takes place' (National Curriculum Development Centre, 2019b, p 43), meaning that fieldwork is not mandatory; teachers are at liberty to adopt it in their lessons or not. This has promoted relaxation in enforcing field-based learning, already coupled with other challenges that disfavour it, such as financial and logistical challenges to undertake it. There are, thus, very limited considerations in the school curricula for Indigenous knowledge, Indigenous pedagogies or attempts to contextualize topics to the place where learners live.

Transitional justice-related school content has a significant share of the 2020 curriculum, where 30 per cent of the entire lower secondary school syllabus for Christian religious education is dedicated to it, up from a meagre 3 per cent in the older 2008 syllabus. Whereas there is a sizeable portion of transitional justice issues in the curriculum, there are no connections of this to the national transitional justice policies in the country. Issues of transitional justice are presented under the topics of peace and conflict resolution in East Africa, and peace, justice and conflict resolution in the old and new curriculum, respectively. However, it is important to note that the topic only appears in the fourth year of the curriculum and that there is no transitional justice-related topic in earlier classes. It would be ideal if transitional justice issues were included throughout the formation stages of young learners rather than only appearing at the terminal stage of this lower secondary education level.

In both the old and new curricula, the issues are framed as a way of maintaining peace and harmonious coexistence in society. Justice is conceived as a way of promoting fairness in society. There is impressive recognition of both formal and informal justice systems in conflict resolution. The informal justice system listed in the learner's book includes the use of informal courts like family courts, clan councils, taboos and divine guidance from ancestral spirits (Isanga and Nsubuga, 2008). In most rural communities, the informal courts are respected and their decisions recognized by the community. It is worthwhile noting that the informal African traditional justice procedural systems are running parallel with the formal legal system, making them plural legal systems (Amone-P'Olak et al, 2017; Skelton and Batley, 2021).

The conflict in northern Uganda involving the LRA and the Government of Uganda (1986–2006) is cited in the 2020 curriculum. One of the learning activities is to guide learners to understand how the victims and the perpetrators of the LRA war were reconciled in the Acholi community based on the traditional justice system of the land. Another one is to guide the learners to appreciate the role played by traditional leaders in the peacebuilding process of many East Africa Community States. The third one is to guide learners to appreciate the role played by African traditional leaders in pursuing transitional justice in resolving conflict in the region. All these scenarios point to the recognition the education system attaches to Indigenous non-formal justice systems in dealing with conflicts and promotion of reconciliation in the region. This recognition also extends to the role of religious leaders in conflict resolution and peacebuilding. However, such recognition of non-formal and Indigenous ways of being and knowing was not consistently seen across the curriculum. Indigenous knowledge is frequently disregarded, treated as 'barbaric' and 'outdated'. In one Christian religious education textbook, African traditional religion is demonized in favour of Christianity and Islam.

While there is a deliberate attempt to trace the causes of conflicts, the curricula present the government's singular narrative as they demonize the LRA for causing massive suffering among the population. By contrast, the government is presented as the victim and 'saviour'. The viewpoint presented is that of the Government of Uganda, while the viewpoint of the LRA is not presented. The learners are not guided to independently discuss the conflict from an exploratory or objective position. For example, the LRA rationale for participating in conflict is not mentioned in either the curricula or in the learning materials, that is, textbooks. The LRA may have pertinent issues that led to its formation and subsequent participation in armed rebellion, one of which is to create political change and protect the Acholi people from persecution by the government, but this is not presented in the text (Vinci, 2007). It is therefore clear that normative ideas of justice are presented with no connection to how these may be built into the relevant and appropriate pedagogies that lead to transformative learning among the learners.

Another important epistemic justice issue in Uganda is the persistent and strict use of only the English language in all curricula and textbooks. Most learners in rural schools are more conversant with the local area mother tongues and have expressed difficulties in comprehending in English, a second or even third language only taught and learned in school (Milligan et al, 2024). This Anglo monolingualism existing in secondary schools is rooted in a government policy document, the Education White Paper (Government of Uganda, 1992, R.7), where it is enshrined that 'English is both the medium of instruction from S1 onwards and a compulsory subject'. It is also noted that 'learners will be encouraged as much as possible to take another foreign language so as to increase their own and the national capacity to communicate at the international level ... one of the major Ugandan languages may also be taught optionally'. Through this, Ugandan languages are placed as inferior and optional, relegating them to the level where schools and learners may not choose to teach or learn them at all. The fact that they are not included in textbook materials – despite the fact that this may support learners to better understand the content – also shows that English alone is deemed the language of instruction. Relatedly, all assessments (in-school and national) are written in English, and not only is English one of the compulsory subjects in lower secondary schools, but it is also used in academic grading for the national exams. When a learner passes all the subjects with distinction but fails English, they are given a lower grade.

Learners' experiences and classroom practice related to the three justices

This section discusses learners' everyday experiences in school. It also explores aspects of the teaching practices, and how the school attempts to navigate environmental, epistemic and transitional justice issues in a twinning interaction between learners and teachers across pedagogy and learner–learner and teacher–learner relationships both in and out of classroom. The extent to which young people's lived experiences of secondary education reflect and embed the three forms of justice was investigated using a mix of methods. Individual interviews, art-based methods and focus group discussions were conducted with the learners of the lower secondary school level. Data collection was structured according to phases, phase one involving four purposively selected schools (two urban boarding and two rural day). The urban/rural character of schools was important to aggregate educational experiences, since urban schools are relatively elite in nature as compared to rural schools, yet they all implement the same curriculum and are regulated by the government.

In-depth interviews were conducted with head teachers of each of the selected secondary schools concerning the administration of teaching and learning. Individual interviews were also conducted with classroom teachers of the geography, biology, agriculture, history and Christian religious education subjects in each of the four schools to explore the classroom pedagogies and the teaching and learning aspects related to the respective specific subjects. In phase two, individual interviews and focus group discussions were conducted with 128 and 32 learners, respectively. Four focus group discussions (one per school) involving 8 learners each undertook arts-based methods to explore learners' every day in- and out-of-school experiences of the three justices and their aspirations for the future. The arts-based methods were designed to engage young people in thoughtful and reflective ways about their experiences of violence both in and out of school, as well as their knowledge of their environment and culture. Firstly, a variety of artistic items (pictures) depicting different forms of violence were displayed. A learner was asked to pick two or three items that resonate with them; they then engaged in a discussion exploring personal experiences about those kinds of violence. Secondly, learners were asked to draw illustrations of any of their valued traditional/cultural practices/items, to be presented after a fortnight. Then, they would be engaged in a discussion of why they value that and if their school curriculum embraces their culture. Finally, in group of at least three, young people were asked to map their communities and school, identifying places that are safe/unsafe, the ones they like/dislike, resources, and any other features/places they feel are important, as well as things they would like to be introduced or removed from their education. All these generated a discussion around the justices.

Since the fieldwork took place during school closures due to the COVID-19 lockdown in the country, classroom observations were not implemented. Learning was largely online; lessons were being delivered on national television, and in other instances the government supplied hard copies of learning materials for learners to do self-study (occasionally helped by a parent-hired private tutor). To make up for classroom observations, teachers were interviewed at school (since they could access school premises), and learners were interviewed from their homes individually. Learners' focus group discussions were conducted at common meeting points. Snowballing was used to identify learners, with initial contacts obtained from classroom teachers about the location of their residences in the community.

This section starts by characterizing the school teaching and learning, then we explore the in- and out-of-school knowledges and how they interact in the context of education. Lastly, learners' views and aspirations about education and the future are presented.

Contextual challenges shaping epistemic injustice

Teacher interviews revealed that learning in most schools is characterized by large classes with an average teacher–learner ratio of 1:60. This ratio is only possible in schools which have enough classroom blocks to divide one class into different streams. In other schools without enough classroom blocks, the ratio can be as high as 1:90. Overcrowded classrooms interfere with learning in such a way that not every learner is given an opportunity to interact with the teacher during the teaching and learning session. The curriculum has structured a unit of time for instruction at 40 minutes. This time is not adequate to ensure every learner gets to interact with the teacher or among themselves, even in the classes with the lowest teacher–learner ratio.

Lack of adequate learner-teacher interactions is a clear form of epistemic injustice because it excludes learners from the dialogical aspects of the teaching–learning processes. This scenario ensures learners do not bring their knowledges and experiences into the classroom, thereby excluding them from knowledge production. The practice described by teachers across the schools in the study is for teachers to interact with high achievers only, who in most cases readily provide responses to the teachers' tasks. At the same time, learners are also excluded from knowledge consumption since learning is limited. Teachers are concerned over the limited time for lesson development, especially in subjects with more content. For example, one teacher (Kitgum) expressed that learners sharing their experiences in class is 'really not much ... [because] the subject is wide and you have to cover so much; even if you give chances for the learners to talk, it is restricted'. The teacher went on to bemoan, 'we really do not have that time enough to get their experience out ... we are time bound, and topic bound'.

To extend the time of classroom interaction during the teaching–learning process, headteachers explained that some schools that participated in this study have stopped implementing single lessons of 40 minutes and made all lessons double (80 minutes). Whereas this has created a little more opportunity for interactions, the learning stations model of classroom organization emphasized by the competence-based curriculum may not benefit from this seemingly additional time.

Firstly, learners are supposed to be organized in learning groups in the class, given tasks, and expected to produce knowledge at learning group level (National Curriculum Development Centre, 2019a). After engaging at learning group level, plenary discussions are to follow where the learners make presentations and the teacher facilitates a discussion. An average class has about six learning groups; and if every group is to discuss and present during the 80 minutes, the time would not be adequate for fruitful discussions. During a focus group discussion, one learner said that 'the way the timetable is, teaching stops till late in the evening and we cannot even get time for group discussion and that hurts us so much'.

Secondly, the crowded nature of the curriculum works against this provision. The lower secondary curriculum prescribes a minimum of 12 subjects a learner must attend. To ensure that all these subjects are timetabled in a week, each day is planned for academic activities from 8 am to 5 pm, violating the official 8 am to 3 pm regulation from the Ministry of Education and Sports which stipulates that academic activities should stop at 3 pm to allow learners to engage in co-curricular activities and projects.

The limited time allocated to learners' projects (individual or collaborative) in favour of academic activities impedes collaborative learning and acquisition of concrete experiences (Kolb, 2014; Paul and Quiggin, 2020), which are at the centre of experiential learning and transformative education. At the same time, constraints occasioned by an overcrowded curriculum do not allow learners' projects to take place across subjects. Teachers explained that schools have adapted to this constraint by engaging learners in at least one project per subject per term. This arrangement limits transdisciplinary transfer of knowledge and promotes the siloing of knowledge (Gaynor, 2016) as if subjects were not related to each other. This may lead to lack of knowledge integration in problem-solving among learners.

Based on teachers' and learners' reflections of the key issues facing the education system – the overloaded curriculum, crowded classrooms and the limited time for school activities – we argue that they interact to produce an axis of a school crash course programme where teachers have to teach multiple classes and learners attend a variety of lessons across a rigid timetable. School therefore is reduced to a maze of endless meanders across curriculum and pedagogical spaces involving learners and teachers on a daily pursuit of a(n) (mis)education, as illustrated in Figure 6.1, which ends with an exit at the end of a four-year cycle. In an attempt to expound on miseducation (Reay, 2017) and what learners go through, Pope (2001) explains a 'grade trap' where there is too much work to do and too little time in which to do it; therefore, learners feel obligated to give up recreation and sleep time, as well as many aspects of a social life, in order to succeed. The scenario may be considered an extended form of what Hutchison et al (2014) refer to as curriculum violence.

The lower secondary school revised curriculum, whose implementation started in 2020, requires a learner to take up to seven compulsory subjects and only two elective subjects in the final year of the cycle. This essentially

Figure 6.1: The axis of miseducation across curriculum, time and classroom size

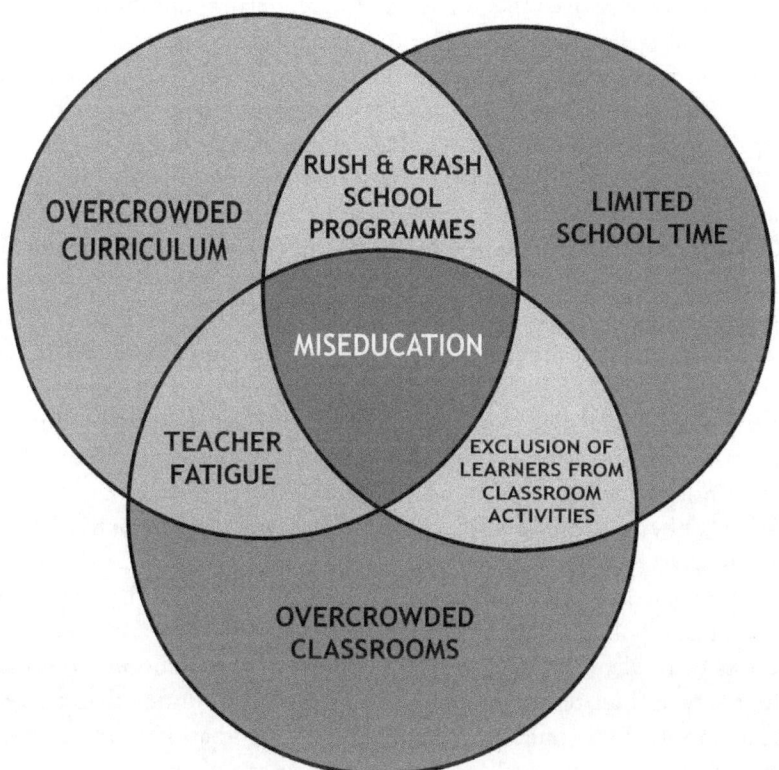

means the learner is not offered a variety of choices because the compulsory subjects limit the choices. This may be a form of 'curriculum coercion'.

Decontextualized education and conflicted knowledges

Another experience learners undergo in their everyday in-school activities relates to conflicted epistemologies (Nuwategeka et al, 2024), where the use of foreign textbook materials that do not relate to their everyday mundane activities and the environments where they live are commonplace. Learners live in communities with a rich collection of Indigenous knowledges. However, this knowledge is sidestepped by formal school knowledge. The learning activities prescribed in the curriculum are in conventional teaching and learning activities typical of formal educational practices, not integrating Indigenous pedagogies which are familiar to the learners.

Assessment of learning is also an avenue where the knowledges are conflicted. For example, in environmental education, teachers shared that the evaluations in schools are based on what learners know about the environment rather than what they do to/in it. Such assessments conflict with the transformative tenets of education, rendering education a potential agent of mal-skilled graduates. The root cause of this scenario is partly the attempt by education systems to implant foreign knowledge systems in areas where they have not been organically developed and therefore do not blend with the local realities of the area. Decontextualized education (Shrestha, 2011; Bisson et al, 2020) inhibits the development of problem-solving skills among learners as it does not relate with their reality.

Conflicted knowledges were clearly seen between learners' experiences of injustices in their daily lives and what they are taught. During the community mapping group discussions, learners expressed their everyday experiences of environmental injustice by citing examples they relate with in the community and the school. The most cited injustices were draining of wetlands for agriculture; deforestation, mainly for charcoal production; indiscriminate and irresponsible disposal of plastic waste (mainly plastic bags or polythene bags); and poor methods of agriculture that cause soil erosion. Other related scenarios included the widespread practice of bush burning carried out to clear fields for ploughing, a practice considered financially cheaper than hiring labour to clear the land. Apart from generating air pollution, the practice leads to other ecological consequences like loss of biodiversity due to fire. Learners in rural schools were more able to cite and relate to examples of environmental justice than those in urban schools. This could be explained by the fact that rural school-going children commute from the communities to school while most urban schools are residential (boarding). The residential nature of most urban schools ensures that learners are dislocated from the community for most of the year (nine months – the school term is three months, and there are three terms in a calendar year).

Teachers and learners both shared that their experiences of these practices were not brought into the classroom when learners are taught about the harmful environmental consequences of deforestation and swamp reclamation, although they live in communities and households where they and their parents undertake deforestation and swamp reclamation to burn charcoal and cultivate crops for sale to raise school fees for their (the learners') education. This paradox exposes the contextual environment in which the formal school education system operates, and how it renders education decontextualized and in a way disconnected from the community.

Conflicted epistemologies inflict an epistemic injustice in the way that learners' place-based knowledges are not recognized and brought into the learning–teaching situation (Fraser, 2009; Masaka, 2019; Ajaps and Forh Mbah, 2022). Lack of recognition of a given knowledge system is expressed in the form of the dominant knowledge system that is a conduit of what Oliveira (2022) refers to as downstream hermeneutic pressure, suffocating other knowledges to give advantage to another different knowledge system. In the schools where the study was conducted, structural hermeneutical injustice (Fricker, 2007) was prevalent, characterized by a strict implementation of a curriculum that makes little room for place-based knowledges. This practice disenfranchizes learners as epistemic agents.

Different forms of violence in learners' everyday experiences of school

A key finding from across the schools was that learners frequently cited significant instances of violence in and out of school. Consistently across the four schools, learners talked about their experiences of corporal punishments and other forms of punishment. Examples of corporal punishment include being beaten or caned, being made to stand holding bricks, being stripped of their clothes when they were not wearing the right uniform, being soaked in water, and being made to sit in the midday sun (when temperatures are often more than 40°C). This is alongside other forms of non-corporal punishment, including being made to clean the toilets, dig the latrine, clean or sweep the compound, fetch water, write lines or write a letter to the head teacher, as well as suspension. Learners expressed that their teachers 'will slap you if you make a mistake' (school in Kitgum) and 'shout and abuse you, saying you are not fit to be in the class' (school in Amuru).

Considering these persistent punishments, learners frequently cited their understanding of 'fairness' or fair treatment of people or anything in situations when there is an issue to be resolved. They generally take justice to mean fairness in, for example, dispensing punishments when they are involved in any form of breaking rules.

The in-school violence is majorly linked to the strict enforcement of English monolingualism as the language of instruction, which is enshrined in school rules and regulations in all the schools that were visited in northern Uganda. As one learner (Kitgum) explained, being caught speaking anything other than English can get learners punished: 'they are made to sweep, or beaten two strokes, or your name will appear in the red book for the vernacular speakers, [if they go in it] twice, they are going to give you one week suspension'. Coupled with these punishments is the fear of being caught and the shame associated with not being able to speak English.

In other writing, we have argued that the violence inflicted on young people goes beyond physical violence, placing them at the intersection of direct, systemic and cultural violence (Milligan et al, 2024). We see cultural violence which reinforces linguistic hegemony of English, and systematic violence where learners' participation in class is limited by their inability to express themselves in English. Persistent devaluing of Indigenous languages and learners' home and community identities constitutes a form of cultural violence. The devaluing of learners' home languages works to uproot them from their identities, and in the long term leads to cultural erosion as more members of the affected communities enrol in the school system. Language is the mirror for every culture because all cultural expressions are built within a language. We argue that schools are sites of violence in northern Uganda, and systematic cultural injustices are inflicted not only on the learners (during their school tenure) but on the larger community (in the long run).

Amid the concerns regarding English monolingualism in school, one policy maker in interview remarked that Uganda is a multilingual country and teachers who qualify to teach are posted in any part of the country regardless of whether they speak the area language or not. This, they argue, leaves the educational policy makers with no choice than to use English as a form of neutral factor in all school communications.

Learning and teaching of the justices

Learners also experience the monotony of classroom-based teaching methods that are rarely punctuated by practical and field-based learning and teaching methods. Because different learners learn differently, there is a requirement for a multiplicity of learning and teaching methods that teachers should implement so that no learner is left behind. The general lack of teaching materials in schools and funds to facilitate fieldwork are cited as reasons learners do not usually get exposed to practical learning activities. With the integration of information and communications technology (ICT) in teaching and learning emphasized in the competence-based lower secondary curriculum, schools are expected to have computer laboratories. Most of the schools visited did not have ICT equipment. One learner (Amuru) retorted that 'with the current curriculum we don't have the facilities for the learners to carry out the research' that they are expected to do. It should be noted that some teachers talked about using locally available materials from the surrounding environment to fill in for the missing materials in schools. This is common with natural science-related subjects like biology, agriculture and chemistry. However, this practice is solely dependent on individual teachers' agency and creativity.

Across the curriculum, learners were exposed to a form of injustice stemming from unharmonized learning activities across the different subjects. In the knowledge-based curriculum, there was no cross-referencing of similar content across the subjects. It was found that related content in different topics is not taught concurrently or merged in one subject by some teachers but is taught independently. There is no initiative from the teachers or the school administration to deliberately coincide with teaching these topics within a specified time period. One teacher (Amuru) explained what (s) he saw as an injustice in the teaching of environmental issues in that 'an

Agriculture teacher comes and teaches the topic ... a Biology teacher also teaches the same topic differently but when the learner attempts to answer the same question maybe in a Biology exam using the knowledge from Agriculture, he will be marked wrong'. However, the new competence-based curriculum has made attempts to clear out repetition of related concepts in different subjects. For example, the topic on soil has been concentrated in agriculture and has not been allocated any time in the new biology and geography syllabi, unlike in the old curriculum where the topic was taught in all three subjects.

Learners also live with remnants of memories of a civil war that ravaged the area for 20 years from 1986 to 2006. Whereas some learners may have experienced the war in their childhood, others are experiencing the after-effects characterized by land conflicts largely stemming from the encampment of entire communities, child abductions and long absence from their land, as well as domestic violence associated with post-traumatic stress disorder (Vindevogel et al, 2013; Amone-P'Olak et al, 2017; Mukasa, 2017; Denov et al, 2023). Whereas memories of the war are fresh in learner's minds, the curriculum and the teaching do not capture a true narrative of it, and learners rely on personal accounts from their families. The teaching of transitional justice issues in school mainly focuses on 'peaceful and harmonious coexistence', where learners are taught how to keep good interpersonal relations rather than being taught about issues of amnesty, reparations and mechanisms of conflict resolution at national level.

Learners' future views, plans and actions related to the three justices

Amid the observed injustices occasioned by the education system, learners aspire to the future that they envision. When asked what they would wish to change in the school system, among other things learners mentioned corporal punishment. The punishments are majorly linked to failure to adhere to a strict observance of English as the medium of communication in the school. However, there are other reasons which lead to corporal punishment, like breaking other school rules and failure to attain minimum academic grades in classroom assignments. It is worth noting that the corporal punishments still go on despite being outlawed by the Ugandan government's teacher professional code of conduct (Government of Uganda, 2012).

Learners also want an end to community violence since it affects them psychologically and inhibits their studies. When there are inter-clan and inter-community land wrangles, learners from the conflicting communities are targeted by the rival groups as they travel to school. It was reported in some schools that some learners have been injured in retaliatory and revenge attacks by rival groups involved in fights over land resources like grazing land, boundaries and cultivation fields.

Learners also shared what things they wanted to be removed from their education. These included: non-recognition of their local language in the teaching and learning process, rude teachers, bullying by fellow learners, too many subjects and extra lessons at night and on weekends. There is an aspiration to learn local cultures through, for example, performing arts or local cuisine. Learners in urban schools expressed their lack of some cultural aspects that urban environments do not embrace. Urban areas are cosmopolitan, and local cultures are masked by a blend of urban culture that seeks to accommodate all the inhabitants. In this way, learners see school as an avenue where local cultures could be promoted through teaching and learning activities.

Learners' aspirations are largely related to epistemic and transitional justice and not environmental justice. Learners feel unjustly treated by curriculum content that is blind to their local knowledges, as well as by the language of instruction that excludes them from knowing in their Indigenous languages. The non-mentioning of any environment-related aspirations points to the diminished role learners think the school system can have in solving environmental issues. This is despite the existence of learners' environmental clubs in schools. It also points to how environmental education is not transformative and may not therefore lead to environmentally responsive citizens fighting issues like climate change (Nuwategeka et al, 2024).

Learners also explained that they expect to have teachers who are approachable. It was observed that some teachers are rude and that they do not give learners a professional reception, especially when learners need to consult them on academic matters. This scenario may relate to the teacher fatigue associated with too much workload resulting from large class sizes, limited staffing and limited time to execute school tasks.

Learning materials were also among the expectations from the learners for the future. They expect the government and the schools to provide sufficient learning materials, especially textbooks and learners' guides, without which they cannot do proper research. In some schools, we observed that most teachers use teacher's guides in the place of learner's guides when teaching the new competence-based curriculum subjects because the learner's guides are not available. Even when the learners are sent to the library to conduct research, they do not find the necessary reference books, or those that are available are inadequate. It is therefore not surprising when this comes about as an expectation.

Conclusions

Based on our analysis of policy, curricula, learners' experiences and our limited insights into classroom practice, we conclude that in the Ugandan education system, justice is conceived in shallow forms of recognition and redistribution. While education may seek to be *for* justice as exemplified in inclusive policies that promote access and equitable quality education, it is not justice due to the way actual curriculum implementation is done. Shallow pedagogies (Balarin and Rodríguez, 2024) characterized by didactic and pedantic methodologies and rote-learning are features of school teaching, reducing education to an activity of memorizing selected content in the name of learning. Assessments aim at grading learners, not embracing their special learning styles. Consequently, education plays the role of excluding citizens from opportunities in life as it 'rewards and sanctions' those who do or do not subscribe to it.

A very significant finding from the Ugandan case study is that the context in which education operates promotes a lot of injustice. Learning and teaching takes place in the context of poverty and limited government funding to education. Whereas schooling is free of tuition at primary and secondary school level due to a deliberate government policy of UPE and USE education, it is not free of other costs. Parents and learners still struggle to afford other school requirements, and often there are dropouts recorded in the system, with low school completion rates. There is more to be done on structural societal issues like poverty to enable education to be an agent of justice so that schools are no longer sites of injustice. Furthermore, despite the wide range of injustices that young people face, we found that these are conspicuously absent in discussions of key justice-related issues. These disconnections and the lack of relevance to the places where the schools are provide clear instances of recognitional (in)justice.

7

Education *as* and *for* Justice: Key Findings from across the Countries

Introduction

Our country case studies provide a number of important insights into the ways that education systems in the Global South are responding to the justice and sustainability agenda articulated in the SDGs. In this chapter, we draw from findings across the three countries to discuss how far education is positioned as an enabler of justice and the ways that education may enact (in)justice. We also draw out some of the major differences across the countries' capacity to respond to justice demands, for example, in their political processes, relations to international global policy agendas, ways of organizing their curricula and pedagogical practices. Through this, we argue that our considerations of education *as* and *for* justice contribute important implications for countries of the Global South.

Across the three cases, although to different degrees in each country, we clearly see that policies have incorporated considerations about what education can or should do for justice. One clear example is in how education should develop young peoples' knowledge, attitudes and behaviours in ways that would enable them to contribute to justice and sustainability; an expectation for education that is widely discussed in the research literature (Olsson et al, 2022). Policies, curricula and textbooks, however, are less clear about how education itself needs to function as a space where justice is practised and about the changes education systems need to undergo to make those other changes possible. By this we mean the changes in pedagogies; school organization; relations between adults and children; and questions of safety, dignity and respect which enable or limit young people's learning. While there may be a more formal commitment to an education *for* justice, this has not fully translated into an education *as* justice. Understanding this gap between education *as* and *for* justice, we argue, is essential to allow us to fully understand what is possible in education's contribution to sustainable development.

Education *for* justice

Policies are the first instance where we can see how different countries are seeking to respond to global demands for education to contribute to justice and sustainability. Policies set each country's intentions and different issues in ways that reflect those countries' understanding and willingness to address different issues. While national policies may reflect global priorities around the role of education *for* justice, they also respond to national demands for justice through greater educational equity and inclusion. As our cases suggest, policies often gain traction when the pull exerted by external policy agendas coincides with the push from internal demands (Kingdon, 1984; Sabatier and Jenkins-Smith, 1993).

Policy intentions and discursive framings

A first look at relevant policies in Perú, Uganda and Nepal suggests a positive commitment in all three countries to address environmental, epistemic and transitional justice concerns, as they all have relevant policies in place. In some cases these are specific education sector policies (for example, Perú's Intercultural and Bilingual Education Policy), while in others they are broader national policies with implications for education (for example, Uganda's National Environment Act). While the three countries share concerns for inclusion, equity and the environment, in Nepal and Uganda these concerns appear within broader sectoral policies (for example, Nepal's School Sector Development Plan). In contrast, Perú seems to have a more developed justice-focused policy landscape that includes sectoral-level policies as well as plans, with the latter indicating more specific implementation commitments and goals (this is the case for both environmental education and intercultural bilingual education). These differences reflect the extent to which the different countries have established grassroots movements leading demands for inclusion that coincide with those of global education policies, as well as the extent to which political processes (such as democratic transitions or processes of decentralization) have coincided with justice-focused agendas.

Environmental education appears to be the area of greatest coincidence for the three countries – with policies, plans and curricular areas in place. This does not necessarily reflect a real prioritization of environmental education in national agendas, nor the incorporation of a justice focus on environmental education policies. On the contrary, such policies seem to be devoid of a justice focus (Sultana, 2021; Wilder et al, 2024). They favour more generic approaches to environmental issues that individualize responsibility for change through an emphasis on environmentally responsible citizens, and make few, if any, distinctions in terms of the different burdens of responsibility and suffering related to environmental change.

Policies for diversity and inclusion offer a complex picture that illustrates some of the challenges that education systems in the Global South may face when trying to promote epistemic justice through a greater recognition of diverse groups and knowledges. The three countries have policies that specifically seek to address this challenge, either through broad intercultural and bilingual education policies (Perú), through policies that seek to cater to the needs of specific groups (like the Alternative Basic Education for Karamoja policy in Uganda), or that seek to better respond to the needs of marginalized groups (like decentralization policies in Nepal). However, and in different ways, these policies often further the persistent othering of such groups, either through the exclusively celebratory approach to diversity (Perú), through their paternalistic take on marginalized populations, or by not recognizing any value in those groups' knowledges (Uganda). Broadly speaking, culturally diverse or marginalized groups are either problems to be solved or expressions of folklore to be celebrated. Rarely is their marginalization seen as the product of historical processes or structural forces whose effects cannot simply be solved through the individual attitudes that recognize only the colourful dimensions of diversity, without problematizing the societal and political processes that reproduce the marginality of culturally diverse groups (Walsh, 2009).

Policy-wise, the greatest challenge for the three countries has been in the development of responses to transitional justice concerns. In Perú, the strong education focus of the recommendations from the Truth and Reconciliation Commission was highly contested, limiting their translation into policies, curricula and classroom practice. In Uganda, national transitional justice policies do not discuss a role for education, while in Nepal, post-conflict political dynamics have rendered transitional justice issues absent in education. As we will discuss later, the difficulties that all three countries have faced in addressing transitional justice concerns through education is likely because of the more explicitly political nature of the problems transitional justice involves and the difficulties in reaching a shared collective understanding of episodes of violence and conflict.

Curricula and textbooks reflect policy discourses and silences

Curricula and textbooks play a key role in the education policy–practice nexus and can be seen as expressions of the pedagogical models that policies seek to promote (Prøitz et al, 2023). We found significant differences in this respect, with Uganda and Nepal leaning to more traditional, content-focused and often overcrowded curricula that tend to imply teacher-centred pedagogies, while Perú has moved to a more minimal competency-based curriculum with much less content specification that seeks to promote more active and learner-centred pedagogies. As we shall see in the next section, despite their very fundamental differences, both these models of curriculum and pedagogy seem to have led to a similar outcome: the predominance of 'shallow pedagogies' that severely limit the potential of education *as* justice and consequently its role *for* justice (see Balarin and Rodríguez 2024).

In terms of content, we generally found that curricula and textbooks maintained the same silences and discursive framings set in policy documents. One clear exception here is the case of transitional justice in Uganda, where there is a conspicuous absence of education in the policy, yet there is content in the school curriculum. Environmental education is the area with the greatest amount of textbook space, but environmental problems are often approached from natural science perspectives, with little discussion of their societal implications and the different burdens of responsibility or impact related to environmental challenges (Singh, 2021). In Perú and Nepal, textbooks from subjects including social studies and citizenship also include content on the environment. Here, the emphasis is on the role of responsible citizenship and individual actions to generate change. When it comes to questions of cultural diversity, there is a similar emphasis on individual responsibility, with little analysis of complex causes beyond human behaviour, or the inequalities that may limit the contributions of individuals to broader societal changes. In some cases, like in social studies textbooks in Nepal, textbook analysis revealed that the language used was problematic and continued to 'other' marginalized groups. We view both these approaches to diversity within the curriculum as very weak articulations of group-based recognition (Young, 1990). Histories of violent conflict are also notably absent from school textbooks in the three countries, reflecting the silence of policies in this area.

The distance between policy, practice and learners' intended actions

The existence of officially sanctioned policies does not always imply an actual commitment in terms of funding and actions. This was emphasized by stakeholders interviewed who often mentioned the scant resources that may be assigned to specify and implement existing policies. Resource allocation may not only reflect the availability of funds in different countries, but also the changing prioritization of different issues over time by changing governments and ministerial administrations – this was clear in the case of Perú. Added to this there are issues around countries' implementation capacities, especially at the local level, which may also get in the way of realizing policy aims. This implementation gap was particularly noticeable in the case of Nepal, where practice differed considerably from policy and curriculum proposals. In Uganda, limited funding to produce adequate teaching and learning materials to guide teachers in the implementation of the new curriculum was also evident and limited the transformative changes among learners that the curriculum envisages. All this means that even when there is a commitment to cater to diversity, sustainability or transitional justice issues at the policy level, the influence of such policies on school practice may be tenuous or even non-existent.

There is a common factor that seems to influence the different countries' commitment to certain policies over time: the extent to which the policies frame different issues in a critical way that may point to the need for broader political and economic changes in the countries. The more critical the framing of an issue, the less chance the policy has of enduring over time and of being implemented. Likewise, the more depoliticized issues are – as when environmental issues are approached from a natural sciences perspective that elides the social and political dimensions of environmental problems, or when cultural diversity is presented only as something to celebrate, but not as something that may lead to injustice – the likelier they are to become acceptable and to influence practice over time. Depoliticization, whether intentional or unintended, has often been associated with the technocratic approaches to policy making that are typical of the neoliberal era (Fawcett et al, 2017), as well as with global citizenship discourses that individualize responsibility for change (Balarin, 2011).

Another common element in justice-related policies was the general emphasis on the need for individual behaviour change and the absence of reflections around broader societal changes that might be needed to achieve just outcomes. This is seen in the emphasis on educating 'environmentally responsible citizens' that we found in the Ugandan National Environment Act (Government of Uganda, 2019a) and the National Forestry and Tree Planting Act (Government of Uganda, 2003). Such discourses are typical in the global citizenship education approaches that dominate approaches to environmental education, civics and citizenship throughout the world (Balarin, 2011; Eaton and Day, 2019; Glackin and King, 2020). Individualizing responsibility for change is in line with the previously mentioned point on the tacit need for depoliticization as a requirement for policy acceptability and real impact on practice.

Our multinational survey provided evidence of how these dominant approaches may limit education systems' contribution to justice and sustainability. The main purpose of the survey was to explore how learners' intended actions in relation to SDGs 13 and 16 related to their knowledge, attitudes and experiences of different forms of justice in education. Results from multilevel modelling analysis showed that both attitudes and experiences were significantly related to learners' intended actions, with the magnitude of the association with experiences (both within and outside of school) being strongest. The relationship between knowledge and intended actions appeared to be much lower. While this could be attributed to fewer questions based on knowledge (Shields et al, 2024), it also calls into question the linear expectations that simply putting some content into the school curriculum will bring about individual and collective change. This suggests that in order to enable an education *for* justice, more thought should be given to the role of education *as* justice; for instance, by attending to young people's experiences of (in)justice within and beyond schooling.

Education *as* (in)justice

Our analysis of school practice in the three countries provides the basis for our understanding of what education *as* justice might mean. While many of our findings reflected important absences we found in pedagogical practice, they have enabled us to formulate a more positive definition of what education *as* justice might require.

Different pedagogical and curricular models, similar shallow pedagogies

Through the participatory activities we developed with learners and teachers, we encountered several key contextual challenges associated with each country's pedagogical and curricular models. In Uganda, the size of the curriculum and the number of children in the classroom clearly limit what teachers can do, including the methods they use and the time they can spend exploring and discussing different issues. Teachers and learners frequently reflected on the challenges of having 60 learners in one class, alongside an expectation for a set amount of content to be covered in each 40-minute lesson. It became evident that the only way in which teachers can manage such expectations is through teacher-centred approaches. Many learners shared that even when they are encouraged to contribute, teachers often focused on a small number of the most academically able learners. These time constraints were also seen in the schools in Nepal. Here, teachers have some more autonomy in terms of what methods they can use, and many offered ideas of how to diversify their classroom practice, including using YouTube, practicals and field trips. However, these were not extensively used, with teachers explaining that there was too much to cover in the curriculum and a lack of financial support for these methods that were deemed 'additional' to core content delivery. In Perú, where the competencies-based curriculum means that teachers have significant autonomy to determine how to teach, we still found quite limited pedagogic choices. Interviews with teachers suggested that this is because they feel unsupported to translate the broad curriculum guidelines into their own developed lessons; they often only use the limited content found in textbooks. But more importantly, their coverage of different content is often superficial and does not involve delving into the complex web of causes and consequences that lead to many of the problems we face today.

We see several similarities that cut across the different curricular and pedagogical models of the three countries. They are all practices that deliver what we have elsewhere referred to as a predominance of 'shallow pedagogies' in schools (Balarin and Rodríguez, 2024). This includes limited attempts to foster young people's capacity for critical thinking or their understanding of complexity; similarly, their ability to problematize and articulate the contradictions between the normative ideals they encounter in school – about individual responsibility for societal and environmental problems and possibilities for change – and the injustices they encounter in their daily lives both in and outside of school. These shallow pedagogies are the result of different processes that inhibit the acquisition and development of knowledge and epistemic capabilities for discernment, deepening understanding and considering ethical standpoints with regards to knowledge.

It is clear that in the three countries there is a need to provide better support for teachers through training, resources and mentoring, and to model better practice that might enable them to develop in young people the critical thinking abilities and capacity to understand complex subjects that are needed for them to be able to contribute to the kinds of changes that current global challenges demand. As we discuss in the next sections, these shallow pedagogies can also be seen as resulting from the depoliticization and individualization of justice and sustainability, as well as from the disconnect between formal knowledge and experience.

Depoliticization of justice concerns in curriculum and classroom practice

Just as policies about the intended contribution of education tend to be framed in depoliticized ways, we also see this very clearly in curriculum and classroom practice. There is evidence of positive attitudes towards justice-related issues among young people across the three countries. In the survey data, learners broadly demonstrated positive responses in relation to the development of certain norms, such as the importance of looking after the environment and respecting cultural diversity. For example, the mean response score (on a scale from 0 to 100) indicated agreement that the children who speak a minoritized language have a right to learn in their language (Nepal: 79.4, Perú: 83.8, Uganda: 79.4). Similarly, and reflecting the shallow pedagogies mentioned earlier, learners in interviews frequently repeated almost sloganistic messaging about it being important to look after the environment, for example, through recycling. In relation to these simplistic and celebratory narratives, we can follow the trajectory of ideas from policy through to curricular content and learners' attitudes. We would argue that this is precisely because of their lack of a justice orientation. This makes them palatable both in terms of the topics included and the uncontroversial ways they are taught. The more depoliticized policy framings are, the more likely they are to shape curricula and school materials, and through that to guide practice.

When it comes to teaching difficult or contentious subjects, like gender equity or histories of violent conflict, we find that these are either not addressed in teaching practice due to fears about potential consequences or due to the lack of guidance that teachers receive about such topics (Perú), or they are presented through simplistic and often one-sided government-sanctioned narratives (Uganda, Nepal) that may include misleading factual information (Nepal). This limits young people's capacity to understand such complex topics as well as the potentially reparative role that education could play in these contexts. In Perú, the attempt to present a balanced history of the Internal Armed Conflict has been met with distrust and resistance. In Uganda, the new curriculum includes teaching about the northern Ugandan conflict but presents a one-sided government-sanctioned narrative. In Nepal, the presentation of recent conflict is reduced primarily to (still potentially contentious) dates and factual information. These different approaches to teaching recent conflict broadly reflect how difficult histories have been taught in many other countries (Bentrovato et al, 2016).

The focal point for debate and disagreements is often assumed to be at the level of policy and curriculum design (Sobe, 2014; Paulson et al, 2020). It is clear, especially from the Peruvian data, that there is also significant discomfort and agency on the behalf of teachers about what they choose to teach, citing a lack of pedagogical resources and guidance to deal with complex and difficult issues. The outcome of this is that Peruvian learners have pieces of what some of them described as 'an incomplete puzzle' for understanding past conflict rather than a larger scope of factual knowledge, including about the structural and historical factors that led to the conflict. This was also often contradicted by what they learned about those conflicts outside of school. Peruvian teachers also discussed how they kept any discussion of conflict to something that happened in the past without discussing the ongoing impact, because they are risky, political and difficult issues to discuss. Similarly in Nepal and Uganda, young people articulated conflict primarily as something in the past, with extremely limited discussion of the ongoing influence and impact of these conflicts for present and future injustices.

Individualization of responses to justice concerns

Justice-related content is also depoliticized through the prevalence of individualistic views in relation to viable solutions to injustice, for example, the inclusion of content on conflict resolution between two individuals. Here again we see a clear route from policy and curriculum through to practice. Young people often talked about solutions to injustices as coming from their own personal effort, rather than through the action of institutions or governments. Similarly, in the curriculum, and echoed in how many young people spoke about injustices, specific problems are discussed as the result of individual practices and attitudes (for example, littering) as well as certain economic practices (for example, illegal logging in Perú). In the teaching of environmental issues in Nepal, while there is an emphasis on action, the way that content is presented is in direct contrast to active participation. Topics are written about in a passive tone that limits connections to what young people could actively do.

This supports the literature that has shown the persistent narrative of individual actions for solving climate change and other global challenges, and related feelings of pressure and anxiety among young people who may feel they are not doing enough (Singh, 2021). This can be seen as a relational injustice given the emotional impact on young people, especially given that most of them are both among the most affected by climate change and those whose actions would bring about the least effect. It is also important to note that such a focus on individual action can be understood as a form of epistemic injustice through the privileging of a Westernized prioritization of the individual, with limited attention given to group or community actions (Smith, 1999; Medina, 2018).

Across the countries, there are extremely limited instances of justice-related issues being addressed in a systemic way that articulates the interaction between different problems and their multiple causes, consequences and possible solutions. This leaves young people feeling disempowered and unsure of how their individual actions could relate to actions at community, national or global levels. Such decontextualization and decoupling of individual actions from broader understandings of whose actions are most likely to bring about transformative change is a clear case of environmental injustice (Macintyre et al, 2020). Together, depoliticization and individualization go against the need for learners to develop the capacity to grasp the complexity of different problems, from those that emerge from historical injustices to the complex and interrelated causes of climate change and environmental degradation.

Contradictions and disconnections between understandings and experiences of (in)justice

While learners could superficially show positive attitudes in relation to a range of justice-related issues, when pushed further, their views often crumbled in the face of contradiction. One scenario in the survey gives clear evidence for this. It started with the following statement:

> A cement factory has opened in the Tinbesi village. As part of this process, the owners of the factory have met with the local government and described the benefits of the factory, including jobs for people in the area. However, people were concerned that the factory would pollute the air and also discharge waste into the river, the main water supply in Tinbesi village and downstream. The river is recognized for its vast diversity of wildlife.

Participants were asked to rate agreement from 0 to 100 with a series of contradictory statements. The results showed many learners agreed that the local population should not lose their jobs just because of air/river pollution (mean response scores – Nepal: 58.6, Perú: 41.9, Uganda, 61.0) and that the rights of the wildlife should not be sacrificed to meet human needs (Nepal: 76.2; Perú: 84.3; Uganda: 78.3). Similarly, the majority of learners, particularly those in Nepal and Uganda, agreed that they would support the building of this sort of business and construction since it would bring development and prosperity to their community (Nepal: 71.0, Perú: 46.8, Uganda: 75.9), but also said that they would organize a peaceful protest with other learners and teachers at their school who love the river/forest/land and don't want to see it destroyed (Nepal: 84.3, Perú: 78.9, Uganda: 88.4).

Such contradictions were also seen in the responses to another scenario about the potential introduction of education in minoritized languages to respect cultural diversity. As noted earlier, the majority response was that children have the right to learn in their own language and that the government should introduce this initiative. However, in the very next question when asked if there are more important things for the government to worry about than introducing teaching in the children's mother tongue, the majority response, at least in Nepal and Uganda, was in agreement (Nepal: 65.4, Perú: 43.5, Uganda: 66.1).

While we were not able to further question learners who agreed with such clearly opposing statements, the qualitative data might offer some answers. Just as learners struggled to discuss causes and consequences of instances of injustice, they also broadly found it difficult to reconcile differing perspectives. In Perú, for instance, learners embraced views about the importance of celebrating diversity and not discriminating against others based on their race or culture but could not fully recognize the contradiction between this normative ideal and the evidence of discriminatory practices that they regularly encountered. This points to the fundamental role of not simply diversifying content and acknowledging alternative viewpoints, but also of supporting young people to understand and evaluate different perspectives and the knowledge claims used to support them (Robertson, 2013; Masaka, 2019). This lack of support for developing critical thinking is a consistent theme across the three countries.

Environmental issues across the three countries are also broadly presented as a singular reality, which affects us all equally and for which we are all individually responsible. This is in direct contrast with what we would see as an environmental justice approach which incorporates climate justice concerns for the unfair impact of human-caused climate change on individuals, communities and countries (Sultana, 2021; Wilder et al, 2024). In the Ugandan curriculum, there is some discussion of how climate change is impacting the national environment, although this is couched in its impact on tourism and economic development. There is almost no mention of the rights of, or impact on, non-human life beyond the impact this will have on human (mainly economic) interests. While these anthropocentric discourses fail to recognize biocentric views of human relations with the non-human world (Schlosberg, 2007), we do see some evidence of learners developing respect for non-human life. A small number of learners in each country, for example, conceptualized environmental justice in terms of justice for the environment.

Another way that we see injustices for the young people across the country contexts is the disconnection between what they learn in school on justice-related issues and how they encounter such issues in their everyday lives. This sits in direct contrast with the consistent messaging in environmental education literature and advocates of critical pedagogies of place that learning about these issues needs to be grounded in learners' experiences of the place where they live (Gruenewald, 2003; Ajaps and Forh Mbah, 2022). This is particularly significant because the qualitative and quantitative data show that most learners live with daily encounters with social and environmental injustices. In the survey, on average, learners agreed that environmental degradation has a negative impact on them and their families. The number was particularly high in Uganda (82.3, compared with 67.5 for Nepal and 63.0 for Perú). However, we found no examples of teachers engaging with learners' experiences of such injustices when they learn about environmental topics. Examples of the disconnection to young people's experience were more common in relation to environmental issues, reflecting the broader literature where experiential learning is advocated (Kalungwizi et al, 2018; Huber et al, 2024). However, the abstraction of issues from daily lives was also present in relation to other justice concerns. For example, learners in Perú spoke at length about the ways that economic precarity impacted their daily lives, and those in Nepal about violence in their homes. These are clear issues of misrecognition, as their experiences of injustices that arise from structural inequalities are sidelined (Young, 1990).

Without situating school-based knowledge in the place where they live, we repeatedly found young people struggled to express the relevance of knowledge they learned in school or how they could translate this into potential routes to action within their own communities. Rather, many discussed justice in normative and often abstract ways – as fairness or equality between individuals. Among Ugandan learners, this was often articulated as fairness when it comes to retribution. Injustice does not come in the prevalence of, say, corporal punishment, but in a perceived unfair distribution of who receives such punishment.

Here we see another distinct contradiction for young people between what learners are taught they ought to be doing and what they and their families would be able to do. As one teacher in Nepal reflected, 'in school we teach to save our natural resources, which is not possible to apply practically as their butter and bread are earned by this. … How does environmental justice weigh-up against human survival/flourishing?' A similar tension was seen in Uganda, where the importance of tree planting takes a prominent role, including in a school-based activity to plant trees. However, many learners live in homes dependent on charcoal production for survival. These disconnections, thus, become particularly stark in the lost learning opportunities to explore what such contradictions mean for the young people, and how they can respond to justice-related issues.

The gaps between school-based knowledge and learners' experiential knowledge can also be seen in the broader epistemic concern for the distinct lack of local or Indigenous knowledges within the school curricula topics that we analysed (Nuwategeka et al, 2024). The clearest example is that from Uganda, where only 4 per cent of the geography syllabus for lower secondary school relates directly or indirectly to locally relevant activities that may bring in learners' Indigenous or local knowledges. This contrasted with learners' positive attitudes towards including Indigenous knowledges and stories in the curriculum (Nepal: 85.8, Perú: 84.7, Uganda: 89.5). However, there is risk that such inclusion is done in superficial ways, reinforcing epistemic misrecognition (Medina, 2018).

(In)justices in schooling experiences

For many of the young people across the three countries, experiences of injustice were also an everyday occurrence in the time that they spent in school, albeit manifested in separate ways across the contexts. Experiences of injustice within school are seen most vividly in the qualitative data from learners in Uganda who reflected on persistent punishment, especially related to enforcing English-only school language policies. These often harrowing narratives of direct violence come in the form of corporal punishment and other instances, such as being made to stand in the midday sun or hold bricks for prolonged periods of time. This is despite the official banning of corporal punishment (Ssenyonga et al, 2022; Milligan et al, 2024). There are clear implications here, particularly for the potential for learning about recent conflict and reparative futures; how can a culture of peace and individual dignity be developed in schooling contexts where there is such violence? Perú offers a more hopeful outlook in this regard. Narratives of corporal punishment were notably absent from learners' and teachers' accounts, in line with other studies that show how such practices, common only a couple of decades ago, have mostly been banished from schools (González, 2018). While stories of bullying and linguistic discrimination did emerge, the latter, especially, were sparse, possibly due to our focus on urban schools, but also, it would seem, due to the incorporation of critical views on the value of linguistic and cultural diversity that can be linked to the role played by intercultural and bilingual education.

Furthermore, this physical and emotional violence in the Ugandan schools works to govern language practices through real – and anticipated – humiliation. The expectations to speak in an unfamiliar language-of-learning-and-teaching – and censoring of other languages – precludes many learners from contributing in class. Here we see a significant difference in the survey data between Ugandan learners and those from Nepal and Perú. In response to the statement 'classmates feel free to use the language they speak at home', the average response was 35.5. This compares with 70.6 in Nepal and 72.4 in Perú. These numbers suggest that there are still learners in different regions of both countries who hide their language(s) in school, which points to structural inequalities based on language. This was supported by the classroom observations and teacher interviews in the Rasuwa district of Nepal, where it was evident that Tamang learners often faced language barriers to access curriculum content and take part in any classroom discussions in Nepali.

Fear, shame and silence have similarly been observed among English medium secondary school learners in Tanzania (Adamson, 2022). Kuchah et al (2022) and Milligan et al (2023) demonstrate how such linguistic barriers and associated feelings of shame hinder epistemic participation in Rwandan secondary school classrooms, with most learners restricted to repetition and limited whole-class responses. Similarly, the Ugandan data show that language-related violence combines with large class sizes and an overburdened curriculum to significantly impede teacher–learner and group-based meaning-making activities. This matters because, as Walker (2019) and Hookway (2010) have argued, an individual's confidence to contribute is crucial in shaping their propensity to participate in epistemic activities. The Nepalese data also show that linguistic minority learners may be more marginalized in class than their Nepali-speaking peers. This suggests that impact on some, many or all learners' ability to consume school-based knowledge and produce new knowledge(s) within and beyond the classroom.

Revisiting redistribution, recognition and representation

In Chapter 2, we proposed Fraser's (2009) 3Rs model as an appropriate foundational framework to explore issues of environmental, epistemic and transitional justice in education. Here we discuss how we have understood our main findings in relation to the 3Rs and consider the ways that looking across different forms of justice enables a richer understanding of 'education as justice'.

It is evident from all three countries that the ways that the national education systems have addressed issues of social justice are more conducive to redistribution (Rawls, 1971; Fraser, 2009). This is seen most markedly in Nepal, where the influence of a rights-based approach to ensuring that all children access quality schooling is most evident. In Perú, where we do find policies that seek to promote the recognition of excluded groups, a similar focus on ensuring the right to quality education through access policies has been even more prominent and less politically contentious than, say, gender equity policies. This focus on access to education, alongside some considerations of quality for those in school, reflects the broader critiques of global educational prioritization and funding in the past 20 years (McCowan, 2010).

If we consider a richer conceptualization of redistribution which cuts across the broader forms of justice, we begin to see some fissures in what each education system provides. In Uganda, violence in different forms is an important aspect of many learners' everyday experiences of schooling. In Nepal, pollution and the risk of landslides affect learners' attendance at school. Learners across the countries were concerned with how natural resources were utilized within and beyond their schools. In Perú, the shallow pedagogies that have emerged in the context of the introduction of a competency-based curriculum and learner-centred pedagogies – which have not been accompanied by adequate support for teachers – leave learners with limited knowledge about most issues in what is a clear case of epistemic injustice (Balarin and Rodríguez, 2024).

We, therefore, argue that distribution must consider access in a broader sense and with considerations of appropriate use of natural resources as well as learners' wellbeing and safety. We further suggest that there is a distributional foundation to how young people can access school knowledge. This includes the availability of learning resources, the opportunity to take part in different learning activities and access to qualified teachers. We see this enhanced conceptualization of redistribution as the foundation from which the other dimensions of justice in education could be realized.

Regarding recognition, education systems in the three countries have made important efforts to promote positive attitudes to cultural diversity and to raise awareness about environmental issues – especially at the level of policy, curricula and textbooks. In Perú there is a clear effort, seen in policies, curricula and practice, to better recognize the value of culturally diverse groups, question discriminatory practices and promote social and gender equity and environmental awareness. Similar efforts can be found in Uganda and Nepal, but with lesser impact due to their limited implementation. These less contentious topics find their way into curricula and from there into classrooms more easily. However, when we look at what is going on in schools, we find several problems in the extent to which topics are taught. At best, this approach of recognition as diversification is an affirmative measure (Hrubec, 2004). But we would argue that the often celebratory – or even problematic – narratives that dominate a lot of such content could also be understood as a form of misrecognition, albeit in more hidden ways.

In all three countries, we also see some clear forms of misrecognition at the curriculum level, with some values, stories and perspectives being backgrounded and rendered invisible (Leibowitz and Bozalek, 2015). This is most clearly seen in relation to more difficult topics – such as content related to recent conflict – and can be seen as an explicit form of misrecognition. By comparison, richer forms of epistemic recognition would be those that go beyond the inclusion of different perspectives or multiple knowledges to include attention to the pedagogic processes that support young people to make sense of and evaluate these different knowledges and perspectives. This echoes the calls in the reparative education literature to support young people to engage with multiplicity when learning about historical and contemporary injustices and violence (Zembylas, 2017; Paulson, 2023; Walker, 2024).

Another significant form of misrecognition comes in the general lack of connection to experience when teaching justice-related topics. This is particularly problematic when teaching happens on topics about which young people have direct experience, and when this experience directly contradicts what they are learning in school. A consistent theme in the critical pedagogy of place literature is the essential role of situating learning in the local realities of where young people live (Gruenewald, 2003; Ajaps and Forh Mbah, 2022). To enable this to happen, we would argue that young people need to be supported to understand the disconnections between what they experience and what they are being taught. Without this, young people across the countries and the contexts within each country were not able to make sense of the issues they are presented with in their everyday lives. Crucially, given the significant relationship between experiences and possible actions in the survey results, we would suggest that this form of misrecognition could be particularly important for how young people will act – individually and collectively – for justice-related issues beyond schooling.

When it comes to representation, we see much less emphasis on this dimension of social justice in policy, curriculum or practice in all three countries. Some of the issues discussed in the previous section regarding recognition are also questions of representation, which is needed for the rights of diverse groups to be guaranteed. We have shown how there is some recognition in curricula and textbooks, for instance of cultural or gender diversity, but there is very little attention paid to the importance of representing the views of distinct groups, including those of young people. This requires not simply providing spaces for representation, but also, and maybe more importantly, enabling young people to make sense of their own experiences and of the different and disconnected perspectives they are presented with. Other relationships are also left entirely unexplored, such as those between individual and community-level actions and the broader structural injustices that perpetuate violence, environmental degradation and group-based discrimination. Advocates for justice-based approaches to environmental education particularly highlight the importance of teaching complexity and systems thinking so that young people can develop understanding of these different relationships and the implications for how they may act on justice-related issues (Tikly, 2019; Singh, 2021).

While we were only able to directly observe lessons in Nepal, the broader qualitative data from learners and teachers suggest that in all countries classrooms are spaces where participation in meaningful learning activities is highly unequal. By contrast, we argue for the essential role of classrooms as spaces where all young people can engage in difficult and complex dialogue and, crucially, be able to produce their own knowledges through such activities (Lara-Steidel and Thompson, 2023; MacDonald and Kidman, 2024).

The defining characteristic of Fraser's (2009) approach to social justice is that economic, cultural and political dimensions of justice cannot be separated. This is where we see the 3Rs most clearly interconnected. For young people to be able to meaningfully participate in classrooms, there is a need for equitable distribution of learning opportunities. This means all children being able to first access school and for inclusive pedagogies and language policies to support them all to feel they can contribute. Secondly, there is the crucial role of recognition of young people's experiences, knowledges, languages and testimonies so that they feel these are valued. If a young person is not recognized, they are unlikely to participate as 'full partners in social interaction' (Fraser, 2009, p 16). As Masaka (2019, p 302) further argues, when there are doubts from peers or teachers about the credibility of learners to assert claims, then the learner may end up doubting their own standing and the knowledge(s) she has which can silence them as 'unreliable sources of knowledge' (see also Fricker, 2007). We, therefore, see issues of representation in the classroom to be fundamentally a question of epistemic justice. We suggest the fundamental role of justice-oriented pedagogies through which young people are supported to become not only consumers of knowledge, but also producers of knowledge. Crucially, such classroom practices model the types of participation young people will engage in beyond schooling, with implications for their contribution to different forms of justice.

Based on these interconnected dimensions of redistribution, recognition and representation, we argue that a just education system:

1. is for all, environmentally and physically safe, and free from discrimination;
2. recognizes and responds to young people's lived experiences and is situated in the place where young people live – including the histories of conflict and inequalities and contemporary experiences of violence, climate change and environmental degradation; and
3. enables all young people to participate fully in the consumption and production of knowledge(s).

It is through this that education for justice may be realized. The survey data particularly highlight the importance of young people's experiences of justice for enabling positive actions in relation to peace, the environment and social justice. Further, the significant qualitative dataset shows that these dimensions of education *as* justice are not visible in secondary schooling in the three countries. This is impacting the ways that education could foster positive attitudes and actions in relation to preventing violent conflict, foster transformative climate action and reduce inequalities.

In Figure 7.1, we expand this framework to show how each of the 3Rs are present in our model of education *as* justice and how they connect to specific aspects in relation to the environmental, epistemic and transitional forms of justice that were the focus of our study. However, as Fraser (2009) argues in relation to the three dimensions of social justice, we also see the different forms of justice as closely linked and frequently interdependent. Environmental justice, for instance, requires a recognition of how diverse groups are unequally impacted by environmental changes and how different forms of knowledge may help establish more sustainable practices (Schlosberg, 2007; Cachelin and Nicolosi, 2022; Wilder et al, 2024). We do not present the framework as a fixed and final entity. While we looked at multiple dimensions and forms of justice and across policy, curriculum and practice, there are elements that we were not able to include. For example, we did not look at broader schooling practices such as how young people are involved in school-level decision-making, how adults and learners relate to each other in schools, or socio-emotional aspects of learning. We hope that other researchers will bring other areas into focus and further enrich this model.

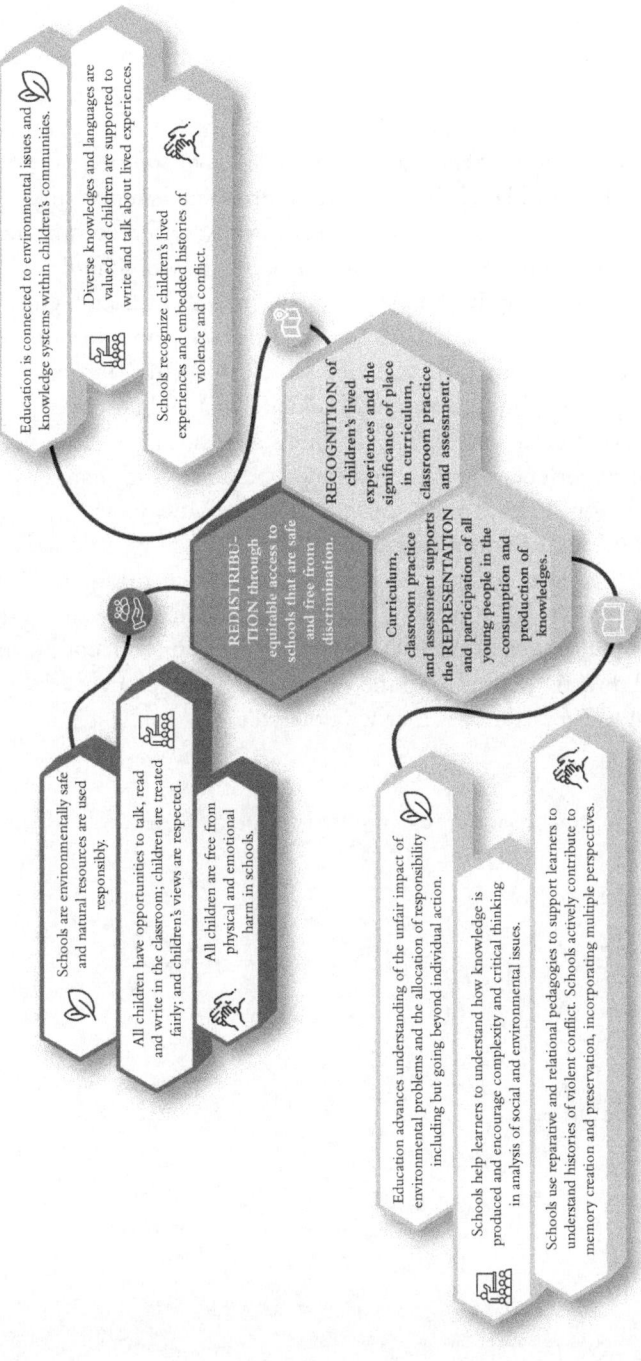

Figure 7.1: The JustEd framework

Conclusions

Comparative findings from JustEd have shown some of the advances and limitations that the justice and sustainability agenda is facing in education systems of the Global South. While we find some promise in the existence of policies that address issues related to different forms of justice, we also find many limitations in the way such policies have endured over time, how they frame the problems they seek to address, the silences they maintain and the difficulties they face for translating discursive commitments into practice. Our findings also present a consistent view of school practices that fall short when attempting to promote justice in and through education, be it because of material constraints (classroom sizes, limited resources), basic conditions (the presence of violence in schools), the lack of support for teaching practices (through training and materials), or because of pedagogical models that limit learners' capacity for thinking critically – for understanding their own experiences and the complex processes that may lead to their marginalization (Balarin and Rodríguez, 2024; Milligan et al, 2024; Paudel et al, 2024). Such findings underscore the urgency of articulating clearer ideas and practices consistent with the normative ideals for justice and sustainability that global policy frameworks present. They also suggest that such ideas and practices need to move beyond thin conceptions of justice that avoid directly confronting the causes and consequences of some of the key global social challenges that we now face.

8

The Central Role of Epistemic Justice in Education to Enable Sustainable Development

Introduction

The claim that education contributes to sustainable development rests on a central assumption that what is placed in school curricula will be taught effectively and translate into relevant skills and attitudes (Bengtsson et al, 2018). As we discussed in Chapter 1, global policies for sustainable development anticipate that through education learners will become citizens who take actions to contribute to justice and sustainable development, both individually and collectively. The complexity of this expectation is often underplayed, with linear trajectories traced between what is written in global and national policy documentation following through to positive outcomes. We saw this very clearly in the analysis of such documentation in Nepal, Perú and Uganda, where we identified multiple references to the role of education as a driver for wider development challenges. By contrast, we have shown that there are complex trajectories – from policy and curriculum design through to classroom practice, assessment and outcomes – that shape the ways that education can equip, or fail to equip, young people to take actions that will enhance progress towards the SDGs.

The central argument of this book has been that for education to enable sustainable development – and more specifically the justice-related outcomes related to it – far more attention needs to be paid to educational practices and schooling experiences. This is what we have called education *as* justice. We have argued that this requires a focus both on different economic, cultural and political dimensions of social justice (Fraser, 2009) and overlapping forms of environmental, epistemic and transitional justice. In Chapter 2, we adapted Anderson's (2012) question to ask: what would it be for educational practices and policies to operate justly? We argue in this chapter that it takes a central focus on epistemic justice since education is a key site where knowledges are consumed, recognized and produced. We also consider the implications of our findings for the transformative education agenda.

Refocusing education as justice around the epistemic core

The main themes discussed in this book – from the marginalization of young people's experiences of injustice to the need for complex articulation of issues to the depoliticization of difficult topics – cut across the different forms of justice. A focus on epistemic justice in this book has helped to interrogate existing practices of knowledge production, interpretation and use in secondary education within policies, in curriculum design, and in and beyond school classrooms. We have seen multiple examples of epistemic injustices, both in interpersonal interactions and through broader institutional practices and policies (Anderson, 2012). The analysis has shown persistent silencing and undervaluing of learners' experiences, knowledges and languages in their everyday interactions in classrooms across the three countries, especially in relation to topics that may be deemed difficult or emotional (Zembylas, 2018; Kuchah et al, 2022; Lara-Steidel and Thompson, 2023). A focus on the global and national knowledge hierarchies related particularly to processes of coloniality have also revealed epistemic injustices embedded in curriculum, policy and pedagogies (Quijano, 2010; Mignolo, 2011).

As Kotzee (2013) has powerfully argued before us, education is both a clear site of multiple epistemic *in*justices and one where a more positive vision of epistemic justice can be realized. Educational spaces are where young people can learn to critique the knowledges presented to them, recognize and value multiple knowledges, and develop their own capacities for participating fully in knowledge production. Schools are just one of these spaces. However, it is evident from our curricular analyses that secondary education is the phase when content becomes more complex and where young people are expected to develop more sophisticated capabilities. We argue that embedding epistemic justice across the curriculum in secondary education is, therefore, particularly important for reconceptualizing the role of education in contributing to justice beyond education.

To operationalize epistemic justice in secondary education to enable other forms of justice, we propose focusing teaching and learning processes around an 'epistemic core' (see Balarin and Milligan, 2024 for an extended discussion of this concept). This idea borrows from that of Elmore's (1996) 'instructional core'. Elmore (1996) argues that the instructional core is made up of the three essential elements of teachers, students and content. It is not one of these individually, but rather the relation between all three that determines high-quality pedagogical practice. Tikly (2019) expands the notion to that of a 'pedagogical core' in line with his arguments that education for sustainable development necessitates a broader conceptualization of pedagogy beyond instruction to include context, theories and values (see also Alexander, 2008). We use the term 'epistemic core' to focus on the explicitly epistemic dimensions of the relationships between teachers, students and content. These dimensions are *openness to students' experiences and the place where they live*, *rich pedagogies* and *a broad range of epistemic resources*.

The first element of the epistemic core is *openness to students' experiences and the place where they live*. Young people spoke at length about these experiences – for example, of environmental degradation and gender-based violence – and with narratives that highlight the precarity and insecurity of their lives in economic, social and environmental terms. However, curricular content has consistently been shown as disconnected from and in contradiction with young people's everyday experiences of injustice. Curricular content in all three countries is presented in quite abstract and decontextualized ways, for example, focusing on technical aspects of conflict resolution or scientific descriptions of climate change. It is also divorced from any sense of continuity through time or relevance to ongoing injustices that young people experience and observe around them. This can be seen as a persistent form of what Fricker (2007) describes as hermeneutical injustice – whereby individuals are prevented from being able to make sense of particular social experiences. By contrast, we argue that in an epistemically just classroom, young people need to be supported to make sense of their experiences. This is particularly important because by mobilizing learners' prior knowledge and experience, transformative learning can be made possible (Lotz-Sisitka et al, 2015, 2017). Openness to students' experiences, then, is not only about creating space for experiences to be discussed. It is also supporting students to understand, question and challenge the tensions between what they are learning and what they are experiencing in their daily lives. There is a central role here for dignity and empathy – between teachers and learners, and to be developed among the learner cohort (Lynch, 2012; Adami, 2021; Miri, 2024).

For young people to learn about the relevance and importance of justice-related issues, it is also clear that learning needs to be situated, at least partly, in the place where they live (Ajaps and Forh Mbah, 2022). This is arguably more important for young people living in sites of significant violence and precarity, because the daily realities of their lives are fundamentally disparate from daily experiences of life in more stable environments. Gruenewald (2003, p 9) writes about the importance of 'learning to live well socially and ecologically in places that have been disrupted and injured'. One potential way to support young people to live well in such places is through reparative pedagogies (Zembylas, 2017; Paulson, 2023; Walker, 2024). These could support young people to respond to violence in their lives, understand the interconnected nature of environmental and social injustices, and support their community-based actions for their futures.

The second element of the epistemic core is *rich pedagogies*, which is the antithesis of the shallow pedagogies that we have discussed in this book. Balarin and Rodríguez (2024, p 63), drawing on the Perú data, theorize shallow pedagogies as those 'that lead to shallow codification of reality, oversimplifying complex phenomena and reducing the understanding of contradictions, which are inherent to social reality'. By contrast, rich pedagogies are those that: deal with difficult issues; enable students to grasp complexity and go beyond individual responsibility; promote analysis, reflection, and critical thinking; and enable connections between school knowledge and students' everyday experiences.

These are pedagogies that share characteristics with critical (Giroux, 1983; hooks, 1994; Freire, 2013) and transformative (Mezirow, 1991; Lotz-Sisitka et al, 2015; Paul and Quiggin, 2020) pedagogies. They are also pedagogies that are fundamentally about how young people can deal with multiple, overlapping and often contradictory knowledges. We have consistently shown throughout this book that the simplistic recognition of different perspectives is not enough. Rather, what is needed is pedagogies that support the 'value of epistemic diversity' in a way that does not lead to relativism (Robertson, 2013). Here, critical thinking is particularly powerful since it can enable young people to make inferences, using different kinds of reasoning to evaluate and make decisions and solve problems (Lai, 2011). Young people across the countries showed limited capacity to discuss the systemic nature of justice-related issues or link the causes and consequences of individual and collective actions. Rich pedagogies can further support examination of societal power relations and the causes and effects of everyday problems, alongside supporting learners to consider solutions. As Walker (2019, p 176) argues, this is both an individual and collective process since 'we learn to think critically not simply through our own efforts but with others in a genuinely collective enterprise in which we recognize each other as worthy interlocutors'.

The third element of the epistemic core is *a broad range of epistemic resources*. By epistemic resources, we refer to the material and discursive means through which young people can access and evaluate different forms of knowledge. The material forms may include textbooks, objects and class visitors, alongside those beyond the classroom, such as those available in community learning spaces or museums. The discursive means include multiple perspectives, epistemic communities and ways of understanding a particular topic. These are particularly important given the propensity seen across the countries for simplistic and singular narratives and the presentation of justice-related issues often in solely abstract and scientific ways. Given the different forms of violence witnessed in relation to language policies in the

Ugandan schools, we would also follow Mkhize (2016), who argues that learners' home languages are essential linguistic and epistemic resources to support access to different knowledges.

The three elements are interconnected, and the realization of epistemic justice in education relies on these connections being maintained. For example, if young people in the mountainous region of Nepal learn about environmental degradation, knowledge learned in school needs to be connected to community experiences, stories and fears of landslides. This relies on pedagogies and epistemic resources that support them to understand the different causes of and potential responses to landslides. This is while recognizing that these exceed what any individual or small community can do and that Nepal's capacity to prevent landslides also depends on broader political and economic power structures. Similarly, if young people in Ayacucho in Perú are going to learn about the Internal Armed Conflict in a way that is not an 'incomplete puzzle', they need to engage with their families' and communities' experiences during the Internal Armed Conflict and access a broad range of epistemic resources alongside pedagogies that promote critical thinking. Learning also necessitates recognition of different narratives, including those contextualized within their own communities' experiences of the violence.

These three elements of the epistemic core – and the relationships between them – are one way that epistemic justice could be realized in schooling. To consider how secondary education could be focused around the epistemic core, it is helpful to return to our definition of epistemic justice as *equality in the consumption, recognition and production of knowledges*, which can map onto Fraser's (2009) 3Rs of redistribution, recognition and representation. Education as epistemic justice could thus be made possible through: redistribution across the education system that supports equality in the consumption of knowledges; recognition of knowledges in curricula and classroom practice; and representation as the equality of the production of knowledges in and beyond the classroom. In Table 8.1 we show how these relate to the epistemic core and offer a set of criteria for understanding how education as epistemic justice could be achieved.

Firstly, we have seen that there is clear maldistribution in terms of how young people can consume knowledges in secondary school classrooms. As Medina (2017, p 43) writes, 'the question is not simply whether or not there are expressive and interpretative resources available for meaning-making and meaning-sharing, but how those resources are used, by whom, and in what ways'. Fricker (2012, p 1318) describes distributive epistemic injustice as 'the unfair distribution of epistemic goods such as education or information'. We would turn this into a positive conceptualization of epistemic justice and expand it. It is about the fair distribution of a broad range of epistemic resources. It is also about the pedagogic methods and learning activities that

Table 8.1: The 3Rs and the epistemic core

	Redistribution across the education system that supports equality in the consumption of knowledges	**Recognition of knowledges in curricula and classroom practice**	**Representation as the equality of the production of knowledges in and beyond the classroom**
Openness to students' experiences and the place where they live	All learners can access teaching, learning and activities (for example, groupwork, debate, school trips) that enable them to understand the knowledge they encounter in schools by grounding it in their own experiences and the place where they live.	Learners' experiences and knowledges (including languages) from where they live are recognized as valuable within the classroom and the school.	Schools view learners as knowledge producers and legitimize a multiplicity in the ways in which students produce knowledge based on their experiences and backgrounds.
Rich pedagogies	All learners have access to teachers and diverse learning methods that enable them to consume knowledges soundly. This includes being able to evaluate, critique and infer from different knowledges.	Diverse ways of knowing are embraced when prescribing pedagogies for schools, including pedagogies that support learners to appreciate multiple truths and perspectives.	Learners can form and communicate their own ideas and arguments, drawing on learning they have engaged with in and outside of school. Learners participate in feedback to teachers to enhance learning and teaching.
A broad range of epistemic resources	A broad range of epistemic resources are distributed equally so that all learners can consume a broad range of knowledges, including in different forms.	Curricula recognize diverse knowledges and perspectives (such as multiple perspectives, communities, theories), and a range of forms (such as objects, class visitors, books, environments).	Learners are supported to produce their own broad range of epistemic resources (such as multiple epistemic perspectives and forms of knowledge).

support them to consume knowledges soundly and understand they relate to their own experiences.

We have also seen clear cases of both epistemic misrecognition and superficial forms of recognition. This is in terms of how certain perspectives and forms of knowledge might be negated and marginalized within policy and curricula as part of broader power structures (Spivak, 1988; Mignolo, 2011) and in classroom interactions (Kerfoot and Bello-Nonjengele, 2023). By contrast, recognition of knowledges in curricula and classroom practice can be realized through recognizing learners' experiential knowledges and languages as valuable and through embracing different ways of knowing, perspectives and material resources.

Most of our qualitative evidence with learners and teachers suggests that schools are spaces where most young people speak very little. When they do, it infrequently leads to learning that supports them to develop, infer or generate new knowledges. Who gets to contribute in the classroom and what experiences and knowledges from outside the classroom are deemed valuable are clearly influenced by what Fricker (2007, p 154) would describe as processes of 'testimonial injustice'. This 'occurs when prejudice on the part of the hearer leads to the speaker receiving less credibility than he or she deserves' and has distinct implications for parity of participation in generating social meanings and new knowledges. Equal opportunities to produce new knowledges can be made possible through supporting young people to be able to form and communicate their own evidence-based arguments and develop their own broad range of resources in diverse forms.

Throughout this book we have argued that a foregrounding of education *as* justice is necessary for education to contribute to justice outcomes. We see a distinct focus on epistemic justice as particularly important for several reasons. The survey data analysis suggested that school-based knowledge alone is not enough for positive attitudes and actions in relation to the environment, peace and reducing inequalities. Rather, education needs to connect what is taught in school with young people's lived experiences of issues related to sustainable development so that the link between multiple knowledges and action can be enabled (Huber et al, 2024). Where young people are not engaged in knowledge production within schooling, it is difficult to envisage how schooling can enable them to become actors in the future who will produce new knowledges that can solve multifaceted problems. If young people are supported to participate fully in decision-making and meaning-making processes within the classroom, this models the ways they can engage and produce new knowledges beyond schooling. By recognizing themselves as knowers, this may enable individuals to have greater epistemic agency throughout their lives (Masaka, 2019; Walker, 2019).

A focus on epistemic justice within education also provides the necessary support for learners to be able to analyse and evaluate justice-related issues and understand the world around them. It provides them with the critical thinking abilities regarding relationships and structural causes to recognize differential power and capacity for reducing climate change and biodiversity loss, social inequalities and peace. These abilities are important for supporting collective behavioural change and the political action that is needed to hold governments and other major contributors to environmental and social injustices to account (Wilder et al, 2024).

While we argue for a refocusing of educational justice efforts around the epistemic core, there are wider necessary conditions that determine if an epistemically just education is possible. As Elmore (1996) argued before us, these other aspects are relevant because they impact on the quality of the elements of the (instructional) core – and the relationships between them. Within the school, some of these elements were laid out in the discussion and the framework presented in Chapter 7. A non-exhaustive list includes non-violence within the school, dignity and non-discrimination, language policies and pedagogies that encourage all young people to talk in class and schools that look after natural resources responsibly. There are also conditions that were not a central feature of our analysis but which we suggest are important, such as anti-bullying school policies. These conditions are no doubt essential if the notion of equality in different forms of knowledge engagement is to be realized.

Tedesco and Lopez (2002, p 7) describe the conditions of educability as 'the entire set of resources, aptitudes or predispositions that make it possible for a child or adolescent to successfully attend school at the same time that it encourages us to analyse the social conditions that make it possible for all children and adolescents to access these resources' (see also Bonal and Tarabini, 2016). While some of these are related to necessary conditions within the school, what is possible in education is also clearly influenced by young people's unequal access to learning opportunities, experiences of (in)justice, and broader social, economic and cultural processes. The wide range of intersecting injustices that the young people in our study encounter in their daily lives include familial financial insecurity, real and feared environmental devastation, bodily violence and social discrimination. As Unterhalter (2021) argues, the inequalities that millions of young people face are profound, multidimensional and intermeshing. The breadth and complexity of the lived experiences of injustices across the nine different districts in the three countries are not issues that education alone can solve. However, there is a vital role that education can play in supporting young people to make sense of, and respond to, their experiences of injustice. This again highlights the importance of looking beyond curricular content as a 'magic bullet' for enabling positive actions and recognizing the contribution of diverse actors and processes.

Conclusions and implications

This book makes a substantial contribution to understandings about the reality of the claims and hopes of how education can contribute to broader development agendas. For education to make such contributions, we have argued for the importance of thinking across different forms (environmental, epistemic, social and transitional) and dimensions (economic, cultural and political) of justice. At a time when transformative education is gaining traction in global agendas for development cooperation – as suggested by UNESCO's (2023) Recommendation for Education for Peace and Human Rights, International Understanding, Cooperation, Fundamental Freedoms, Global Citizenship and Sustainable Development and its new vision for education worldwide (UNESCO, 2022) – this knowledge and insight will be invaluable in informing policy change and enactment. Countries and regional authorities need rigorous evidence to underpin the decisions they make in revising education policies and investments to reinforce the contribution of education to sustainable development.

We have methodically examined the pathways from global to national policy to curriculum design and content through to classroom practice and to assessment and outcomes. This work demonstrates that policy enactment and realization of policy objectives is a complex, layered process, typically complicated by multiple interruptions and disruptions over time, and which interacts with diverse webs of relationships, histories, technologies, bureaucracy and the available resources to fund education. Our research suggests that the ways in which young people experience schooling – in particular, the extent to which they experience justice in their schooling – has a profound bearing on the development of their capacities to take positive actions for the SDGs.

We, the authors of this book, continue to work together in several ways to bring about educational reform, including developing in-service teacher training for secondary school teachers in Nepal and Uganda. We also look to develop new ways to extend the research in new directions. While our findings have suggested significant congruences across the diverse contexts of Nepal, Perú and Uganda, one limitation to our study is the lack of a case study in the Global North. We are mindful of drawing conclusions or advocating for an education that may overburden young people in Global South countries with the responsibility of action, especially since our findings have shown the significant and intersecting injustices they face in their daily lives. Transformed education in countries that are more responsible for the global climate crisis and economic inequalities may have a greater impact on the types of societal transformations needed.

We have argued that a refocusing of educational justice efforts around epistemic justice is just one of the ways that secondary education could be 're-imagined' and 'transformed' (UNESCO, 2022) as a catalyst for the facilitation of transformed attitudes and actions towards the SDGs and beyond. There is little doubt based on our extensive data generation and analysis that educational policies, curricula and processes need a much stronger justice focus. Our findings suggest that the distance between the education that we have outlined in this chapter and what we found in schools in Nepal, Perú and Uganda is currently vast. We do not, therefore, make these calls for transformation lightly and recognize the scale of the task for education systems, especially sitting within such powerful global discourses that focus on outcomes and efficiency (Unterhalter, 2019; Schweisfurth, 2023).

However, the urgency and complexity of the global challenges we face – and which young people will particularly be burdened with responding to throughout their lives – demands a shift from what Fraser (in Hrubec, 2004) describes as affirmative measures to structural transformations. We argue that the need to centre education on principles of equality in the consumption, recognition and production of knowledges is now more important than ever. With the increasing presence of artificial intelligence and the intensification of social and political polarization, education can play a vital role in supporting young people to handle knowledge and understand what sources of information are trustworthy and just (Robertson, 2013). Our arguments also come at a timely moment – particularly in relation to environmental justice – as there are multiple non-governmental organizations and multi-country partnerships orienting towards justice. For example, the Greening Education Partnership – a global alliance with over 80 country members – has established justice as one of four central pillars of a quality environmental education curriculum (United Nations, nd). Similarly, academics and practitioners are increasingly coming together to push for educational change. In the introduction to a recent NORRAG special issue organized by the Alternatives Project (Adamson et al, 2024), the editors write:

> Co-existing and inter-related global crises are pushing humanity and the living planet towards political, social, economic, and ecological collapse. These crises – seen in the worldwide coronavirus pandemic, structural inequalities, police brutality and racism, entrenched patriarchy, accelerating climate chaos, and the constant threat of wars – are driven globally by capitalism and militarism. We must seize this unique historical moment to reconceive and radically change public education as an entry point for deeper transformations that will build human solidarity and cooperation bringing an end to racism, patriarchy, and capitalism. (Adamson et al, 2024, p 11)

As the Moloko song persistently reminded us at the turn of the century, 'the time is now'.

Appendix

Additional background information about each of the countries

In this appendix we provide some further contextual information about each of the countries in the JustEd study. We particularly focus on the country's experiences that resonate with environmental, epistemic and transitional justice. Each author from Nepal, Perú and Uganda, respectively, chose what specific information they thought was most important for the reader to have as background information.

Nepal

Nepal is a multilingual, multicultural and multi-religious country in South Asia, sharing its territorial borders with China to the north and India to the east, west and south. Linguistic, religious and cultural diversity has been the defining characteristic of the country, and it has been acknowledged and promoted by the current Constitution (Government of Nepal, 2015). Nepal is also globally noted for its geodiversity and biodiversity. Geographically, it is divided into the Himalayan, middle-hill and Terai regions, with the world's highest peak, Mount Everest, at 8,848 metres above sea level and the lowest point in the Terai at an elevation of 60 metres above sea level. Ecologically, it is divided into three belts, namely mountains, hills and Terai (or plains). According to the recent census, Nepal's population has reached 29.1, million of which 51.13 per cent are females and 48.87 per cent are males. The country's annual average population growth rate was 0.92 per cent in 2021 (National Statistics Office, 2023). The population by ecological belt comprises 53.61 per cent of the total population living in Terai region, 40.31 per cent in the hill region and 6.08 per cent in the mountain region. The proportion of the population living in urban municipalities is 66.17 per cent, while the proportion in rural municipalities is 33.83 per cent. One fifth (20.27 per cent) of the population in Nepal lives below the poverty line, with a poverty gap index of 4.52 per cent, and the Gini index for consumption inequality was estimated to be 0.30 in 2023 (National Statistics Office, 2024;

World Bank, 2024). There are 142 castes/ethnicities speaking about 124 languages belonging to 4 major language families (National Statistics Office, 2023). Of them, Nepali is the most widely spoken first and second language, which has been constitutionally recognized as the official language of the nation, other national languages in addition to Nepali may be determined as official languages by State law. The country's total literacy rate for the population aged 5 years and above was 76.2 per cent in 2021, with a male literacy rate of 83.6 per cent and a female literacy rate of 69.4 per cent. Among the literate population, only 19.5 per cent have completed higher levels of education (above school leaving certificate or equivalent), with high unemployment across all education levels (National Statistics Office, 2023; World Bank, 2024).

Following the end of the Maoist insurgency in 2008, and particularly with the promulgation of the 2015 Constitution, Nepal adopted a three-tier government model: federal, provincial and local, with each level entrusted with defined powers, responsibilities and resources. Politically, Nepal practises the federal, democratic and republican system of governance and is constitutionally committed to socialism based on democratic norms and values including fundamental rights, social equity, social justice and inclusion, as well as equal distribution of socio-economic and cultural opportunities and natural resources (Government of Nepal, 2015). Nepal is experiencing increasing climate risks, ranking 10th globally among countries most impacted by past climate hazards, while it is ranked 44th in terms of vulnerability to future climate risks (World Bank, 2024). As a geographically diverse country, Nepal faces a wide range of extreme weather-related natural hazards due to climate change and environmental degradation, including rising temperatures, irregular rainfall patterns, floods, landslides, droughts, avalanches and glacier lake outburst floods (Vaidya et al, 2019; Central Bureau of Statistics, 2022).

Perú

Perú is a multicultural and multilingual country of more than 30 million inhabitants, 80 per cent of whom now live in urban areas – up from 34.5 per cent during the 1940s. Geographically, it is divided into three main regions: the desertic coast, the mountainous Andean region and the Amazon – which hold, respectively, 55 per cent, 32 per cent and 13 per cent of the country's population. Perú, where 26 per cent of the population is Indigenous, is the country with the second largest Indigenous population in Latin America (Godenzzi, 2007). While 70 per cent of the population speaks Spanish, the official language, 4.2 million Peruvians speak Quechua or Aymara, the Andean Indigenous languages, and 230,000 Peruvians speak one of nearly 40 different Indigenous Amazonian languages (INEI, 2017).

During the past three decades Perú experienced important social and economic changes. At the end of 1980s the country was in the throes of a violent internal armed conflict and was experiencing unprecedented record levels of hyperinflation that plunged millions into poverty and severely limited the State's capacity to provide basic services. In 1990 the newly elected government of Alberto Fujimori implemented a programme of structural reforms that stabilized the economy, but at the cost of deepening the poverty and precarity of millions of people. The government also managed to contain the armed conflict, but at the expense of severe human rights violations. After closing and reorganizing Congress in 1992, Fujimori's government became increasingly authoritarian and corrupt, co-opting institutions, including the judiciary and the media, to back his attempt to keep himself in power through a second, unconstitutional re-election. Fujimori's regime fell in 2001 after widespread evidence of corruption was leaked to the media.

As the country recovered its democracy, a one-year transition government was established and charged with organizing democratic elections. Fujimori's fall revealed the country's precarious institutions and democratic commitments, and the transition government sought to re-establish and reinvigorate the country's democratic system, creating deliberative institutions to reach agreements around national policy priorities. It also established the Truth and Reconciliation Commission (CVR, for its name in Spanish) to investigate the crimes committed between 1980 and 2000. Education was central to this democratic and transitional justice agenda.

Between 2002 and 2013, Perú became one of the fastest-growing economies in Latin America, with a growth rate of around 6.1 per cent. This led to a substantial reduction in monetary poverty, which dropped from 52.2 per cent to 26.1 per cent between 2005 and 2013 (World Bank, 2017). Economic growth was mostly the result of a favourable international economic environment (namely, a supercycle of raw materials in the global economy) paired with the adoption of macroeconomic policies that contributed to create a scenario of high growth and low inflation (World Bank, 2017).

Economic growth was built mainly on extractive and export industries, mainly mining, but also fishery and export-oriented agriculture. Deregulation measures established during the 1990s and early 2000s led to a growth in informal and illegal activities in those same sectors, as well as in the drug trade. All these activities have added to the environmental impacts of global warming, making Perú a country highly vulnerable to climate change. Perú has 70 per cent of the world's tropical glaciers, which are now melting at a very fast pace, affecting the regulation of the water cycle. This impacts the availability of water for the population and crops, as well as the incidence of natural disasters like landslides and floods. Deforestation in the Amazon – for crops, logging and mining activities – has only added to this problem.

While economic growth has benefited many inhabitants of Perú, such gains have not benefited all groups equally and the country remains a deeply unequal society. Poverty 'remains disproportionately rural' (World Bank, 2017, p 8), and there are profound inequalities between the vast majority of workers employed in often precarious informal jobs (around 75 per cent of the total workforce) and formal sector workers. While socio-economic marginalization in Perú is closely intertwined with the population's ethnic background, other forms of inequality, like those based on gender, are also very profound, with women not only faring worse than men in both employment and salaries, but also being exposed to pervasive forms of violence (Hernández, 2019).

Inequalities are also evident in education. The years of economic growth also led to important improvements in access (with now universal enrolments in primary schooling and 86 per cent access to secondary schooling among the school-age population), the reduction of drop-out and repetition rates, and improvements in national and international standardized test results (Cueto et al, 2016; Balarin and Rodríguez, 2019). However, educational inequalities persist, especially among learners who grow up poor, live in rural areas, have a mother with little education, or are members of an Indigenous group (Cueto et al, 2018). In addition, urban schools offer better infrastructure and education quality than rural schools; some Indigenous children attend schools where Spanish is the only language of instruction (thus impacting on their right to learn in their mother tongue); the most skilled teachers are assigned to classrooms with learners of higher socio-economic status; and learners from urban areas are more likely to access higher education than those from rural areas (Cueto et al, 2016, 2018). As stated by Balarin & Escudero (2018), the Peruvian school system is now much more unequal than Peruvian society as a whole.

Uganda

Uganda is in East Africa. There are over 40 Indigenous languages spoken in the country (Ssempuuma, 2013) across over 40 ethnic groups, potentially setting the stage for ethnocultural conflicts stemming from competition for resources and positions of power (Kibanja et al, 2012). The population has an annual growth rate of 2.9 per cent (Uganda Bureau of Statistics, 2024) and is young, with a median age of 16.7, and largely rural, yet with a growing urban population at 29.3 per cent (Worldometer, 2024). The country is listed among low-income countries (World Bank, 2023), with the incidence of poverty quoted at 20.3 per cent of the population (Uganda Bureau of Statistics, 2024). The country's recent history is marked by colonial legacies, having been colonized by Britain. Currently, the country faces development challenges characterized by environmental, economic and social problems.

The main issue related to environmental degradation is wetland and natural forest encroachment by settlements and industrial developments. The country's natural forest cover is declining at an alarming rate. According to the National Forestry Authority (2008), Uganda's forest and woodland cover dropped from 4.9 million hectares (20 per cent of Uganda's land area) in 1990 to 3.6 million (14 per cent) in 2005, representing a deforestation rate of 1.9 per cent. By 2020, this rate had increased to 12 per cent, accounting for the release of 413t of CO_2, and to 14 per cent in 2023, representing 500t of CO_2 (Global Forest Watch, nd). These rates of deforestation have correspondingly been accompanied by reductions in wetland cover in the country. By the year 2000, an estimated 2,376km² of wetland area had been reclaimed for agricultural and industrial activities in Uganda (National Environment Management Authority, 2001). Although the wetland coverage is estimated at 13 per cent of Uganda's surface area, only 8.9 per cent (21,526km²) of this is intact, while 4.1 per cent (9,885km²) is under some form of degradation owing to a number of factors, including urbanization, population increase, uncoordinated planning and demand for more arable land (Ministry of Water and Environment, 2021).

Economically, poverty in the country is pervasive, where rural poverty is more prevalent than urban poverty (Hassan and Birungi, 2011). There are conflict hotspots in the country, most especially in northern Uganda, where a combination of cattle rustling and civil armed rebellions have been prevalent. Between 1987 and 2007 Uganda resembled a 'war with peace' model, suggesting that the government in power embraced the antagonisms of conflict in the north at the same time as peaceful coexistence and development in the south (Shaw and Mbabazi, 2007). The country also faces challenges with the education system, especially issues to do with underfunding associated with low budgetary allocations. The system is not responsive to the multidimensional needs of the society, like addressing the rampant poverty (Datzberger, 2018) when education is nearly an uncontested development strategy to tackle several forms of social, economic and environmental challenges.

The country is still grappling with the armed rebellion of the Allied Democratic Forces (ADF) rebel group in the west, as well as the legacies of armed conflict involving the Lord's Resistance Army (LRA) in the north, and insecurity caused by the armed Karamojong cattle rustlers in the northeast. The insecurity and conflict precipitated by the Karamojong manifests in the form of intra-ethnic armed raids among the Matheniko, Tepeth and Jie, as well as inter-tribal warfare between the Karamojong and the neighbouring communities in Uganda, Kenya and South Sudan (Hopwood et al, 2015). This conflict has persisted despite the governments of Uganda and Kenya deliberately disarming the Karamojong and giving amnesty in exchange for voluntary disarmament (Mkutu, 2008; Marigat, 2023). Amnesty was also granted to ex-combatants of the LRA war who voluntarily denounced rebellion, and they were reintegrated into the community (Yarbrough, 2014; Bradfield, 2017; Akello, 2019).

In Uganda, education is regulated by the government; it prescribes the curriculum for primary, post-primary and secondary levels; pays teachers' salaries; and supplies educational materials. The government also regulates private educational institutions. The country is implementing universal primary and secondary education, as well as post-primary education. The seeming extension of education to the masses at this level works to create an awareness among school-going children that they will be change agents in addressing environmental, epistemic and transitional justice issues.

References

Adami, R. (2021) 'Revisiting the past: human rights education and epistemic justice', *Human rights education review*, 4(3), pp 5–23. Available at: https://doi.org/10.7577/hrer.4486

Adamson, L. (2021) 'Language of instruction: a question of disconnected capabilities', *Comparative education*, 57(2), pp 187–205. Available at: https://doi.org/10.1080/03050068.2020.1812236

Adamson, L. (2022) 'Fear and shame: students' experiences in English-medium secondary classrooms in Tanzania', *Journal of multilingual and multicultural development*, 45(8), pp 3275–3290. Available at: https://doi.org/10.1080/01434632.2022.2093357

Adamson, F., Benatar, R., Gibbons, M., Ginsburg, M., Klees, S.J., Lipari, G. et al (eds) (2024) *Education for societal transformation: alternatives for a just future. NORRAG special issue*, 10. NORRAG.

Adhikari, B.R. and Poudel, P.P. (2024) 'Countering English-prioritised monolingual ideologies in content assessment through translanguaging practices in higher education', *Language and education*, 38(2), pp 155–172. Available at: https://doi.org/10.1080/09500782.2023.2217804

Aikman, S. (1997) 'Interculturality and intercultural education: a challenge for democracy', *International review of education*, 43(5), pp 463–479. Available at: https://doi.org/10.1023/A:1003042105676

Ajaps, S. and Forh Mbah, M. (2022) 'Towards a critical pedagogy of place for environmental conservation', *Environmental education research*, 28(4), pp 508–523. Available at: https://doi.org/10.1080/13504622.2022.2050889

Ake, C. (1979) *Social science as imperialism: the theory of political development*. University of Ibadan Press.

Akello, G. (2019) 'Reintegration of amnestied LRA ex-combatants and survivors' resistance acts in Acholiland, northern Uganda', *International journal of transitional justice*, 13(2), pp 249–267. Available at: https://doi.org/10.1093/ijtj/ijz007

Alcázar, L., Balarin, M., Glave, C. and Rodríguez, M.F. (2020) 'Fractured lives: understanding urban youth vulnerability in Perú', *Journal of youth studies*, 23(2), pp 140–159. Available at: https://doi.org/10.1080/13676261.2019.1587154

Alexander, R. (2008) *Essays on pedagogy*. Routledge.

Aman, R. (2015) 'Why interculturalidad is not interculturality: colonial remains and paradoxes in translation between indigenous social movements and supranational bodies', *Cultural studies*, 29(2), pp 205–228. Available at: https://doi.org/10.1080/09502386.2014.899379

Amsden, J. and VanWynsberghe, R. (2005) 'Community mapping as a research tool with youth', *Action research*, 3(4), pp 357–381. Available at: https://doi.org/10.1177/1476750305058487

Amone-P'Olak, K., Dokkedahl, S.B. and Elklit, A. (2017) 'Post-traumatic Stress Disorder among child perpetrators and victims of violence from the northern Uganda civil war: findings from the WAYS study', *Journal of psychology in Africa*, 27(3), pp 235–242. Available at: https://doi.org/10.1080/14330237.2017.1321849

Anderson, E. (2012) 'Epistemic justice as a virtue of social institutions', *Social epistemology*, 26(2), pp 163–173. Available at: https://doi.org/10.1080/02691728.2011.652211

Anderson, K., Elder-Robinson, E., Howard, K. and Garvey, G. (2023) 'A systematic methods review of photovoice research with Indigenous young people', *International journal of qualitative methods*, 22, p 16094069231172076. Available at: https://doi.org/10.1177/16094069231172076

Arellano Salazar, A. (2022) *The politics of anti-gender campaigns: an analysis of congressional debates in Peru regarding the educational curriculum reform*. Doctoral thesis. Université d'Ottawa/University of Ottawa.

Ayorekire, J. and Twinomuhangi, R. (2012) 'Uganda: educational reform, the rural–urban digital divide, and the prospects for GIS in schools', in A.J. Milson, A. Demirci, and J.J. Kerski (eds) *International perspectives on teaching and learning with GIS in secondary schools*. Springer Netherlands, pp 283–289.

Azzarito, L. (2023) 'Photo-elicitation to amplify and elevate the voices of research participants', in L. Azzarito (ed) *Visual methods for social justice in education*. Springer International Publishing, pp 55–73. Available at: https://doi.org/10.1007/978-3-031-25745-2_4

Bacchi, C. and Goodwin, S. (2016) *Poststructural policy analysis: a guide to practice*. Palgrave Macmillan.

Bagnoli, A. (2009) 'Beyond the standard interview: the use of graphic elicitation and arts-based methods', *Qualitative research*, 9(5), pp 547–570. Available at: https://doi.org/10.1177/1468794109343625

Bailey-Rodriguez, D. (2021) 'Qualitatively driven mixed-methods approaches to counselling and psychotherapy research', *Counselling and psychotherapy research*, 21(1), pp 143–153. Available at: https://doi.org/10.1002/capr.12383

Balarin, M. (2011) 'Global citizenship and marginalisation: contributions towards a political economy of global citizenship', *Globalisation, societies and education*, 9(3–4), pp 355–366. Available at: https://doi.org/10.1080/14767724.2011.605321

REFERENCES

Balarin, M. (2025) 'The making and unmaking of education reforms in countries with weak state institutions: lessons from Peru', in D.B. Edwards Jr, M. Moschetti, and C. Díaz-Ríos (eds) *The state and education in Latin America: foundations, fault-lines and alternatives*. Brill-Sense.

Balarin, M. and Benavides, M. (2010) 'Curriculum reform and the displacement of knowledge in Peruvian rural secondary schools: exploring the unintended local consequences of global education policies', *Compare: a journal of comparative and international education*, 40(3), pp 311–325. Available at: https://doi.org/10.1080/03057920903374440

Balarin, M. and Escudero, A. (2018) 'Evaluación del diseño e implementación de la intervención de soporte pedagógico intercultural del Ministerio de Educación del Perú'.

Balarin, M. and Milligan, L.O. (2024) 'Education as justice: articulating the epistemic core of education to enable just futures', *Global social challenges journal*, 3(3), pp 125–141. Available at: https://doi.org/10.1332/27523349Y2024D000000013

Balarin, M. and Rodríguez, M.F. (2019) 'Endurance and absences in Peru's reform: the challenge of second-order reforms in the core of educational practice', in M. Balarin and M.F. Rodríguez (eds) *Politics of education in Latin America*. Brill, pp 116–133.

Balarin, M. and Rodríguez, M.F. (2024) 'Shallow pedagogies as epistemic injustice: how uncritical forms of learning hinder education's contribution to just and sustainable development', *Global social challenges journal*, 3, pp 49–67. Available at: https://doi.org/10.1332/27523349Y2024D000000007

Balarin, M., Monge, C. and Sarmiento, P. (2021) 'Country profile: Peru: JustEd: education as and for environmental, epistemic and transitional justice'. Available at: https://doi.org/10.5281/zenodo.5518029

Balarin, M., Alcázar, L., Rodriguez, M.F. and Glave, C. (2017) *Transiciones inciertas: una mirada a los jóvenes de contextos urbanos vulnerables de Lima*. Grupo de Análisis para el Desarrollo.

Balarin, M., Paudel, M., Sarmiento, P., Singh, G.B. and Wilder, P. (2021) 'Exploring epistemic justice in educational research'. JustEd. Available at: https://doi.org/10.5281/zenodo.5502143

Baldwin, C., Pickering, G. and Dale, G. (2023) 'Knowledge and self-efficacy of youth to take action on climate change', *Environmental education research*, 29(11), pp 1597–1616. Available at: https://doi.org/10.1080/13504622.2022.2121381

Barrett, A.M., Milligan, L.O., Sane, E. and Bowden, R. (2025) 'Multilingual education for sustainable development in sub-Saharan Africa: towards epistemic inclusion', *Prospects*. Available at: https://doi.org/10.1007/s11125-025-09731-1

Bartlett, L. and Vavrus, F. (2017) *Rethinking case study research*. Routledge.

Bartlett, R., Koncul, A., Lid, I.M., George, E.O. and Haugen, I. (2023) 'Using walking/go along interviews with people in vulnerable situations: a synthesized review of the research literature', *International journal of qualitative methods*, 22, p 16094069231164606. Available at: https://doi.org/10.1177/16094069231164606

Batanda, J. (2009) *The role of civil society in advocating for transitional justice in Uganda*. Institute for justice and reconciliation, African Programme.

Bellino, M.J., Paulson, J. and Anderson Worden, E. (2017) 'Working through difficult pasts: Toward thick democracy and transitional justice in education', Comparative education, 53(3), pp 313–332. Available at: https://doi.org/10.1080/03050068.2017.1337956

Bengtsson, S.E., Barakat, B. and Muttarak, R. (2018) *The role of education in enabling the sustainable development agenda*. Routledge.

Bentrovato, D., Korostelina, K. and Schulze, M. (eds) (2016) *History can bite: history education in divided and postwar societies*. V&R unipress.

Biesta, G. (2015) *Good education in an age of measurement: ethics, politics, democracy*. Routledge.

Billingsley, K. (2018) 'Intersectionality as locality: children and transitional justice in Nepal', *International journal of transitional justice*, 12(1), pp 64–87. Available at: https://doi.org/10.1093/ijtj/ijx032

Bisson, M.-J., Gilmore, C., Inglis, M. and Jones, I. (2020) 'Teaching using contextualised and decontextualised representations: examining the case of differential calculus through a comparative judgement technique', *Research in mathematics education*, 22, pp 284–303. Available at: https://doi.org/10.1080/14794802.2019.1692060

Bonal, X. and Tarabini, A. (2009) 'Global solution for global poverty? The World Bank education policy and the anti-poverty agenda', in *Re-reading education policies: a handbook studying the policy agenda of the 21st century*. Brill, pp 96–111.

Bonal, X. and Tarabini, A. (2016) 'Being poor at school: exploring conditions of educability in the favela', *British journal of sociology of education*, 37(2), pp 212–229. Available at: https://doi.org/10.1080/01425692.2014.924394

Borràs, S. (2016) 'New transitions from human rights to the environment to the rights of nature', *Transnational environmental law*, 5(1), pp 113–143. Available at: https://doi.org/doi:10.1017/S204710251500028X

Bradfield, P. (2017) 'Reshaping amnesty in Uganda: the case of Thomas Kwoyelo', *Journal of International Criminal Justice*, 15(4), 827–855.

Bradbury-Jones, C., Isham, L. and Taylor, J. (2018) 'The complexities and contradictions in participatory research with vulnerable children and young people: A qualitative systematic review', *Social science & medicine*, 215, pp 80–91. Available at: https://doi.org/10.1016/j.socscimed.2018.08.038

REFERENCES

Branch, A. (2018) 'From disaster to devastation: drought as war in northern Uganda', *Disasters*, 42, pp 306–327. Available at: https://doi.org/10.1111/disa.12303

Branch, A. and Martiniello, G. (2018) 'Charcoal power: the political violence of non-fossil fuel in Uganda', *Geoforum*, 97, pp 242–252. Available at: https://doi.org/10.1016/j.geoforum.2018.09.012

Brighouse, H. (2004) *Justice*. Polity Press.

Cachelin, A. and Nicolosi, E. (2022) 'Investigating critical community engaged pedagogies for transformative environmental justice education', *Environmental education research*, 28(4), pp 491–507. Available at: https://doi.org/10.1080/13504622.2022.2034751

Caldani, F., Ferrer, G., Gysling, J. and Tapia, C. (2013) *Estudio diagnóstico y propositivo sobre las necesidades de alineamiento entre los componentes del sistema curricular del Perú*. Proyecto FORGE. Available at: http://www.grade.org.pe/forge/descargas/Informe%20diagn%C3%B3stico%20Curricular%20Caldani%20y%20otros.pdf

Central Bureau of Statistics (2022) *Climate change related indicators of Nepal*. National Planning Commission, Government of Nepal. Available at: https://unstats.un.org/unsd/envstats/compendia/Nepal_ClimateChangeRelatedIndicatorsofNepal_2022.pdf

Chesnut, C.E., Hitchcock, J.H. and Onwuegbuzie, A.J. (2018) Using mixed methods to inform education policy research, in C.R. Lochmiller (ed) *Complementary research methods for educational leadership and policy studies*, pp 307–324.

Chisholm, L. (2018) 'Representations of class, race, and gender in textbooks', in *the Palgrave handbook of textbook studies*. Palgrave Macmillan, pp 225–237.

Chow, L., Mohammed, R. and Szabo, G. (2024) 'Racing against time: achieving the sustainable development goals with and for children'. Save the Children. Available at: https://resourcecentre.savethechildren.net/pdf/Racing-Against-Time-2024.pdf/

Cole, E.A. (2007) 'Transitional justice and the reform of history education', *The international journal of transitional justice*, 1(1), pp 115–137. Available at: https://dx.doi.org/10.1093/ijtj/ijm003

Costa, M.V. (2010) *Rawls, citizenship and education*. Routledge.

Consejo Nacional de Educación (2006) *Proyecto Educativo Nacional al 2021: La educación que queremos para el Perú*. CNE.

Consejo Nacional de Educación (2007) *Proyecto Educativo Nacional al 2021*.

Constitution of the Republic of Uganda (1995) Uganda, ULII. Available at: https://ulii.org/akn/ug/act/statute/1995/constitution/eng@2018-01-05

Creswell, J. and Plano Clark, V. (2018) *Designing and conducting mixed methods research*. 3rd edn. SAGE publications.

Cueto, S., León, J., Ramírez, C. and Guerrero, G. (2016) 'Oportunidades de aprendizaje y rendimiento escolar en matemática y lenguaje: resumen de tres estudios en Perú', *REICE: Revista Iberoamericana sobre Calidad, Eficacia y Cambio en Educación*, 6(1), pp 29–41. Available at: https://grade.org.pe/publicaciones/455-oportunidades-de-aprendizaje-y-rendimiento-escolar-en-matematica-y-lenguaje-resumen-de-tres-estudios-en-peru/

Cueto, S., Penny, M. and Sanchez, A. (2018) 'What have we learned from the Young Lives study in Peru?', *Young Lives* [Preprint].

Curriculum Development Centre (2014) *Secondary education curriculum: Part 1 Compulsory subjects*. Curriculum Development Centre, Ministry of Education.

Curriculum Development Centre (2017) *Social Studies Grade 10*. Curriculum Development Centre, Ministry of Education.

Curriculum Development Centre (2019) *National curriculum framework for school education in Nepal 2019*. Curriculum Development Centre, Ministry of Education, Science and Technology.

Curriculum Development Centre (2021) *Secondary education curriculum 2021: Grade 9 and 10*. Curriculum Development Centre, Ministry of Education, Science and Technology, https://www.moecdc.gov.np/storage/gallery/1687153367.pdf

CVR (2003) *Informe final. Recomendaciones. reformas institucionales*. Comisión de la Verdad y la Reconciliación Perú.

CVR (2010) *Informe final: comisión de la verdad sobre los hechos del Palacio de Justicia*. Comisión de la Verdad y la Reconciliación Perú.

Datzberger, S. (2018) 'Why education is not helping the poor. Findings from Uganda'. *World development*, 110, 124–139.

Davies, L. (2017) 'Justice-sensitive education: The implications of transitional justice mechanisms for teaching and learning', *Comparative Education*, 53(3), pp 333–350. Available at: https://doi.org/10.1080/03050068.2017.1317999

DeJaeghere, J. (2020) 'Reconceptualizing educational capabilities: A relational capability theory for redressing inequalities', *Journal of human development and capabilities*, 21(1), pp 17–35. Available at: https://doi.org/10.1080/19452829.2019.1677576

Denov, M., Cadieux Van Vliet, A., Mosseau, N. and Lakor, A.A. (2023) 'The meaning of land and place for children born of war in northern Uganda', *Children's geographies*, 21(4), pp 693–707. Available at: https://doi.org/10.1080/14733285.2022.2113857

Destrooper, T. and Gissel, L.E. (eds) (2023) *Transitional justice in aparadigmatic contexts: accountability, recognition, and disruption*. Taylor & Francis.

Devries, K., Ward, C.H., Naker, D., Parkes, J., Bonell, C., Bhatia, A. et al (2022) 'School violence: where are the interventions?', *The Lancet child and adolescent health*, 6(1), pp 5–7. Available at: https://doi.org/10.1016/s2352-4642(21)00329-1

REFERENCES

Dewey, J. (1938) *Experience and education*. Macmillan.

Durrani, N. (2008) 'Schooling the "other": the representation of gender and national identities in Pakistani curriculum texts', *Compare: a journal of comparative and international education*, 38(5), pp 595–610. Available at: https://doi.org/10.1080/03057920802351374

Eaton, E. and Day, N. (2019) 'Petro-pedagogy: fossil fuel interests and the obstruction of climate justice in public education', *Environmental education research*, 26(4), pp 457–473. Available at: https://doi.org/10.1080/13504622.2019.1650164

Education (Pre-Primary, Primary and Post-Primary) Act (2008) Uganda. Available at: https://ulii.org/akn/ug/act/2008/13/eng@2023-12-31

Elfert, M. and Ydesen, C. (2023) 'UNESCO, the OECD and the World Bank: a global governance perspective', in M. Elfert and C. Ydesen (eds) *Global governance of education*. Springer International Publishing (Educational Governance Research), pp 23–50.

Elmore, R. (1996) 'Getting to scale with good educational practice', *Harvard educational review*, 66(1), pp 1–27. Available at: https://doi.org/10.17763/haer.66.1.g73266758j348t33

Fairclough, N. (2013) 'Critical Discourse Analysis', in N. Fairclough (ed) *Critical discourse analysis*. Routledge, pp 9–20.

Fawcett, P., Flinders, M., Hay, C. and Wood, M. (eds) (2017) *Anti-politics, depoliticization, and governance*. Oxford University Press.

Ferrer, G. (2004) *Las reformas curriculares de Perú, Colombia, Chile y Argentina, ¿Quién responde por los resultados?* GRADE (Documentos de Trabajo).

Fetters, M.D., Curry, L.A. and Creswell, J.W. (2013) 'Achieving integration in mixed methods designs – principles and practices', *Health services research*, 48(62), pp 2134–2156. Available at: https://doi.org/10.1111/1475-6773.12117

Finnegan, W. (2023) 'Educating for hope and action competence: a study of secondary school students and teachers in England', *Environmental education research*, 29(11), pp 1617–1636. Available at: https://doi.org/10.1080/13504622.2022.2120963

Floresta, J.K. (2021) 'Undoing a culture of violence in schools by hearing the subalterned students who experience war in Mindanao', *Journal of peace education*, 18(3), pp 260–281. Available at: https://doi.org/10.1080/17400201.2021.1940113

Fraser, N. (1995) 'Recognition or redistribution? A critical reading of Iris Young's justice and the politics of difference', *Journal of political philosophy*, 3(2), pp 166–180. Available at: https://doi.org/10.1111/j.1467-9760.1995.tb00033.x

Fraser, N. (2009) *Scales of justice: reimagining political space in a globalizing world*. Columbia University Press.

Fraser, N. and Honneth, A. (2003) *Redistribution or recognition? A political-philosophical exchange*. Verso.

Freire, P. (2013) *Pedagogy of the oppressed*. 30th anniversary edition. Bloomsbury.

Fricker, M. (2007) *Epistemic injustice: power and the ethics of knowing*. Oxford University Press.

Fricker, M. (2012) 'Epistemic justice as a condition of political freedom?', *Synthese*, 190(7), pp 1317–1332. Available at: https://doi.org/10.1007/s11229-012-0227-3

Fricker, M. (2015) 'Epistemic contribution as a central human capability', in G. Hull (ed) *The equal society: essays on equality in theory and practice*. Lexington Books, pp 73–90.

Galtung, J. (1969) 'Violence, peace, and peace research', *Journal of peace research*, 6(3), pp 167–191. Available at: https://doi.org/10.1177/002234336900600301

Gandolfi, H. (2022) 'Environmental challenges & social justice', *BERA Research Intelligence*, pp 12–13. Available at: BERA Research Intelligence 150 - Spring 2022

Gaynor, N. (2016) 'Round pegs in square holes? Development education, the formal sector and the global knowledge economy', *Policy and practice: a development education review*, 23, pp 1–15. Available at: https://www.developmenteducationreview.com/issue/issue-23/round-pegs-square-holes-development-education-formal-sector-and-global-knowledge

Gewirtz, S. (1998) 'Conceptualizing social justice in education: mapping the territory', *Journal of education policy*, 13(4), pp 469–484. Available at: https://doi.org/10.1080/0268093980130402

Giroux, H. (1983) 'Theories of reproduction and resistance in the new sociology of education: A critical analysis', *Harvard educational review*, 53(3), pp 257–293. Available at: https://doi.org/10.17763/haer.53.3.a67x4u33g7682734

Glackin, M. and King, H. (2020) 'Taking stock of environmental education policy in England – the what, the where and the why', *Environmental education research*, 26(3), pp 305–323. Available at: https://doi.org/10.1080/13504622.2019.1707513

Global Forest Watch (nd) *Global Forest Watch Uganda dashboard. Uganda deforestation rates & statistics*. Available at: https://www.globalforestwatch.org/dashboards/country/UGA

Global Partnership for Education (2014) *250 million reasons to invest in education*. Global Partnership for Education. Available at: https://www.globalpartnership.org/sites/default/files/2014-04-GPE-Case-for-investment_0.pdf

Godenzzi, J.C. (2007) 'Ciudadanía intercultural y política de lenguas: perspectiva latinoamericana', *Signo y seña* (18), pp 19–39. Available at: https://doi.org/10.34096/sys.n18.5785

González, M.P. (2018) 'La historia escolar y los profesores. Una mirada desde el Mercosur', in G.Á.d. Amézola and L.F. Cerri (eds) *Los jóvenes frente a la historia: Aprendizaje y enseñanza en escuelas secundarias*. La Plata: Facultad de Humanidades y Ciencias de la Educación, Universidad Nacional de La Plata.

González, N., Eguren, M. and Belaunde, C. de (2017) *Desde el aula: una aproximación a las prácticas pedagógicas del maestro peruano*. Instituto de Estudios Peruanos.

Goody, J. (2006) *The theft of history*. Cambridge University Press.

Government of Nepal (2015) 'The constitution of Nepal'. Government of Nepal. Available at: https://www.moljpa.gov.np/public/uploads/238f7219-492b-40af-a919-c94c35f9c269.pdf

Government of Nepal (2017) 'Local government operation act, 2017', *Nepal Gazette*, pp 1–119. Available at: https://www.moljpa.gov.np/public/uploads/36793035-f160-4b82-a050-9143b6badf28.pdf

Government of Nepal (2018) 'Compulsory and free education act'. Government of Nepal. Available at: https://giwmscdnone.gov.np/media/app/public/275/posts/1720161886_32.pdf

Government of Uganda (1992) *Government White Paper on the Education Policy Review Commission report*. Government of Uganda.

Government of Uganda (2000) *Amnesty Act*. Available at https://mia.go.ug/sites/default/files/resources/The%20Amnesty%20Act%2C%202000.pdf

Government of Uganda (2001) *Universities and other Tertiary Institutions Act*. Government of Uganda. Available at: https://policies.mak.ac.ug/sites/default/files/policies/001_UNIVERSITIES_%20AND_OTHER_TERTIARY_INSTITUTIONS_ACT.pdf

Government of Uganda (2002) *The Education Service Act*. Government of Uganda. Available at: https://www.ugandalaws.com/statutes/principle-legislation/education-service-act

Government of Uganda (2003) *National Forestry and Tree Planting Act*. Government of Uganda.

Government of Uganda (2006a) *Employment Act*. Available at https://ulii.org/akn/ug/act/2006/6/eng@2006-06-08

Government of Uganda (2006b) *Refugee Act*. Available at: https://ulii.org/akn/ug/act/2006/21/eng@2006-08-04

Government of Uganda (2008) *The Business, Technical, Vocational Education and Training Act*. Government of Uganda.

Government of Uganda (2012) 'The Education Service Act 2002 (Act No. 13 of 2002): The education service (teachers' professional code of conduct), legal notice No. 11 of 2012'. Government of Uganda. Available at: https://www.scribd.com/document/642975889/TEACHERS-PROFESSIONAL-CODE-OF-CONDUCT-2012

Government of Uganda (2014) *Higher Education Students Financing Act*. Government of Uganda.

Government of Uganda (2015) *Public Private Partnership Act*. Available at: https://ulii.org/akn/ug/act/2015/13/eng@2015-09-16

Government of Uganda (2018) 'Ministry of Education and Sports: the national teacher policy'. Government of Uganda.

Government of Uganda (2019a) *The National Environment Act*. Government of Uganda. Available at: https://nema.go.ug/sites/all/themes/nema/docs/National%20Environment%20Act,%20No.%205%20of%202019.pdf

Government of Uganda (2019b) *Transitional Justice Policy*. Government of Uganda.

Government of Uganda (2021) *The Uganda National Examinations Board Act*. Government of Uganda.

Grieve, T. and Mitchell, R. (2020) 'Promoting meaningful and equitable relationships? Exploring the UK's Global Challenges Research Fund (GCRF) funding criteria from the perspectives of African partners', *The European journal of development research*, 32(3), pp 514–528. Available at: https://doi.org/10.1057/s41287-020-00274-z

Gruenewald, D. (2003) 'The best of both worlds: a critical pedagogy of place', *Educational researcher*, 32(4), pp 3–12. Available at: https://doi.org/10.3102/0013189X032004003

Guerrero, L. (2013) *Informe completo sobre la reforma curricular*. FORGE.

Hajir, B. (2023) 'Between "the paradox of liberalism" and "the paradox of decoloniality": education for peacebuilding in conflict settings', *Globalisation, societies and education*, 22(3), pp 433–445. Available at: https://doi.org/10.1080/14767724.2022.2160971

Hall, B.L., Godrie, B. and Heck, I. (2020) 'Knowledge democracy and epistemic in/justice: reflections on a conversation', *The Canadian journal of action research*, 21(1), pp 27–45. Available at: https://doi.org/10.33524/cjar.v21i1.516

Hassan, R. and Birungi, P. (2011) 'Social capital and poverty in Uganda', *Development Southern Africa*, 28(1), 19–37.

Hernández, W. (ed) (2019) *Violencias contra las mujeres: la necesidad de un doble plural*. GRADE y PNUD. Available at: https://grade.org.pe/publicaciones/violencias-contra-las-mujeres-la-necesidad-de-un-doble-plural/

Hoadley, U. (2017) *Pedagogy in poverty: lessons from twenty years of curriculum reform in South Africa*. Routledge.

Honneth, A. (1992) 'Integrity and disrespect: principles of a conception of morality based on the theory of recognition', *Political Theory*, 20(2), pp 187–201. Available at: https://doi.org/10.1177/0090591792020002001

Honneth, A. (1995) *The struggle for recognition: the moral grammar of social conflicts*. Cambridge: MIT press.

hooks, bell (1994) *Teaching to transgress*. Routledge.

Hookway, C. (2010) 'Some varieties of epistemic injustice: reflections on Fricker', *Episteme*. 2012/01/03 edn, 7(2), pp 151–163. Available at: https://doi.org/10.3366/epi.2010.0005.

Hopwood, J., Porter, H. and Saum, N. (2015) 'Karamojong women and the extremes of insecurity'. Justice and Security Research Programme, Paper 27.

Horsthemke, K. (2009) 'Learning for the natural environment: the case against anthropocentrism', *US–China education review*, 6(10), pp 22–30. Available at: https://www.thefreelibrary.com/Learning+for+the+Natural+Environment%3a+The+Case+against...-a0237843045

Hrubec, M. (2004) 'Towards global justice: an interview with Nancy Fraser', *Czech sociological review*, 40(6), pp 879–889. Available at: https://sreview.soc.cas.cz/pdfs/csr/2004/06/07.pdf

Huaman, E.S. (2017) 'Indigenous rights education (IRE): Indigenous knowledge systems and transformative human rights in the Peruvian Andes', *International journal of human rights education*, 1(1), pp 1–34. Available at: https://repository.usfca.edu/ijhre/vol1/iss1/5

Huber, M., Jabot, M. and Heath, C. (2024) *Experiential learning and community partnerships for sustainable development: a foundational model for climate action*. Routledge. Available at: https://doi.org/10.4324/9781003489337

Hutchison, C., Wiggan, G. and Starker, T. (2014) 'Curriculum violence and its reverse: The under-education of teachers in a pluralistic society and its implications for the education of minority students', *Insights on learning disabilities: from prevailing theories to validated practices*, 11(1), pp 85–111. Available at: https://link.gale.com/apps/doc/A368380203/AONE?u=anon~e3d606b7&sid=googleScholar&xid=afa8be4f

ILO (1989) *Indigenous and Tribal Peoples Convention (No. 169)*. International Labour Organization.

INEI (2017) *Censo Nacional*. Instituto Nacional de Estadística del Perú.

Isanga, E. and Nsubuga, G.E.N. (2008) *Ordinary level Christian religious education*. MK Publishers.

Jave, I. (2021) *La humillación y la urgencia: políticas de reparación posconflicto en el Perú*. Pontificia Universidad Católica del Perú, Fondo Editorial.

Jave, I., Reategui, F. and Hurtado, E. (2018) 'El proceso de justicia transicional en Perú-2018', in *Informes Anuales de la Red Latinoamericana de Justicia Transicional: verdad, justicia, reparaciones y memoria*. Red Latinoamericana de Justicia Transicional.

Jencks, C. (2002) 'Does inequality matter?', *Daedalus*, 131(1), pp 49–65. Available at: https://www.jstor.org/stable/20027737

Jessop, B. (2010) 'Cultural political economy and critical policy studies', *Critical policy studies*, 3(3–4), pp 336–356. Available at: https://doi.org/10.1080/19460171003619741

JustEd (2023) 'JustEd evidence brief 1: key findings'. JustEd Project. Zenodo.

Kakupa, P. and Shayo, H.J. (2021) 'Implementing Sustainable Development Goal on Education (SDG4) amid donor fatigue: challenges for the Global South', *Advances in social sciences research journal*, 8(11), pp 20–28. Available at: https://doi.org/10.14738/assrj.811.11132

Kahlke, R., Maggio, L.A., Lee, M.C., Cristancho, S., LaDonaa, K., Abdallah, Z. et al (2024) 'When words fail us: An integrative review of innovative elicitation techniques for qualitative interviews', *Medical education*, 59(4), pp 1–13. Available at: https://doi.org/10.1111/medu.15555

Kahn, R.V. (2010) *Critical pedagogy, ecoliteracy, & planetary crisis: the ecopedagogy movement*. Peter Lang.

Kalungwizi, V.J., Krogh, E., Gjøtterud, S.M. and Mattee, A. (2018) 'Experiential strategies and learning in environmental education: lessons from a teacher training college in Tanzania', *Journal of adventure education and outdoor learning*, 20(2), pp 95–110. Available at: https://doi.org/10.1080/14729679.2018.1555047

Keddie, A. (2020) 'Schooling and social justice through the lenses of Nancy Fraser', in C. Vincent (ed) *Nancy Fraser, social justice and education*. Routledge, pp 40–56.

Keet, A. (2014) 'Epistemic "othering" and the decolonisation of knowledge', *Africa Insight*, 44(1), pp 23–37. Available at: https://journals.co.za/doi/epdf/10.10520/EJC161966

Kerfoot, C. and Bello-Nonjengele, B. (2023) 'Towards epistemic justice: Constructing knowers in multilingual classrooms', *Applied linguistics*, 44(3), pp 462–484. Available at: https://doi.org/10.1093/applin/amac049

Kezabu, K.L. (2022) 'Intersections of Indigenous knowledge and place-based education: possibilities for new visions of sustainability education in Uganda', *Australian journal of environmental education*, 38(2), pp 192–194. Available at: https://doi.org/10.1017/aee.2022.15

Kibanja, G.M., Kajumba, M.M. and Johnson, L.R. (2012) 'Ethnocultural conflict in Uganda: politics based on ethnic divisions inflame tensions across the country', in D. Landis and R.D. Albert (eds) *Handbook of ethnic conflict: international perspectives*. Springer US, pp 403–435.

Kingdon, J.W. (1984) *Agendas, alternatives, and public policies*. Pearson.

Klees, S.J. (2022) 'UNESCO's futures of education report: what is missing?', *NORRAG Blog*, 21 February. Available at: https://www.norrag.org/unescos-futures-of-education-report-what-is-missing-by-steven-j-klees/

Kohli, R.K.S. (2011) 'Working to ensure safety, belonging and success for unaccompanied asylum-seeking children', *Child abuse review*, 20(5), pp 311–323. Available at: https://doi.org/10.1002/car.1182

Kolb, D. (2014) *Experiential learning: experience as the source of learning and development*. FT Press.

Kopnina, H. (2020) 'Education for the future? Critical evaluation of education for sustainable development goals', *The journal of environmental education*, 51(4), pp 280–291. Available at: https://doi.org/10.1080/00958964.2019.1710444

Kotzee, B. (2013) 'Educational justice, epistemic justice, and leveling down', *Educational theory*, 63(4), pp 331–350. Available at: https://doi.org/10.1111/edth.12027

Kuchah, K., Adamson, L., Dorimana, A., Uwizeyemariya, A., Uworwabayeho, A. and Milligan, L.O. (2022) 'Silence and silencing in the classroom: Rwandan girls' epistemic exclusion in English medium basic education', *Journal of multilingual and multicultural development*, pp 1–15. Available at: https://doi.org/10.1080/01434632.2022.2159031

Küfeoğlu, S. (2022) *Emerging technologies: value creation for sustainable development*. Springer.

Kushnir, I. and Nunes, A. (2022) 'Education and the UN development goals projects (MDGs and SDGs): definitions, links, operationalisations', *Journal of research in international education*, 21(1), pp 3–21. Available at: https://doi.org/10.1177/14752409221088942

Lai, E. (2011) *Critical thinking: a literature review research report*. Parsons Publishing.

Langole, S. (2010) 'Peace education for inter-ethnic and inter-cultural solidarity in Uganda: A curriculum agenda'. Available at: https://api.semanticscholar.org/CorpusID:155927851

Lara-Steidel, H. and Thompson, W.C. (2023) 'Epistemic injustice? Banning "critical race theory", "divisive topics", and "embedded racism" in the classroom', *Journal of philosophy of education*, 57(4–5), pp 862–879. Available at: https://doi.org/10.1093/jopedu/qhad069

Leibowitz, B. (2008) 'Towards a pedagogy of possibility: teaching and learning from a 'social justice' perspective', in E. Bitzer (ed) *Higher Education in South Africa: a scholarly look behind the scenes*. SUN MeDIA, pp 85–101.

Leibowitz, B. and Bozalek, V. (2015) 'The scholarship of teaching and learning from a social justice perspective', *Teaching in higher education*, 21(2), pp 109–122. Available at: https://doi.org/10.1080/13562517.2015.1115971

Local Government Act (1997) Uganda. Available at: https://ngobureau.go.ug/staging/sites/default/files/laws_regulations/2020/12/The%20Local%20Governments%20Act.pdf

Logan, T. and Murphy, K. (2017) 'Reflections on education and transitional justice: notes from the field', *Comparative Education*, 53(3), pp 483–494. Available at: https://doi.org/10.1080/03050068.2017.1339424

López, L.E. and Küper, W. (1999) 'La educación intercultural bilingüe en América Latina: balance y perspectivas', *Revista Iberoamericana de educación*, 20 [Preprint].

Lotz-Sisitka, H., Wals, A.E.J., Kronlid, D. and McGarry. D. (2015) 'Transformative, transgressive social learning: rethinking higher education pedagogy in times of systemic global dysfunction', *Current opinion in environmental sustainability*, 16, pp 73–80. Available at: https://doi.org/10.1016/j.cosust.2015.07.018

Lotz-Sisitka, H., Mukute, M., Chikunda, C., Baloi, A. and Pesanayi, T. (2017) 'Transgressing the norm: transformative agency in community-based learning for sustainability in southern African contexts', *International review of education*, 63(6), pp 897–914. Available at: https://doi.org/10.1007/s11159-017-9689-3

Lupinacci, J. and Happel-Parkins, A. (2016) '(Un)learning anthropocentrism: an ecojustice framework for teaching to resist human-supremacy in schools', in S. Rice and A.G. Rud (eds) *The educational significance of human and non-human animal interactions: blurring the species line.* Palgrave Macmillan US, pp 13–30.

Lynch, K. (2012) 'Affective equality as a key issue of justice: A comment on Fraser's 3-dimensional framework', *Social justice series*, 12(3), pp 45–64. Available at: http://hdl.handle.net/10197/4400

MacDonald, L. and Kidman, J. (2024) 'Uncanny pedagogies: teaching difficult histories at sites of colonial violence', in G. Vass and M. Hogarth (eds) *Critical studies and the international field of Indigenous education research.* Routledge, pp 31–46.

Macintyre, T., Tassone, V. and Wals, A. (2020) 'Capturing transgressive learning in communities spiraling towards sustainability', *Sustainability*, 12(12), p 4873. Available at: https://doi.org/doi:10.3390/su12124873

Manyike, T.V. and Shava, S. (2018) 'The decolonial role of African indigenous languages and indigenous knowledges in formal education processes', *Indilinga: African journal of Indigenous knowledge systems*, 17(1), pp 36–52. Available at: https://hdl.handle.net/10520/EJC-fe647aa43

Marigat, S.K. (2023) 'Managing cattle rustling by enhancing police–community cooperation in the Karamoja Cluster: Lessons from Baringo, Kenya', *African security review*, 32(1), 81–98. Available at: https://doi.org/10.1080/10246029.2022.2141129

Masaka, D. (2019) 'Attaining epistemic justice through transformation and decolonisation of education curriculum in Africa', *African identities*, 17(3–4), pp 298–309. Available at: https://doi.org/10.1080/14725843.2019.1681259

Mason, J. (2006) 'Mixing methods in a qualitatively driven way', *Qualitative research*, 6(1), pp 9–25. Available at: https://doi.org/10.1177/1468794106058866

Mbah, M., Ajaps, S. and Molthan-Hill, P. (2021) 'A systematic review of the deployment of Indigenous knowledge systems towards climate change adaptation in developing world contexts: implications for climate change education', *Sustainability*, 13(9), p 4811. Available at: https://doi.org/10.3390/su13094811

Mbembe, A. (2021) *The paths of tomorrow: contribution to thinking commensurate with the planet*. 32. UNESCO. Available at: https://unesdoc.unesco.org/ark:/48223/pf0000387026_eng

McCowan, T. (2010) 'Reframing the universal right to education', *Comparative education*, 46(4), pp 509–525. Available at: https://doi.org/10.1080/03050068.2010.519482

McIntyre, J. and Abrams, F. (2021) *Refugee education: theorising practice in schools*. Routledge.

Medina, J. (2017) 'Varieties of hermeneutical injustice', in I.J. Kidd, J. Medina and G. Pohlhaus, Jr (eds) *The Routledge handbook of epistemic injustice*. Routledge, pp 41–52. Available at: https://www.taylorfrancis.com/books/mono/10.4324/9781315212043/routledge-handbook-epistemic-injustice?refId=dc8989c1-5640-4d3f-8a4e-582bb0482202&context=ubx

Medina, J. (2018) 'Misrecognition and epistemic injustice', *Feminist philosophy quarterly*, 4(4), pp 1–20. Available at: https://ojs.lib.uwo.ca/index.php/fpq/article/view/6233

Menton, M., Larrea, C., Latorre, S., Martinez-Alier, J., Peck, M., Temper, L. and Walter, M. (2020) 'Environmental justice and the SDGs: from synergies to gaps and contradictions', *Sustainability Science*, 15, pp 1621–1636. Available at: https://doi.org/10.1007/s11625-020-00789-8

Meredith, M. (2024) 'Approaches to epistemic justice', in M. Meredith (ed) *Universities and epistemic justice in a plural world: knowing better*. Springer Nature Singapore, pp 35–45.

Mezirow, J. (1991) *Transformative dimensions of adult learning*. Jossey-Bass.

Mignolo, W. (2011) *The darker side of Western modernity: global futures, decolonial options*. Duke University Press.

Miles, S. and Singal, N. (2010) 'The Education for All and inclusive education debate: conflict, contradiction or opportunity?', *International journal of inclusive education*, 14(1), pp 1–15. Available at: https://doi.org/10.1080/13603110802265125

Milligan, L.O. (2022) 'Towards a social and epistemic justice approach for exploring the injustices of English as a Medium of Instruction in basic education', *Educational review*, 74(5), pp 927–941. Available at: https://doi.org/10.1080/00131911.2020.1819204

Milligan, L.O., Ajok, P., Balarin, M., Espinal, S., Karki, M., Kornakech, D. et al (2021) 'Education at the intersection of environmental, epistemic and transitional justices: an initial scoping review'. Available at: https://zenodo.org/records/5558839#.ZA9C53bP2Uk

Milligan, L.O., Dorimana, A., Uwizeyemariya, A., Uworwabayeho, A., Sprague, T., Adamson, L. and Kuchah, K. (2023) 'Umuzigo w'inyongera: girls' differential experiences of the double-burden of language and gender in Rwandan English medium secondary education', *Language and education*, pp 1–16. Available at: https://doi.org/10.1080/09500782.2023.2288635

Milligan, L.O., Isingoma, B., Aciro, T., Mirembe, D.D., Krause, N. and Nuwategeka, E. (2024) 'Learners' everyday experiences of violence in English medium secondary education in Uganda', *Global social challenges journal*, 3, pp 31–48. Available at: https://doi.org/10.1332/27523349Y2024D000000008

MIMP (Ministerio de la Mujer y Población Vulnerables) (2019) *Decreto Supremo N° 008–2019-MIMP. Política de Igualdad de Género*. Available at: https://siteal.iiep.unesco.org/sites/default/files/sit_accion_files/peru_-_politica-nacional-igualdad-de-genero.pdf

Ministry of Education (2009) 'School sector reform plan 2009-2015'. Ministry of Education, Government of Nepal. Available at: https://planipolis.iiep.unesco.org/sites/default/files/ressources/nepal_school_sector_reform_2009.pdf

Ministry of Education (2011) 'SZOP national framework and implementation guideline, 2068'. Available at: https://resourcecentre.savethechildren.net/pdf/np_moe_szopguidelines.pdf

Ministry of Education (MoE) (2016) *School sector development plan 2016/2017–2022/23*, Ministry of Education, Government of Nepal. Available at: https://www.doe.gov.np/assets/uploads/files/3bee63bb9c50761bb8c97e2cc75b85b2.pdf

Ministry of Education, Science and Technology (MoEST) (2019a) *Sustainable development goal 4: Education 2030, Nepal National Framework*. Ministry of Education, Science and Technology, Government of Nepal. Available at: https://tinyurl.com/4rn2sc2e

Ministry of Education, Science and Technology (MoEST) (2019b) National education policy 2019. Ministry of Education Science and Technology, Government of Nepal. Available at: https://moest.gov.np/content/10155/10155/

Ministry of Education, Science and Technology (MoEST) (2022) *School education sector plan, 2022/23–2031/32*. Ministry of Education, Science and Technology. Government of Nepal.

MINEDU (Ministerio de Educación) (1972) 'Ley general de educación'. Decreto-Ley N°19326. Lima.

MINEDU (Ministerio de Educación del Perú) (2002) 'Ley para la Educación Bilingüe Intercultural'.

MINEDU (Ministerio de Educación del Perú) (2003) *Ley Nro. 28044 Ley General de Educación*.

MINEDU (Ministerio de Educación del Perú) (2016) *Política sectorial de Educación Intercultural y Educación Intercultural Bilingüe.*

MINEDU (Ministerio de Educación del Perú) (2016a) 'Plan Multianual de Reparaciones en Educación para las Víctimas de la Violencia en el Perú – REPAEDUCA 2016-2021'.

MINEDU (Ministerio de Educación del Perú) (2016b) 'Currículo Nacional de la Educación Básica'.

MINEDU (Ministerio de Educación del Perú) (2016c) 'Plan Nacional de Educación Ambiental 2017–2022'.

Ministerio del Ambiente (2012) *Política Nacional de Educación Ambiental – PNEA.*

Ministry of Environment and Forests (2019) *The Environment Protection Act, 2019 (2076).* Ministry of Environment and Forests, Government of Nepal, 2019(9), pp 1–24.

Ministry of Water and Environment (2021) *Natural resources, environment, climate change, land and water management programme: programme performance report 2021.* Government of Kenya.

Mkutu, K. (2008) 'Disarmament in Karamoja, northern Uganda: is this a solution for localised violent inter and intra-communal conflict? *The round table*, 97(394), 99–120. Available at: https://doi.org/10.1080/0035853070 1844718

Miri, M.A. (2024) 'An integrated conceptual model for enhancing refugee education', *British educational research journal*, 50(4), pp 1857–1877. Available at: https://doi.org/10.1002/berj.4005

Mitchell, R. and Milligan, L.O. (2023) 'Lesson observations in sub-Saharan Africa: bringing learners into focus', *Cambridge journal of education*, 53, pp 627–644. Available at: https://doi.org/10.1080/0305764X.2023.2206788

Mkhize, D. (2016) 'Mediating epistemic access through everyday language resources in an English language classroom', *Southern African linguistics and applied language studies*, 34(3), pp 227–240. Available at: https://doi.org/10.2989/16073614.2016.1250355

Mkwananzi, F. and Cin, M. (2021) 'Equal research partnerships are a myth – but we can change that', *Times Higher Education*, 10 June. Available at: https://www.timeshighereducation.com/campus/equal-research-partnerships-are-myth-we-can change

Mookherjee, M. (2023) *Global justice and recognition theory: dignifying the world's poor.* Routledge.

Mukasa, N. (2017) 'War-child mothers in northern Uganda: the civil war forgotten legacy', *Development in practice*, 27(3), pp 354–367. Available at: https://doi.org/10.1080/09614524.2017.1294147

Musara, E., Grant, C. and Vorster, J.-A. (2021) 'Inclusion as social justice: Nancy Fraser's theory in the South African context', in C.A. Mullen (ed) *Handbook of social justice interventions in education.* Springer, pp 39–58.

Muñoz, F. (2017) 'Las políticas educativas y la incorporación de género en la educación (1990–2016): un campo en disputa', *Tarea*, 94, pp 14–24. Available at: Tarea94_14_Fanni_Munoz.pdf

Muñoz, F., Ruiz-Bravo, P. and Rosales, J.L. (2006) 'El género y las políticas educativas en el Perú', in Ames, P. (ed) *Las brechas invisibles del Perú*, IEP, pp 71–100.

National Curriculum Development Centre (2019a) *Lower secondary Curriculum: curriculum framework*. National Curriculum Development Centre.

National Curriculum Development Centre (2019b) *Lower secondary curriculum: geography Syllabus*. National Curriculum Development Centre.

National Curriculum Development Centre (2000) Uganda. Available at: https://ulii.org/akn/ug/act/decree/1973/7/eng@2000-12-31

National Environment Management Authority (2001) *State of the environment report for Kampala*. National Environment Management Authority.

National Forestry Authority (2008) *Strategic action plan for the period 2008/9 to 2012/13 with priorities for the first five years*. Government of Uganda.

National Planning Authority (2020) *Third National Development Plan (NDPIII) 2020/21–2024/25*. Kampala.

National Planning Commission (2020) 'The fifteenth plan 2019/20–2023/24'. Government of Nepal. Available at: https://npc.gov.np/content/4487/4487-the-fifteenth-plan-fiscal-yea/

National Statistics Office (2023) *National population and housing census 2021: national report*. Office of the Prime Minister and Council of Ministers. Available at: https://censusnepal.cbs.gov.np/results/downloads/national

National Statistics Office (2024) *Nepal living standards survey IV, 2022–23: summary report*. Office of the Prime Minister and Council of Ministers, Government of Nepal. Available at: https://nepalindata.com/media/resources/items/0/b1707800524_89_pdf.pdf

Ndlovu-Gatsheni, S.J. (2021) 'Epistemic injustice', in F.J. Carrillo and G. Koch (eds) *Knowledge for the Anthropocene*. Edward Elgar Publishing, pp 167–177.

Ndofirepi, A.P. and Gwaravanda, E.T. (2018) 'Epistemic (in)justice in African universities: a perspective of the politics of knowledge', *Educational review*, 71(5), pp 581–594. Available at: https://doi.org/10.1080/00131911.2018.1459477

Ngidi, N.D. and Moletsane, R. (2023) 'Geographies of school-related gender-based violence: children's visual accounts of school toilets', *Children's geographies*, 21(6), pp 1119–1135. Available at: https://doi.org/10.1080/14733285.2023.2201671

Novelli, M., Lopes Cardozo, M.T.A. and Smith, A. (2017) 'The 4RS framework: analyzing education's contribution to sustainable peacebuilding with social justice in conflict', *Journal on education in emergencies*, 3(1), pp 14–43. Available at: https://doi.org/10.17609/N8S94K

REFERENCES

Novelli, M., Lopes Cardozo, M. and Smith, A. (2019) 'The "4 Rs" as a tool for critical policy analysis of the education sector in conflict affected states', *Education and conflict review*, 2, pp 70–75. Available at: Novelli_Article_12_Novelli.pdf

Nussbaum, M. (2000) *Women and human development: the capabilities approach.* Cambridge University Press.

Nussbaum, M. (2003) 'Capabilities as fundamental entitlements: Sen and social justice', *Feminist Economics*, 9(2–3), pp 33–59. Available at: https://doi.org/10.1080/1354570022000077926

Nussbaum, M. (2011) *Creating capabilities: the human development approach.* The Belknap Press of Harvard University Press.

Nuwategeka, E., Komakech, D. and Ajok, P. (2021a) 'Country profile: Uganda: JustEd: Education as and for environmental, epistemic and transitional justice'. Available at: https://doi.org/10.5281/zenodo.5517536

Nuwategeka, E., Monge, C., Shields, R. and Singh, A. (2021b) 'Exploring environmental justice in educational research'. Available at: https://doi.org/10.5281/zenodo.5517300

Nuwategeka, E., Mirembe, D.D., Milligan, L.O. and Aciro, T. (2024) 'Conflicted epistemologies in secondary school environmental education: implications for sustainable climate action in Uganda', *Compare: a journal of comparative and international education*, pp 1–18. Available at: https://doi.org/10.1080/03057925.2024.2378295

Nwako, Z., Grieve, T., Mitchell, R., Paulson, J., Saeed, T., Shanks, K. and Wilder, R. (2023) 'Doing harm: the impact of UK's GCRF cuts on research ethics, partnerships and governance', *Global social challenges journal*, 2(2), pp 64–85. Available at: https://doi.org/10.1332/GJSZ3052

Odora Hoppers, C. (2021) 'Research on Indigenous knowledge systems: the search for cognitive justice', *International journal of lifelong education*, 40(4), pp 310–327. Available at: https://doi.org/10.1080/02601370.2021.1966109

Office of the Prime Minister (2021) *Sustainable Development Goals (SDGs) progress report 2021.* SDGs Secretariat.

Oliveira, L. (2022) 'Hermeneutic injustices: practical and epistemic', in *Interpretation und geltung series:* (hermeneutik und interpretationstheorie, 3), pp 107–123. Available at: https://doi.org/10.30965/9783657703227_008

Olsson, D., Gericke, N. and Boeve-de Pauw, J. (2022) 'The effectiveness of education for sustainable development revisited – a longitudinal study on secondary students' action competence for sustainability', *Environmental education research*, 28(3), 405–429. https://doi.org/10.1080/13504622.2022.2033170

Parkes, J., Heslop, J., Johnson Ross, F., Westerveld, R. and Unterhalter, E. (2016) *A rigorous review of global research evidence on policy and practice on school-related gender-based violence.* UNICEF.

Parkes, J., Bhatia, A., Datzberger, S., Nagawa, R., Naker, D. and Devries, K. (2023) 'Addressing silences in research on girls' experiences of teacher sexual violence: insights from Uganda', *Comparative education*, 59(2), pp 193–213. Available at: https://doi.org/10.1080/03050068.2022.2133861

Paudel, M., Singh, A., Sharma, S., Bahadur Singh, G. and Wilder, W. (2024) '(Dis)connection between curriculum, pedagogy and learners' lived experience in Nepal's secondary schools: an environmental (in)justice perspective', *Global social challenges journal*, 3, pp 9–30. Available at: https://doi.org/10.1332/27523349Y2024D000000010

Paul, L.A. and Quiggin, J. (2020) 'Transformative education', *Educational theory*, 70(5), pp 561–579. Available at: https://doi.org/10.1111/edth.12444

Paulson, J. (2023) 'Reparative pedagogies', in Y. Hutchinson, A.A. Cortez Ochoa, J. Paulson and L. Tikley (eds) *Decolonizing education for sustainable futures*. Bristol University Press, pp 220–240.

Paulson, J. and Bellino, M. (2017) 'Truth commissions, education, and positive peace: an analysis of truth commission final reports (1980–2015)', *Comparative Education*, 53(3), pp 351–378. Available at: https://doi.org/10.1080/03050068.2017.1334428

Paulson, J. and Tikly, L. (2023) 'Reconceptualizing violence in international and comparative education: revisiting Galtung's framework', *Comparative education review*, 67(4), pp 771–796. Available at: https://doi.org/10.1086/726372

Paulson, J., Abiti, N., Bermeo Osorio, J., Charria Hernández, C.A., Keo, D., Manning, P. et al (2020) 'Education as site of memory: developing a research agenda', *International studies in sociology of education*, 29(4), pp 429–451. Available at: https://doi.org/10.1080/09620214.2020.1743198

Paulson, J., Espinal, S., Karki, M., Komakech, D., Kurawa, G., Ranabhat, S. and JustEd (2021) 'Exploring transitional justice in educational research (Version 1)'. JustEd. Available at: https://doi.org/10.5281/zenodo.5533918

Pherali, T. (2021) 'Social justice, education and peacebuilding: conflict transformation in southern Thailand', *Compare: a journal of comparative and international education*, 53(4), pp 710–727. Available at: https://doi.org/10.1080/03057925.2021.1951666

Phillips, A. (2004) 'Defending equality of outcome', *Journal of political philosophy*, 12(1), pp 1–19. Available at: https://doi.org/10.1111/j.1467-9760.2004.00188.x

Phyak, P. (2021) 'Epistemicide, deficit language ideology, and (de)coloniality in language education policy', *International journal of the sociology of language*, 267–268, pp 219–233. Available at: https://doi.org/10.1515/ijsl-2020-0104

Phyak, P. and Sah, P. (2022) 'Epistemic injustice and neoliberal imaginations in English as a medium of instruction (EMI) policy', *Applied linguistics review*, AOP, 15(4), pp 1321–1343. Available at: https://doi.org/10.1515/applirev-2022-0070

Pilapil, R. (2020) 'Beyond redistribution: Honneth, recognition theory and global justice', *Critical Horizons*, 21(1), pp 34–48. Available at: https://doi.org/10.1080/14409917.2020.1744281

Piscitelli, A. and D'Uggento, A.M. (2022) 'Do young people really engage in sustainable behaviors in their lifestyles?', *Social Indicators Research*, 163(3), pp 1467–1485. Available at: https://doi.org/10.1007/s11205-022-02955-0

Pope, D.C. (2001) *'Doing school': how we are creating a generation of stressed out, materialistic, and miseducated students*. Yale University Press.

Portugal, T. and Uccelli, F. (2018) 'Memorias, temores y silencios: El conflicto armado interno y su tratamiento en la escuela', *Tarea, Revista de Educación y Cultura*, 98, pp 18–24. Available at: https://hdl.handle.net/20.500.14660/1156

Prentice, C.M., Vergunst, F., Minor, K. and Berry, H.L. (2024) 'Education outcomes in the era of global climate change', *Nature Climate Change*, 14, pp 214–224. https://doi.org/10.1038/s41558-024-01945-z

Prøitz, T.S., Aasen, P. and Wermke, W. (2023) *From education policy to education practice: unpacking the nexus*. Springer Nature.

Quijano, A. (2010) 'Coloniality and modernity/rationality', in W. Mignolo and A. Escobar (eds) *Globalization and the decolonial option*. Routledge, pp 22–32.

Rawls, J. (1971) *A theory of justice*. Oxford University Press.

Reay, D. (2017) *Miseducation: inequality, education, and the working classes*. Policy Press.

Reid, A. (2019) 'Blank, blind, bald and bright spots in environmental education research', *Environmental education research*, 25(2), pp 157–171. Available at: https://doi.org/10.1080/13504622.2019.1615735

Robertson, E. (2013) 'The epistemic value of diversity', in B. Kotzee (ed) *Education and the growth of knowledge: perspectives from social and virtue epistemology*. Wiley-Blackwell, pp 166–178.

Robeyns, I. (2005) 'Selecting capabilities for quality of life measurement', *Social indicators research*, 74, pp 191–215. Available at: https://doi.org/10.1007/s11205-005-6524-1

Robeyns, I. (2017) *Wellbeing, freedom and social justice: the capability approach re-examined*. Open Book Publishers.

Rodríguez-Gómez, D., Foulds, K. and Sayed, Y. (2016) 'Representations of violence in social science textbooks: rethinking opportunities for peacebuilding in the Colombian and South African post-conflict scenarios', *Education as change*, 20(3), pp 76–97. Available at: https://doi.org/10.17159/1947-9417/2016/1532

Sabatier, P.A. and Jenkins-Smith, H.J. (eds) (1993) *Policy change and learning: an advocacy coalition approach*. Westview Press.

Schlosberg, D. (2007) *Defining environmental justice: theories, movements, and nature*. Oxford University Press.

Schmidt, R. (2006) 'Value-critical policy analysis', in *Interpretation and methods: empirical research methods and the interpretive turn*. M.E. Sharpe, pp 300–315.

Schweisfurth, M. (2011) 'Learner-centred education in developing country contexts: from solution to problem?', *International journal of educational development*, 31(5), pp 425–432. Available at: https://doi.org/10.1016/j.ijedudev.2011.03.005

Schweisfurth, M. (2023) 'Disaster didacticism: pedagogical interventions and the 'learning crisis'', *International journal of educational development*, 96, p 102707. Available at: https://doi.org/10.1016/j.ijedudev.2022.102707

Selim, Y. (2018) 'Contestation and resistance: the politics of and around transitional justice in Nepal', *Conflict, Security & Development*, 18(1), pp 39–60. Available at: https://doi.org/10.1080/14678802.2017.1420314

Sen, A. (1992) *Inequality reexamined*. Harvard University Press.

Sen, A. (1999) *Development as freedom*. Oxford University Press.

Sharma, S., Paudel, M., Singh, A., Milligan, L. and Singh, G.B. (2024) 'Environmental justice education in Nepal: policies and practices', *Prithvi academic journal*, 7, pp 41–56. Available at: https://doi.org/10.3126/paj.v7i1.65762

Shaw, T. and Mbabazi, P. (2007) 'Two Ugandas and a "Liberal Peace"? Lessons from Uganda about conflict and development at the start of a new century', *Global society*, 21(4): 567–578.

Shrestha, I.M. (2011) *My journey of learning and teaching: a trans/formation from culturally decontextualised to contextualised mathematics education*. Master's Thesis. Kathmandu University.

Skelton, A. and Batley, M. (2021) 'A comparative review of the incorporation of African traditional justice processes in restorative child justice systems in Uganda, Lesotho and Eswatini', in T. Gavrielides (ed) *Comparative restorative justice*. Springer International Publishing, pp 245–264.

Shields, R., Muratkyzy, A., Paudel, M., Singh, A., Nuwategeka, E., Rodriguez, M.F. and Paulson, J. (2024) 'From experience to actions for justice: learners' views on epistemic, environmental and transitional justice in Nepal, Peru and Uganda', *Global social challenges journal*, 3, pp 68–83. Available at: https://doi.org/10.1332/27523349Y2024D000000011

Silova, I., Rappleye, J. and You, Y. (2020) 'Beyond the Western horizon in educational research: toward a deeper dialogue about our interdependent futures', *ECNU review of education*, 3(1), pp 3–19. Available at: https://doi.org/10.1177/2096531120905195

Singh, G.B., Karki, M., Paudel, M., Ranabhat, S. and Singh, A. (2021) 'Country profile: Nepal: JustEd: Education as and for environmental, epistemic and transitional justice'. Tribhuvan University Working paper. Available at: https://researchportal.bath.ac.uk/en/publications/country-profile-nepal-justed-education-as-and-for-environmental-e

Singh, V. (2021) 'Toward a transdisciplinary, justice-centered pedagogy of climate change', in R. Iyengar and C. Kwauk (eds) *Curriculum and learning for climate action*. Brill, pp 169–187.

Smit, B. and Onwuegbuzie, A.J. (2018) 'Observations in qualitative inquiry: when what you see is not what you see', *International journal of qualitative methods*, 17(1), p 1609406918816766. Available at: https://doi.org/10.1177/1609406918816766

Smith, L.T. (1999) *Decolonizing methodologies: research and Indigenous peoples*. Zed Books and Otago University Press.

Sobe, N. (2014) 'Textbooks, schools, memory, and the technologies of national imaginaries', in J.H. Williams (ed) *(Re)constructing Memory*. Brill, pp 311–318.

Soysal, N. and JustEd (2023) 'Embedding a justice approach in secondary education: a practical guide for teachers and teacher educators in Uganda'. JustEd. Available at: https://doi.org/10.5281/zenodo.8399947

Spivak, G.C. (1988) 'Can the subaltern speak?', in L. Grossberg and C. Nelson (eds) *Marxism and interpretations of culture*. University of Illinois Press, pp 271–313.

Sriprakash, A. (2023) 'Reparations: theorising just futures of education', *Discourse: studies in the cultural politics of education*, 44(5), pp 782–795. Available at: https://doi.org/10.1080/01596306.2022.2144141

Sriprakash, A., Nally, D., Myers, K. and Ramos-Pinto, P. (2020) 'Learning with the past: racism, education and reparative futures'. Paper commissioned by UNESCO for the Futures of Education Initiative.

Sriprakash, A., Tikly, L. and Walker, S. (2020) 'The erasures of racism in education and international development: re-reading the "global learning crisis"', *Compare: a journal of comparative and international education*, 50(5), pp 676–692. Available at: https://doi.org/10.1080/03057925.2018.1559040

Srivastava, P. and Hopwood, N. (2009) 'A practical iterative framework for qualitative data analysis', *International journal of qualitative methods*, 8(1), pp 76–84. Available at: https://doi.org/10.1177/160940690900800107

Ssempuuma, J. (2013) 'Ugandan English', in *The Mouton world atlas of variation in English*. De Gruyter Mouton, pp 475–482.

Ssenyonga, J., Hermenau, K., Nkuba, M. and Hecker, T. (2022) 'Reducing teachers' use of violence toward students: a cluster-randomized controlled trial in secondary schools in southwestern Uganda', *Children and youth services review*, 138, pp 15–26. Available at: https://doi.org/10.1016/j.chiabu.2019.04.012

Stevens, D.M., Brydon-Miller, M. and Raider-Roth, M. (2016) 'Structured ethical reflection in practitioner inquiry: theory, pedagogy, and practice', *The educational forum*, 80(4), pp 430–443. Available at: https://doi.org/10.1080/00131725.2016.1206160

Sultana, F. (2021) 'Critical climate justice', *The geographical journal*, 188(1), pp 118–124. Available at: https://doi.org/10.1111/geoj.12417

Táíwò, O.O. (2022) *Reconsidering reparations*. Oxford University Press.

Tapia, J. and Cueto, S. (2017) 'El apoyo de FORGE al desarrollo del Currículo Nacional de la Educación Básica del Perú'. GRADE.

Tedesco, J. (2010) 'Educar para la justicia social. Nuevos procesos de socialización, ciudadanía y educación en América Latina', *Revista IIDH*, 52, pp 231–246. Available at: https://repositorio.iidh.ed.cr/handle/123456789/1259

Tedesco, J.C. and Lopez., N. (2002) 'Desafíos a la educación secundaria en América Latina', *Revista de la CEPAL*, 76, pp 55–69. Available at: https://unesdoc.unesco.org/ark:/48223/pf0000370509

Tejero, L. (2014) '"Nosotros, las víctimas": violencia, justicia transicional y subjetividades políticas en el contexto peruano de recuperación posconflicto', *Papeles del CEIC* [Preprint].

wa Thiong'o, N. (1986) *Decolonizing the mind: the politics of language in African literature*. James Currey.

Tikly, L. (2019) *Education for sustainable development in the postcolonial world: towards a transformative agenda for Africa*. Routledge.

Tikly, L. and Barrett, A.M. (2011) 'Social justice, capabilities and the quality of education in low-income countries', *International journal of educational development*, 31(1), pp 3–14. Available at: https://doi.org/10.1016/j.ijedudev.2010.06.001

Tito, S.O. (2013) *Peace education in Uganda: educators' perceptions of a peace education curriculum*. Doctoral thesis. Simon Fraser University.

Trapnell, L. and Neira, E. (2004) 'Situación de la educación intercultural bilingüe en el Perú', *Consultancy for the World Bank. Working document* [Preprint].

Uccelli, F. Agüero, J.C., Pease, M.A. and Portugal, T. (2017) *Atravesar el silencio: Memorias sobre el conflicto armado interno y su tratamiento en la escuela*. Instituto de Estudios Peruanos.

Uganda Bureau of Statistics (2022) 'Multidimensional poverty index report'. Uganda Bureau of Statistics.

Uganda Bureau of Statistics (2024) 'National population and housing census 2024: Preliminary results'. Uganda Bureau of Statistics.

UN Department of Economic and Social Affairs (nd) Available at: https://sdgs.un.org/goals/goal13

UNESCO (nd) *Greening Education Partnership.* UNESCO. Available at: https://www.unesco.org/en/sustainable-development/education/greening-future

UNESCO (2005) *Convention against Discrimination in Education (1960): awareness-raising and ratification.* UNESCO Digital Library.

UNESCO (2015) *Education for All 2000–2015: achievements and challenges; EFA global monitoring report, 2015.* UNESCO. Available at: https://www.unesco.org/gem-report/en/publication/education-all-2000-2015-achievements-and-challenges

UNESCO (2020) *Inclusion and education: all means all.* 2020. UNESCO. Available at: https://www.unesco.org/gem-report/en/node/168

UNESCO (2022) *Reimagining our futures together: a new social contract for education.* UNESCO.

UNESCO (2023) 'Records of the general conference, 42nd session. Volume 1 Resolutions'. UNESCO. Available at: https://unesdoc.unesco.org/ark:/48223/pf0000388394/PDF/388394eng.pdf.multi.page=68

United Nations (2010) 'Guidance note of the Secretary-General: United Nations approach to transitional justice'. United Nations.

United Nations Nepal (2020) 'Literature review on harmful practices in Nepal'. United Nations Nepal. Available at: https://nepal.unfpa.org/sites/default/files/pub-pdf/Literature%20Review%20on%20Harmful%20Practices%20in%20Nepal.pdf

United Nations Suriname (2010) 'The sustainable development goals in Suriname: quality education'. United Nations Suriname. Available at: https://suriname.un.org/en/sdgs/4

Unterhalter, E. (2019) 'The many meanings of quality education: Politics of targets and indicators in SDG 4', *Global policy*, 10, pp 39–51. Available at: https://doi.org/10.1111/1758-5899.12591

Unterhalter, E. (2021) 'Addressing intersecting inequalities in education', in T. McCowan and E. Unterhalter (eds) *Education and international development: an introduction.* 2nd edn. Bloomsbury, pp 127–149.

Vaidya, R.A., Shrestha, M.S., Nasab, N., Gurung, D.R., Kozo, N., Pradhan, N.S. and Wasson, R.J. (2019) 'Disaster risk reduction and building resilience in the Hindu Kush Himalaya', in P. Wester, A. Mishra, A. Mukherji and A. Shrestha (eds) *The Hindu Kush Himalaya assessment.* Springer, pp 389–419. Available at: https://doi.org/10.1007/978-3-319-92288-1_11

Vally, S., Dolombisa, Y. and Porteus, K. (1999) 'Violence in South African schools', *Current issues in comparative education*, 2(1), pp 80–90. Available at: https://doi.org/10.52214/cice.v2i1.11325

Vanner, C., Akseer, S. and Levi, T.K. (eds) (2022) *Teaching peace and conflict: the multiple roles of school textbooks in peacebuilding.* Springer Nature Switzerland.

Vinci, A. (2007) 'Existential motivations in the Lord's Resistance Army's continuing conflict', *Studies in conflict and terrorism*, 30(4), pp 337–352. Available at: https://doi.org/10.1080/10576100701200173

Vincent, C. (ed) (2020) *Nancy Fraser, social justice and education*. Routledge.

Vindevogel, S., de Schryver, M., Broekaert, E. and Derluyn, I. (2013) 'War-related experiences of former child soldiers in northern Uganda: comparison with non-recruited youths', *Pediatrics and international child health*, 33(4), pp 281–291. Available at: https://doi.org/10.1179/2046905513Y.0000000084

Vladimirova, K. and Le Blanc, D. (2016) 'Exploring links between education and Sustainable Development Goals through the lens of UN flagship reports', *Sustainable development*, 24(4), pp 254–271. Available at: https://doi.org/10.1002/sd.1626

Walker, M. (2006) 'Towards a capability-based theory of social justice for education policy-making', *Journal of education policy*, 21(2), pp 163–185. Available at: https://doi.org/10.1080/02680930500500245

Walker, M. (2016) 'Context, complexity and change: education as a conversion factor for non-racist capabilities in a South African University', *Race, ethnicity and education*, 19(6), pp 1275–1287. Available at: https://doi.org/10.1080/13613324.2015.1095176

Walker, M. (2019) 'Why epistemic justice matters in and for education', *Asia Pacific education review*, 20(2), pp 161–170. Available at: https://doi.org/10.100//s12564-019-09601-4

Walker, M. (2020) 'Failures and possibilities of epistemic justice, with some implications for higher education', *Critical studies in education*, 61(3), pp 263–278. Available at: https://doi.org/10.1080/17508487.2018.1474774

Walker, M. (2024) 'Repair in education spaces', *Journal of human development and capabilities*, 25(1), pp 1–20. Available at: https://doi.org/10.1080/19452829.2023.2297917

Walker, M. and Unterhalter, E. (eds) (2007) *Amartya Sen's capability approach and social justice in education*. Palgrave Macmillan.

Wals, A. (2019) 'Sustainability-oriented ecologies of learning: a response to systemic global dysfunction', in *Ecologies for learning and practice: emerging ideas, sightings, and possibilities*. Routledge, pp 61–78.

Wals, A. and Jickling, B. (2002) '"Sustainability" in higher education: from doublethink and newspeak to critical thinking and meaningful learning', *Higher education policy*, 15(2), pp 121–131. Available at: https://doi.org/10.1016/S0952-8733(02)00003-X

Walsh, C. (2009) 'Interculturalidad crítica y pedagogía de-colonial: apuestas (des) de el in-surgir, re-existir y re-vivir', *Educação Online*, 15. Available at: https://educacaoonline.edu.puc-rio.br/index.php/eduonline/article/view/1802

Wang, C.C. (2006) 'Youth participation in photovoice as a strategy for community change', *Journal of community practice*, 14(1–2), pp 147–161. Available at: https://doi.org/10.1300/J125v14n01_09

Wilder, R. Nuwategeka, E., Monge, C. and Talavera, A.B. (2024) 'Environmental justice in education for climate action: case studies from Perú and Uganda', *Children and society*, 00. Available at: https://doi.org/10.1111/chso.12899

Wilson-Strydom, M. (2015) 'University access and theories of social justice: Contributions of the capabilities approach', *Higher education*, 69, pp 143–155. Available at: https://www.jstor.org/stable/43648778

World Bank (2017) 'Systematic country diagnostic – Peru'. World Bank.

World Bank (2018) *World Development Report 2018: learning to realize education's promise.* World Bank. Available at: https://doi.org/10.1596/978-1-4648-1096-1

World Bank (2023) 'Poverty and equity brief: Uganda'. World Bank.

World Bank (2024) 'Poverty and equity brief: Nepal'. The World Bank Group. Available at: https://www.worldbank.org/en/topic/poverty/publication/poverty-and-equity-briefs

Worldometer (2024) *Population of Uganda: current and historical.* Available at: https://www.worldometers.info/world-population/uganda-population/#google_vignette

Yarbrough, S. (2014) 'Amnesty or Accountability: The Fate of High-Ranking Child Soldiers in Uganda's Lord's Resistance Army', *Vanderbilt journal of transnational law*, 47, 531.

Young, I.M. (1990) *Justice and the politics of difference.* Princeton University Press.

Zembylas, M. (2017) 'Love as ethico-political practice: inventing reparative pedagogies of aimance in "disjointed" times', *Journal of curriculum and pedagogy*, 14(1), pp 23–38. Available at: https://doi.org/10.1080/15505170.2016.1277572

Zembylas, M. (2018) 'Affect, race, and white discomfort in schooling: decolonial strategies for "pedagogies of discomfort"', *Ethics and education*, 13(1), pp 86–104. Available at: https://doi.org/10.1080/17449642.2018.1428714

Index

References to figures and photographs appear in *italic* type; those in **bold** type refer to tables. References to endnotes show both the page number and the note number (231n3).

A

ABEK *see* Alternative Basic Education for Karamoja (ABEK)
Abrams, F. 18, 32
Alternative Basic Education for Karamoja (ABEK) 108, **109**, 130
Amnesty Act (Uganda) 109, **109**, 111
Amuru (Uganda) 45, 52, **53**, 123, 124–125
Anderson, E. 17, 27, 147
author's research *see* JustEd
Ayacucho (Perú) 44, 52, **53**, 95, 96, 97–98, 99, 151

B

Bagnoli, A. 49
Balarin, M. 150, 160
Barrett, A.M. 24, 36
Bartlett, L. 41
Basic Education for the Urban Poor (BEUPA) 108
biocentric justice 28, 114
Bozalek, V. 24

C

Cachelin, A. 36
capabilities 21–22
Capabilities Approach 21, 22, 24
Cin, M. 13–14
climate change
 climate justice and 7–8, 28–29, 138
 curricula, and 61, 66–67, 74, 97, 114
 epistemic injustice and 136
 epistemic justice and 153–154
 impacts of 38, 42
 Nepal, in 158
 Perú, in 159
 policy, and 63
 SDG 13 (Climate Action) 3, 7, 9–10, 74, 132
climate justice 7–8, 28–29, 138

Cole, E.A. 35
Conflict, the *see* Internal Armed Conflict (Perú)
conscientization 35–36, **37**
corporal punishment 38, 123, 125, 139–140
COVID-19 pandemic *see* JustEd
critical discourse analysis (CDA) 48
critical thinking
 importance of 37
 pedagogies, characteristics of rich **37**, 150, 153–154
 policy, and 86
 shallow pedagogies, and 100, 105, 134, 137–138
cultural diversity 79, 82, 85, 91, 98, 99–100, 101, 131, 132
curricula
 author's overview of 33–35
 climate change, and 61, 66–67, 74
 findings, JustEd research 130–131
 Nepal, in 65–69, **66**, 130, 131
 Perú, in 47, 88–92, **89**, 131
 transversal approaches to 84–85, 89, 90, 100
 Uganda, in 112–117, **113**, 130, 131, 132
curriculum coercion 120–121
curriculum violence 120
CVR *see* Truth and Reconciliation Commission (CVR) (Perú)

D

Davies, L. 30, 33, 73
Day, N. 33
decontextualized education 121–123, 136, 149
depoliticization 80. 87–88, 100–101, 105, 132, 134–136
development cooperation *see* global development cooperation
Devries, K. 38

INDEX

distribution 17–19, 20–21, 22 *see also* maldistribution; redistribution; social justice
distributive justice 17–19, 28–29
diversity *see* cultural diversity

E

Eaton, E. 33
education
  author's overview of 2–6
  decontextualized education 121–123, 136, 149
  right to 2, 3, 19, 60, 107, 141
  see also education *as* justice; education *for* justice; environmental education; JustEd; learners; schools; teachers
Education Act (Nepal) **61**, 63
Education Act (Uganda) 108, 109, **109**, 111
education *as* justice
  author's overview of 1, 6–7
  author's summary of 147, 153–154
  findings, JustEd 133–140, 144
  importance of 14
  3Rs framework, and 25, 27, 56, 141
Education for All (UNESCO) 84
education *for* justice
  author's overview of 1, 6, 7
  author's summary of 144
  findings, JustEd 129–133
  how to achieve 14
  3Rs framework, and 25, 27, 56
Education Reform Law (Perú) 83
Educational Reparations Plan for Victims of Violence in Perú 82, **82**, 84, 86
Elmore, R. 148, 154
Environment Protection Act (Nepal) 62–63
environmental education
  findings, JustEd research 129–130, 131
  Nepal, in 66
  Perú, in 79–80, 82, 84, 86–87, 90–91
  Uganda, in 110–111, 112, 114, 121–122
environmental justice
  author's overview of 8, 28
  author's summary of 144, 156
  biocentric justice 28, 114
  curricula and 34
  curricular documents, in **47**
  in-person activities on 69
  Nepal, in 60–61, **61**, 62–63
  Perú, in 82, **82**, 88
  social justice, and 28–30
  Uganda, in **109**, **113**, 114, 122, 126, 138, 139
  youth movements 39
epistemic core 148–151, **152**, 154
epistemic injustice
  author's overview of 106
  climate change, and 136

curricula, and 34, 35
distributive 151–152
findings, JustEd research 141, 148
miseducation 120, *121*
Nepal, in 27, 70, 75–76, 78
Perú, in 80–81
scholarship on 26–27
shallow pedagogies and 86, 103
Uganda, in 119–121, *121*, 122–123, 124–125
epistemic justice
  author's overview of 8, 15, 106
  author's summary of 143–144, 147, 148–149, 151, 153–154, 155–156
  collaboration and 13
  curricular documents, in **47**, 48
  definitions of 8, 27
  factors that affect 27, 75–76, 143–144
  futures, multiple 33
  Indigenous knowledge, and 36
  in-person activities on 69
  JustEd, in 49–50
  Nepal, in 63–64, 67, 70, 72, 77
  Perú, in 82, **82**, 88
  scholarship on 26
  3Rs framework, and 28
  Uganda, in 108, **109**, 115, 117
epistemic misrecognition *see* misrecognition
equity 7, 18–19, 104 *see also* gender equity
Escudero, A. 160

F

Fifteenth Plan (Nepal) 62–63, 64, 65, 77–78
Floresta, J.K. 38
4th R (reconciliation) 31–32
Fraser, N.
  distributive justice 19
  recognition 20, 28
  3Rs framework of social justice 22, 23–25, 28, 31, 141, 143, 144, 151
  transformative approach 31, 32, 156
Freire, P. 19, 24, 35–36
Fricker, M. 26, 27, 149, 151, 153

G

Gandolfi, H. 34
Gender Equality Policy (Perú) **82**, 85
gender equity 81–82, **82**, 83–84, 85, 89–90, 91, 96–97, 98–99
General Education Law (Perú) 104
Gewirtz, S. 19
Giroux, H. 35
Glackin, M. 33
global development cooperation 2, 4, 6, 155
Global Partnership for Education 3
Gruenewald, D. 36, 149
Gulu (Uganda) 45

H

Hajir, B. 31
Hall, B.L. 8
hermeneutical injustice 123, 149
Honneth, A. 19, 20, 23, 32
hooks, b. 19
Hookway, C. 140
Hopwood, N. 57
Huaman, E.S. 35
human rights *see* rights
Hutchison, C. 120

I

IBE *see* Sectoral Policy on Intercultural Education and Intercultural Bilingual Education (IBE) (Perú)
Indigenous knowledge 34–35, 36, 111, 115, 116, 121, 139
inequity 19
injustice *see* epistemic injustice; hermeneutical injustice
instructors *see* teachers
Internal Armed Conflict (Perú) 43, 44, 79, 86, 89–90, 91–92, 96–100, 101–102, 135, 151
interviewees *see* learners; teachers

J

Jickling, B. 37
JustEd
  author's overview of 9–13, 41–42
  author's summary of 59, 146, 155–156
  challenges faced during 13–14
  COVID-19 on, impact of 11, 14, 45, 47, 49, 51, 59, 92, 118
  critical policy analysis 45–46
  curricular documents 46–48, **47**
  data analysis 52, **53**, 53–54
  data generation 48–52, **51**, 92–95, *94*
  ethics 58
  findings 76–78, 103–106, 126–127, 129–133, 133–140
  framework 144, *145*
  in-person activities with learners *69*, 69–70
  observations 70–73, 73–74, 75–76, 96–100, 100–103
  sampling 52
  surveys **54**, 54–56
  theory development 56–58, **57**
  see also learners; Nepal; Perú; schools; teachers; 3Rs framework (redistribution, recognition, representation); Uganda
justice
  biocentric justice 28, 114
  climate justice 7–8, 28–29, 138
  in education 4–5, 6–7, 40
  see also education *as* justice; education *for* justice; environmental justice; epistemic justice; social justice; transitional justice

justice principles 7

K

Kalungwizi, V.J. 38
Keddie, A. 20, 23
Keet, A. 28
King, H. 33
Kitgum (Uganda) 45, 52, **53**, 119, 123
Kohli, R.K.S. 32
Kotzee, B. 18, 148
Kuchah, K. 140

L

Lai, E. 37
Lalitpur district (Nepal) 43, 44, 52, **53**
Langole, S. 112
languages
  English, epistemic injustice of 27, 117, 123–124, 126, 139–140
  of instruction 53
  right to learn in own 134, 137, 160
  spoken in research sites 53
learners
  aspirations of 125–126
  on barriers to education 75–76
  on challenges faced 133
  data generation with 92–95, *94*
  epistemic core and 149–151, **152**
  findings, JustEd 133–140
  on gaps in knowledge 72–73
  on injustice 95
  in-person activities with *69*, 69–70
  on justice-related issues 96–97, 98, 99–100, 134, 136–137, 138
  learning–practice gap 73–74
  observations on, JustEd research 70, 71, 96–100, 124–125
  on school environments 71, 102
  violence, experiences of 123–124, 125, 139–140
Leibowitz, B. 24
Lima (Perú) 44–45, 52, **53**, 90, 95, 96, 97
Local Government Operation Act (Nepal) 60, **61**, 62, 64, 65
Lopez, N. 154
Lord's Resistance Army (LRA) (Uganda) 43, 45, 116–117, 161–162
Lotz-Sisitka, H. 37
LRA *see* Lord's Resistance Army (LRA) (Uganda)
Lynch, K. 31–32

M

Mahottari district (Nepal) 43, 44, 52, **53**
maldistribution 19, 23–24, 27, 29, 151
Masaka, D. 143
Mbembe, A. 29
McCowan, T. 19

INDEX

McIntyre, J. 18, 32
Medina, J. 151
Menton, M. 87
Meredith, M. 26
Mignolo, W. 33
Millennium Development Goals (MDGs) 18
Milligan, L.O. 27, 140
Miri, M.A. 31
miseducation 120, *121*
misrecognition 20, 24, 28, 138–139, 142, 152–153
Mkwananzi, F. 13–14
monolingualism 117, 123–124
Mookherjee, M. 20, 22
Musara, E. 24

N

National Curriculum (Perú) 79, 81, 85, 86, 88, **89**, 89–92, 101–102
National Curriculum Development Centre (NCDC) (Uganda) 110
National Curriculum Framework (NCF) (Nepal) 61, **61**, 63, 67
National Development Plan (NDP) (Uganda) 107
National Education Policy (NEP) (Nepal) 62, 64
National Education Project (Perú) 104
National Environment Act (Uganda) **109**, 109–110, 111, 129, 132
National Environmental Education Policy (Perú) **82**, 86
National Forestry and Tree Planting Act (Uganda) **109**, 109–110, 111, 132
National Intercultural and Bilingual Education Policy (Perú) 83, 129, 130
National Policy for Bilingual Education (Perú) 83
National Transitional Justice Policy (Uganda) 109, **109**, 111
NCDC *see* National Curriculum Development Centre (NCDC) (Uganda)
NCF *see* National Curriculum Framework (NCF) (Nepal)
Ndlovu-Gatsheni, S.J. 26
NEP *see* National Education Policy (NEP) (Nepal)
Nepal
  author's overview of 10–11, 42, 43–44, 157–158
  author's summary of 76–78, 133–140
  climate change 158
  curricula in 65–69, **66**, 130, 131
  data generation methods in 50, **51**
  education in 60–61, 62
  environmental education in 66
  environmental justice in 60–61, **61**, 62–63
  epistemic injustice in 27, 70, 75–76, 78
  epistemic justice in 63–64, 67, *69*, 70, 72, 77
  in-person activities *69*, 69–70
  observations, JustEd research 70–73, 73–74, 75–76
  policies in, education and justice **61**, 61–65, 129, 130–131
  right to education in 60
  sampling in 52, **53**
  schools in 11
  secondary education in 10
  transitional justice in 64–65, 67–69, 72, 130
Nicolosi, E. 36
Novelli, M. 31
Nussbaum, M. 21

O

OECD 3
Oliveira, L. 122–123
oppression 19–20, 36

P

Paulson, J. 38, 39
pedagogies
  author's overview of 35–38, **37**
  rich pedagogies 150, **152**
  shallow pedagogies 80–81, 100, 102–103, 105, 127, 131, 134, 141, 150
pedagogy of possibility 24
Perú
  author's overview of 10–11, 42, 43, 44–45
  author's summary of 103–106, 133–140, 158–160
  climate change 159
  COVID-19 in, impact on JustEd 47
  curricula in 47, 88–92, **89**, 131
  data generation methods in 50, **51**, 92–95, *94*
  education in 79–81, 84–85, 85n1
  environmental education in 79–80, 82, 84, 86–87, 90–91
  environmental justice in 82, **82**, 88
  epistemic injustice in 80–81
  epistemic justice in 82, **82**, 88
  gender equity 81–82, **82**, 83–84, 85, 89–90, 91, 96–97, 98–99
  Internal Armed Conflict 43, 44, 79, 86, 89–90, 91–92, 96–100, 101–102, 135, 151
  policies in, education and justice 81–82, **82**, 83–88, 129, 130, 131
  redistribution in 79, 87–88, 103
  sampling in 52, **53**
  schools in 11
  secondary education in 10
  transitional justice in 82, **82**, 84, 88, 130

193

Truth and Reconciliation Commission
  (CVR) (Perú) 81, 82, **82**, 84, 86, 87, 92,
  103, 159
petro-pedagogy 33
Pherali, T. 31
Phillips, A. 18
Phyak, P. 27, 37–38
Plan Nacional de Educación Ambiental
  (Perú) 86
policies *see* education for justice; Nepal;
  Perú; Uganda
Pope, D.C. 120
Portugal, T. 99

Q
Quijano, A. 26

R
Rasuwa district (Nepal) 43–44, 52, **53**,
  75, 140
Rawls, J. 7, 18, 21
recognition
  author's summary of 141–142, 143–144,
    150, 151, 152–153
  JustEd framework *145*
  as justice principle 7, 8, 19–20, 30
  misrecognition 20, 24, 28, 138–139, 142,
    152–153
  scholarship on 20
  3Rs framework 23, 24, 25, 151, **152**
Recommendation on Education for
  Peace, Human Rights and Sustainable
  Development (UNESCO) 5–6
reconciliation 30, 31–32, 92, 109, 111, 116
redistribution
  author's summary of 141, 144, 151
  JustEd framework *145*
  as justice principle 7
  Perú, in 79, 87–88, 103
  3Rs framework 23, 25, **152**
  transitional justice, and 30
reinhabitation 36
reparation
  education for 33
  Educational Reparations Plan for Victims of
    Violence in Perú 82, **82**, 84, 86
  importance of 32
  JustEd framework *145*
  pedagogies of 36, **37**, 57–58, 73, 149–150
reparative turn 33
representation
  author's summary of 143–144
  epistemic justice, and 28
  JustEd framework *145*
  as justice principle 7
  participation, *vs.* 29
  3Rs framework, and 23, 24, 25, 30–31,
    151, **152**

research by author *see* JustEd
rich pedagogies 150, **152**
rights
  curricula, in 30, 67, 68
  education, to 2, 3, 19, 60, 107, 141
  environment, of the 110
  language, to learn in own 134, 137, 160
  non-human life, of 28, 137, 138
  of young people 30, 65
Robertson, E. 37
Robeyns, I. 22
Rodríguez, M.F. 150
Rodríguez-Gómez, D. 34

S
Sah, P. 27
Schlosberg, D. 29–30, 31, 40
Schmidt, R. 46
scholarship
  on capabilities 21–22
  on curricula 33–35
  on environmental justice 28–30
  on epistemic injustice 26–27
  on oppression 19
  on pedagogies 35–38
  on recognition 20
  on school environments 38–39
  on social justice 17–19
  on 3Rs (redistribution, recognition,
    representation) 24–25, 30–32
  on transformations 33
  on transitional justice 30
School Education Sector Plan (SESP)
  (Nepal) 61, **61**, 62, 63, 64–65, 77
School Sector Development Plan (SSDP)
  (Nepal) **61**, 63, 64, 77
School Sector Reform Plan (SSRP)
  (Nepal) 64, 77
schools
  monolingualism in 117, 123–124
  observations on, JustEd research 75–76,
    100–103
  school environments 38–39
  violence in 38–39, 123–124, 125
  see also learners; teachers
SDG 4 (Quality Education) 7, 10, 18, 20–21,
  61, 62, 63, 74, 107, 114
SDG 10 (Reduced Inequalities) 7, 9–10
SDG 13 (Climate Action) 3, 7, 9–10,
  74, 132
SDG 16 (Peace, Justice and Strong
  Institutions) 3, 7, 9–10, 132
SDGs (Sustainable Development Goals) 3,
  7, 87
Sectoral Policy on Intercultural Education
  and Intercultural Bilingual Education
  (IBE) (Perú) **82**, 83, 84, 104
Sen, A. 21, 24

INDEX

SESP *see* School Education Sector Plan (SESP) (Nepal)
shallow pedagogies 80–81, 100, 102–103, 105, 127, 131, 134, 141, 150
Silova, I. 33
Singh, Ashik 15–16
Sobe, N. 38
social justice
 author's summary of 141, 143–144
 capabilities and 21–22
 conscientization 35–36
 definitions of 23
 distributive models of 7, 17–19
 environmental justice, and 28–30
 epistemic justice and 26–28
 transitional justice, and 30–32
 youth movements 39
 see also recognition; redistribution; representation; 3Rs framework (redistribution, recognition, representation)
Soysal, Nese 57
Spivak, G.C. 26
Sriprakash, A. 33, 34, 36
Srivastava, P. 57
SSDP *see* School Sector Development Plan (SSDP) (Nepal)
SSRP *see* School Sector Reform Plan (SSRP) (Nepal)
students *see* learners
Sultana, F. 29
Sustainable Development Goals (SDGs) 3, 7, 87 *see also specific SDGs (e.g., SDG 4)*

T

teachers
 on challenges faced 133–134, 135
 on curricula challenges 70–71
 data generation with 92–95, *94*
 on epistemic injustice 119–120, 124–125
 findings, JustEd 133–140
 on justice-related issues 96–97, 98–99
 observations on, JustEd research 70, 71–72, 74, 96–100
 on school environments 75, 76, 102
Tedesco, J.C. 154
3Rs framework (redistribution, recognition, representation)
 author's overview of 23–26
 author's use of 25–26, 141–144
 critiques of 31–32
 epistemic core, and **152**
 epistemic justice and 28
 4th R (reconciliation) 31–32
 limitations of 30–31
Tikly, L. 24, 30, 39, 148–149
transformations 31, 32–33, **37**
transitional justice
 author's overview of 9, 30

curricular documents, in **47**
definitions of 9
in-person activities on *69*
Nepal, in 64–65, 67–69, 72, 130
Perú, in 82, **82**, 84, 88, 130
reconciliation, and 30, 31–32, 92, 109, 111, 116
reparation and 57–58
social justice, and 30–32
Uganda, in 108–109, **109**, 111–112, **113**, 115–116, 125, 130, 131
violence, and 39
Truth and Reconciliation Commission (CVR) (Perú) 81, 82, **82**, 84, 86, 87, 92, 103, 159

U

Ucayali (Perú) 44, 52, **53**, 97, 101
Uccelli, F. 99
Uganda
 author's overview of 10–11, 42, 43, 45, 160–162
 author's summary of 126–127, 133–140
 COVID-19 in, impact on JustEd 51
 curricula in 112–117, **113**, 130, 131, 132
 data generation methods in 50, 51, **51**, 117–118
 decontextualized education in 121–123
 education in 107–108
 environmental education in 110–111, 112, 114, 121–122
 environmental justice in **109**, **113**, 114, 122, 126, 138, 139
 epistemic injustice in 119–121, *121*, 122–123, 124–125
 epistemic justice in 108, **109**, 115, 117
 language of instruction in 117, 123–124
 Lord's Resistance Army (LRA) 43, 45, 116–117, 161–162
 policies in, education and justice **109**, 109–112, 129, 130–131, 132
 sampling in 52, **53**
 schools in 11–12
 secondary education in 10
 transitional justice in 108–109, **109**, 111–112, **113**, 115–116, 125, 130, 131
 violence in schools 123–124, 125
UN *see* United Nations
UNESCO 3, 5–6, 33, 40, 83, 84, 107, 155
United Nations 3, 9
United Nations Declaration of Human Rights 2, 67
Unterhalter, E. 18, 20, 154

V

Vanner, C. 34
Vavrus, F. 41

violence
  art-based reflections of 118
  author's summary of 149, 150–151
  corporal punishment 38, 123, 125, 139–140
  cultural violence 123–124
  curricula, and 34, 68, 79
  curriculum violence 120
  definitions of 39
  epistemic violence 26
  gender-based 67, 85, 96–97, 98
  reparations, and 32, 36, 57–58, 82, 86
  schools, in 38–39, 123–124, 125
  transitional justice and 39, *69*

W

Walker, M. 33, 35, 40, 140, 150
Wals, A. 37
Wilson-Strydom, M. 21–22
World Bank 3, 5

Y

Young, I.M. 19–20, 21, 23